I FOUND IT!

EVIDENCE OF THE HUMAN CONDITION

VOLUME ONE

ACCUMULATED BY **DAVID ANTHONY**

PULP!
SEATTLE USA

Dedicated to **Charles R. Cross**

Thank You...
Rew and Amy for working so hard to make this happen, Pepper Kaye for being an angel, Nina Pearlman and Chris Phillips for editorial assistance, JillEllyn Reilly, Vickie Nauman for invaluable support, and lastly, everyone who's ever contributed to "I Found It!" one way or another.

PULP!
P.O. Box 70584
Seattle WA 98107
1-877-723-PULP
naked@pulpnet.com
www.pulpnet.com

Digital photographs of artifacts by Earl Harper of Harper Studios, Seattle
Background photographs by Pepper Adams
Photograph of David Anthony by Joe Ehrbar

ISBN 0-9667339-1-6

Printed in the United States of America

First Edition
99 00 01 02 03 10 9 8 7 6 5 4 3 2 1

Required Disclaimer
Artifacts pictured in this book are provided anonymously and for entertainment purposes only, and therefore contain no recipes, recommendations or advice that may be injurious to the reader. PULP! makes no claims to these materials nor any guarantees to their authenticity. Names and places mentioned in artifacts pictured in this book are non-fictitious and have been intentionally eliminated to preserve the anonymity of the parties involved. Likewise, names of submittors and locations describing where items were found have been abbreviated to protect their identities. Any similarities to specific persons, places and events are purely coincidental. The ideas, views and opinions expressed herein by the creators of such artifacts do not necessarily reflect the views of the editor, the photographers, the employees of PULP!, or their associates, families and friends.

Email David Anthony at **eyefoundit@aol.com**

Portions of this book have been previously published in *The Rocket* magazine.

…goddamn motherfucking sonofabitch asshole!…you fucking ripped me off, jerk!… Get a life, bitch… …my love, I am nothing without you…we will be together always and forever… …I hate this fucking class…do you like Suzie? She is, like, so totally fake!… …your worthless existence has made my life miserable! Fuck off!!!… …we did some disgusting shit and now every-one knows about it. Wanna do it again?… …Dear Diary, I sure hope no one reads this!… …you're my best friend forever, or at least until somebody better than you comes along… …let me smell your panties and I'll pay you well, but you'll have to wait 'til next week…

It started with **my personal little fetish** concerning those notes, photos, letters and other personal jetsam one finds littering the streets and sidewalks. I collected them. It was this uncomplicated doorway into someone's secret history that was something of a privilege, though I never could figure out why anyone would *ever* let some of this stuff get out in public. I had a feeling others did the same thing. Admit it, **we're all voyeurs in one way or another**. We can't help bending an ear to eavesdrop on someone else's conversation in the coffee shop, pretending to read; as we pass by apartment windows at night we stare a little longer than we should when we catch a glimpse of flesh; we watch in fascinated horror as someone has an argument in public. It's none of our goddamn business. Still, we can't help but feel a little more than turned on or smug when we see someone's secret side or find out about how **fucked** somebody else's life is—*we think we have* our *shit together.*

I decided to start a column devoted to publishing this lost glory. People started sending me stuff. I'd pick the best and run a small picture of it with a written translation or explanation. Simple enough.

So it goes that in the almost five years since "I Found It!" first started appearing in the Seattle magazine *The Rocket*, hundreds if not thousands of letters have arrived regularly; some in hastily sealed envelopes, others on the stationery of notable businesses. I would have never imagined "I Found It!" achieving the cult status it has today. Really, I'm still amazed at how many people are actually willing, like myself, to pick up this mostly filthy crap lying on the ground, read it, look at it, and then keep it; finding themselves gleefully titillated with the highlights or nightmares of someone else's life. It's beautiful. It's the very reason I've never commented on anything that's ever run: the reaction should be personal—yours, not some insipid remark I get to make.

It should be noted I've always made a point to keep it all confidential. Care has always been taken to protect the identity of whomever this stuff belongs to, even if they were **stupid** enough to lose it. I guess that's the deal: they lost it, someone found it, I published it, and no one knows who it's about but me, my assistant Pepper Kaye and the contributor.

Many have asked if I question the credibility of these submissions. My answer is to say I've developed this latent sense for authenticity, and to be honest, I've never really questioned any of them. Their validity rests in the very spontaneous nature that prevails in their informal and candid revelations, never meant for any other audience except the one (usually) person at which they were directed.

From humble beginnings springs this first collection, culled from previously-published columns, plus other pieces that just wouldn't have been appropriate in a family paper. This book you have in your hands would not exist without the generous submissions of those who have contributed to the column over the years, and if it weren't for you, me and some poor slob dropping, tossing or just plain losing something—somewhere.

"Look Closer"

...or something like that...

David Anthony, September 1999

COMPLAINT DEPT.

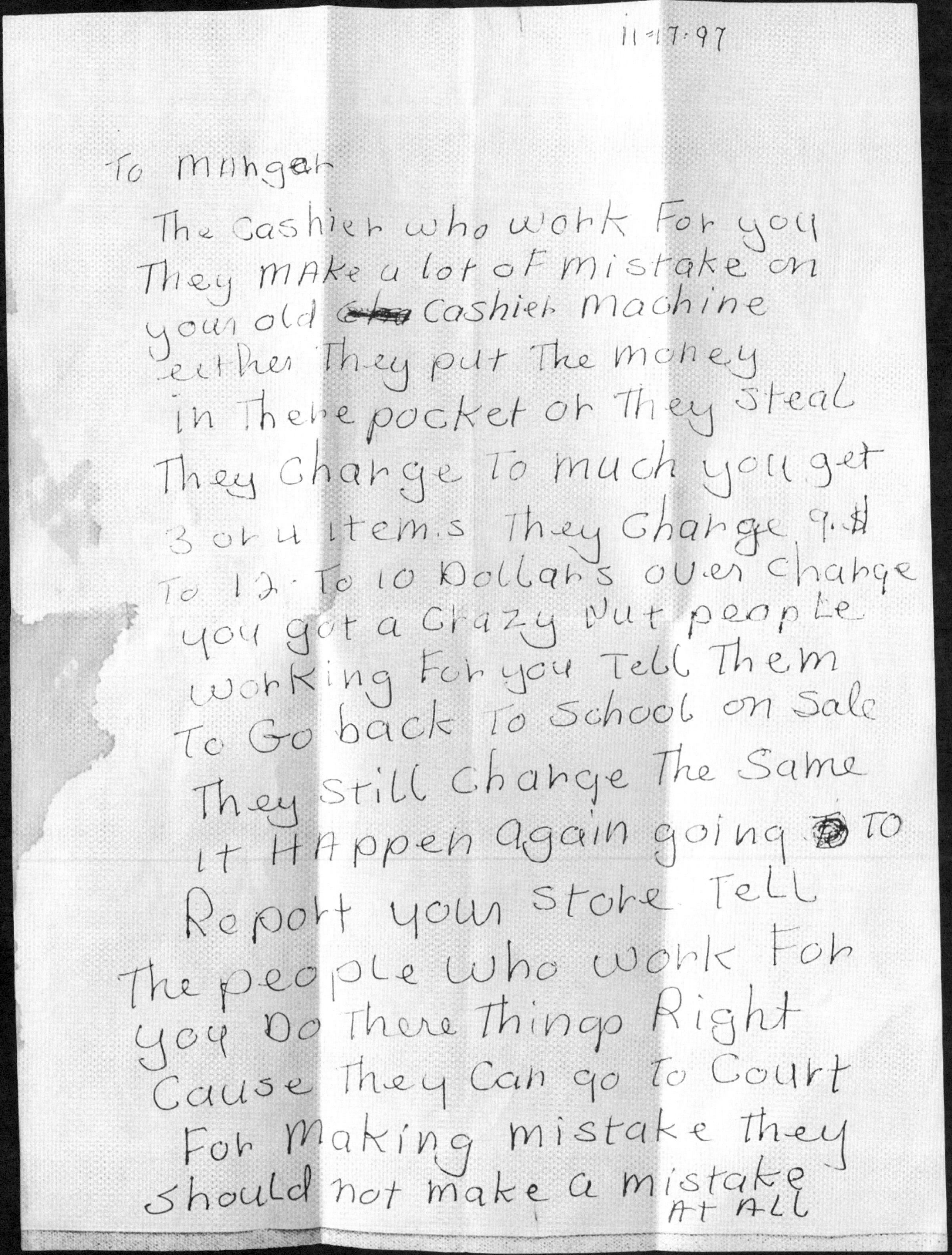

11-17-97

To Mangar

The cashier who work For you
They MAke a lot of mistake on
your old cashier machine
either They put The money
in There pocket or They steal
They charge To much you get
3 or 4 items They Charge 9.$
To 12. To 10 Dollars over charge
you got a crazy Nut people
working For you Tell Them
To Go back To School on Sale
They still charge The Same
it HAppen again going TO
Report your store Tell
The people who work For
you Do There Things Right
Cause They Can go To Court
For Making mistake they
should not make a mistake
At ALL

Found by Sunny in a thrift store in Seattle's sunny neighborhood of Ballard on November 22, 1997.

8½" x 11", black ballpoint pen on white paper

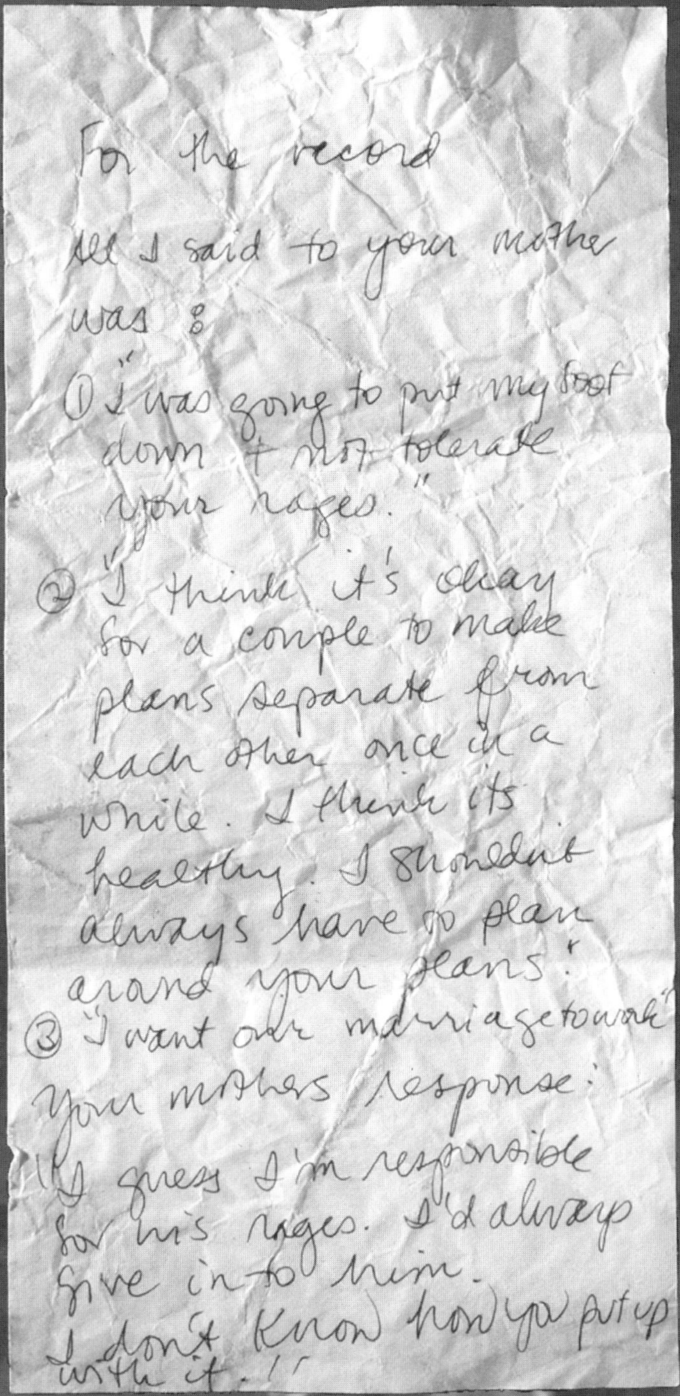

For the record

All I said to your mother was:

① "I was going to put my foot down + not tolerate your rages."

② "I think it's okay for a couple to make plans separate from each other once in a while. I think it's healthy. I shouldn't always have to plan around your plans."

③ "I want our marriage to work"

Your mothers response:
"I guess I'm responsible for his rages. I'd always give in to him.
I don't know how you put up with it."

For the record

All I said to your mother was:

① "I was going to put my foot down + not tolerate
your rages."

② "I think it's okay for a couple to make plans
separate from each other once in a while.
I think it's healthy. I shouldn't always have to
plan around your plans."

③ "I want our marriage to work"

Your mothers response:
"I guess i'm responsible for his rages. I'd always
give in to him.
I don't know how you put up with it."

Found by Laura S. on the sidewalk near the corner of NE 75th Street and 20th Avenue NE in Seattle.
4⅛" x 8⅜", black rollerball ink on white paper

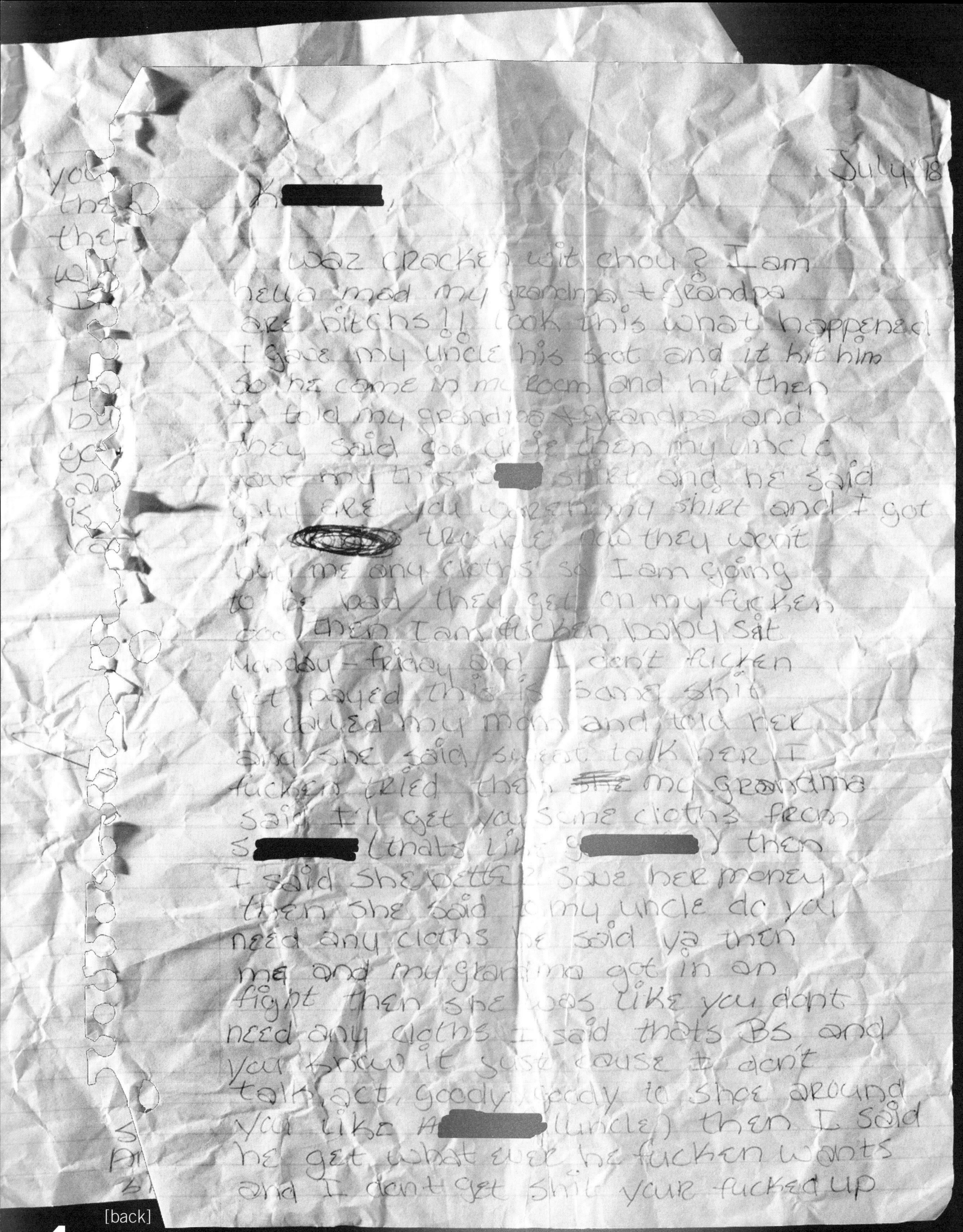

July '98

K[redacted],

Waz cracken wit chou? I am
hella mad my grandma + grandpa
are bitchs!! look this what happened
I gave my uncle his scot and it hit him
so he came in my room and hit then
I told my grandma + grandpa and
they said go circle then my uncle
saw my this [redacted] shirt and he said
why are you wearing my shirt and I got
in [redacted] trouble now they won't
buy me any cloths so I am going
to be bad they get on my fucken
cool then I am fucken baby sit
Monday - friday and I don't fucken
get payed this is some shit
I called my mom and told her
and she said sweet talk her I
fucken tried then ~~she~~ my grandma
said I'll get you some cloths from
S[redacted] (thats like g[redacted]) then
I said she better save her money
then she said to my uncle do you
need any cloths he said ya then
me and my grandma got in an
fight then she was like you dont
need any cloths I said thats BS and
you know it just cause I don't
talk, act, goody goody to shoe around
you like A[redacted] (uncle) then I said
he get what ever he fucken wants
and I dont get shit your fucked up

[back]

[front]

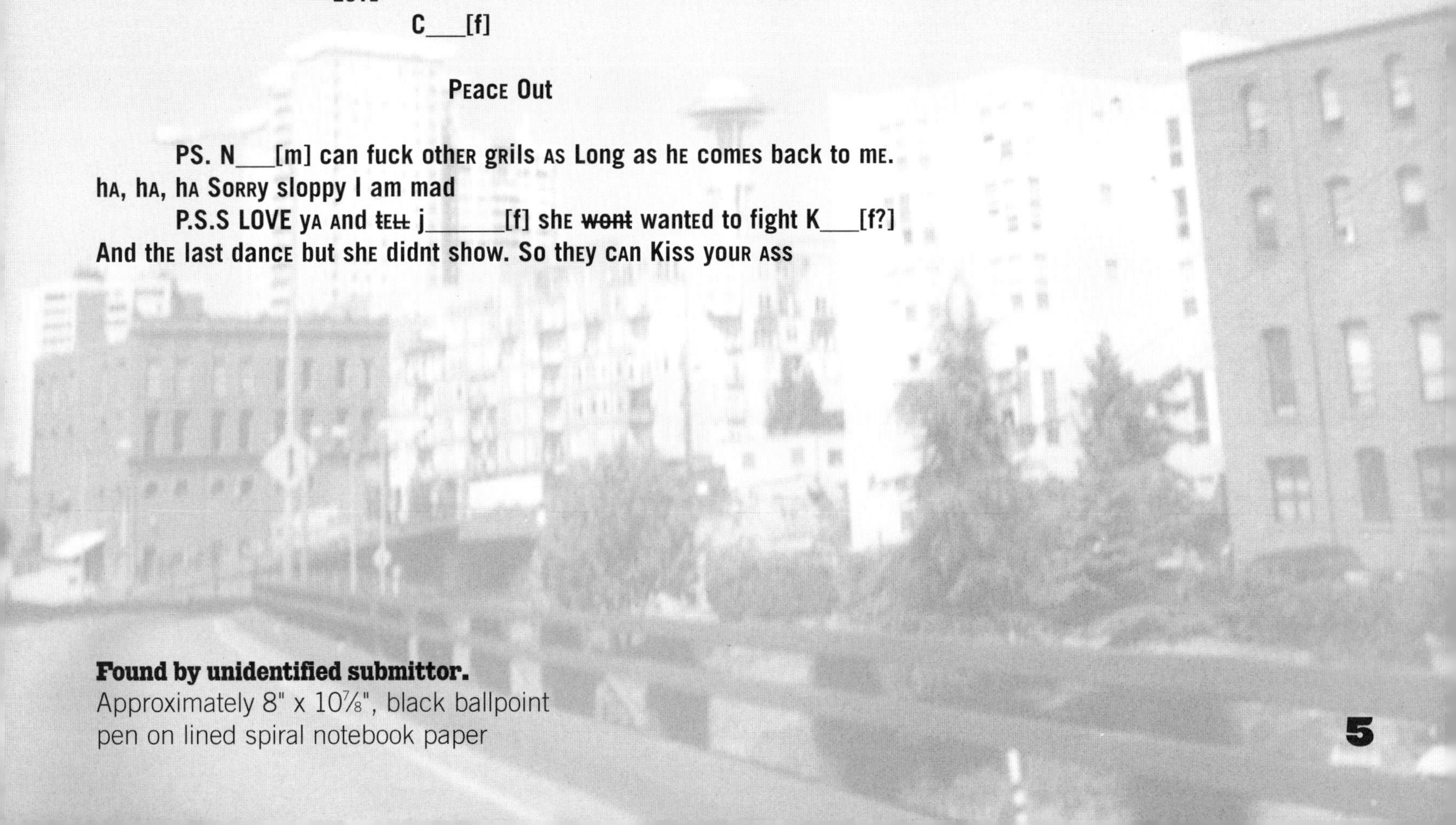

[front]

July "98"

K______[f],

waz cracken wit chou? I am hella mad my grandma + grandpa are bitchs!! LooK this what happened I gave my uncle his scot and it hit him so he came in my room and hit then I told my grandma + grandpa and they said ooo ciccie then my uncle gave my this N___[brand] shirt and he said why are you waren my shirt and I got in ~~tr~~[misspelling scribbled out] trouble now they won't buy me any cloths so I am going to be bad they get on my fucKen ooo then I am fucKen baby s~~e~~it Monday – friday and I don't fucKen get payed this is some shit I called my mom and told her and she said sweat talk her I fucKen tried then ~~she~~ my grandma said I'll get you some cloths from S_____[thrift store] (thats like g_______[thrift store chain]) then I said She better save her money then she said to my uncle do you need any cloths he said ya then m~~ye~~ and my grandma got in an fight then she was liKe you dont need any cloths I said thats BS and you know it just cause I don't talk, act, goody, goody to shoe around you like A______[m] (uncle) then I said he get what ever he fucKen wants and I dont get shit your fucked up

[back]
you fucKen treat the dog better then me your really fucked up then she Left and when she was closen the door I said Bitch!!.

I cant wait to come home this is fucKed up they wont buy me any film but they ~~boight~~ got my fucken uncle 4 or 5 rolls and hes going to Mexico this is messed up well I have to vacuom my grand~~s~~mas house.

Love

C___[f]

Peace Out

PS. N___[m] can fuck other grils as Long as he comes back to me. ha, ha, ha Sorry sloppy I am mad

P.S.S LOVE ya and ~~tell~~ j______[f] she ~~wont~~ wanted to fight K___[f?] And the last dance but she didnt show. So they can Kiss your ass

Found by unidentified submittor.
Approximately 8" x 10⅞", black ballpoint pen on lined spiral notebook paper

~~CARE~~ O - GRAM
HATE

TO: P [redacted]

FROM: J [redacted]

T[redacted] LUTHERAN CHURCH

[outside]

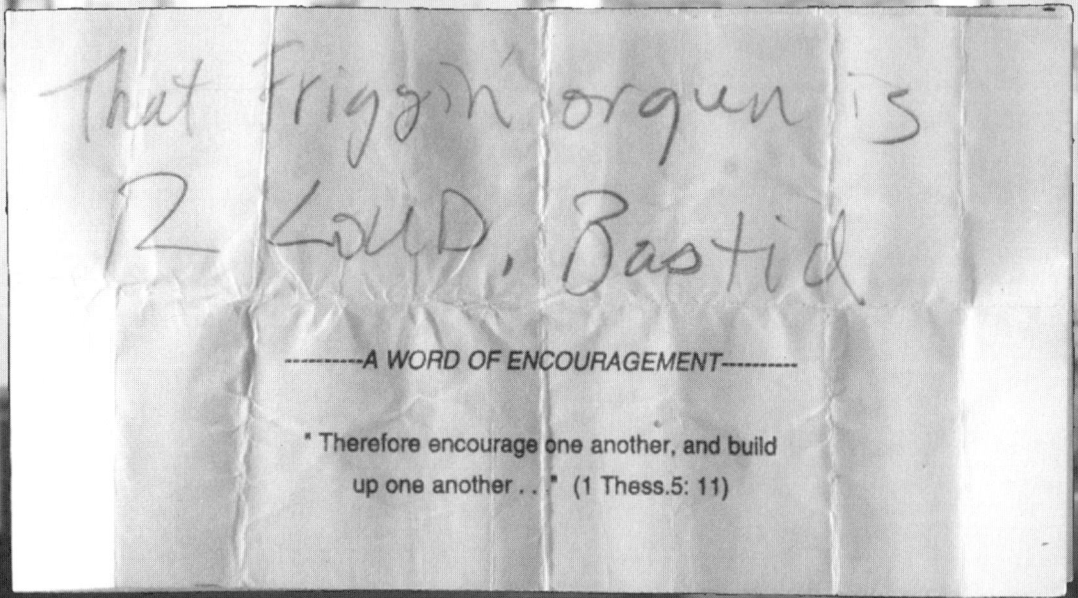

That Friggin' orgun is 2 LOUD, Bastid

----------A WORD OF ENCOURAGEMENT----------

" Therefore encourage one another, and build up one another . . ." (1 Thess.5: 11)

[inside]

[outside]
~~CARE~~ HATE - O - GRAM

TO: P___[m]
FROM: J___[m]

T______ LUTHERAN CHURCH

[inside]
That Friggin' orgun is 2 LOUD. Bastid

----------A WORD OF ENCOURAGEMENT----------
"Therefore encourage one another, and build up one another..." (1 Thess.5: 11)

Found by Bill at a restaurant in Albany, OR.
Folded size: 5 7/16" x 2 7/8", pencil and photocopy on yellow paper

Found by Jason J. in the Seattle apartment complex where he lives.
8½" x 11", black marker on typing paper

OK Laundry Detergent theif...

This is war! I can easily understand dipping into a full box, nothing noticable. But what goes through a persons mind when they empty a minature 4 load box of tide that was tucked carefully away. Might they think the reason that person bought such a small box was because he might be running a bit short on money? How did it feel throwing my empty box of detergent in the trash can? Did you feel like a winner! Who knows next time you dip into a strange box of detergent it might contain silver nitrate or some other odd chemical that will turn all you're clothes dark purple. Ah ha! Make me go to the store spending money I could use to eat will ya? Will see who's laughing when all you're friends refer to you as "The Grape"

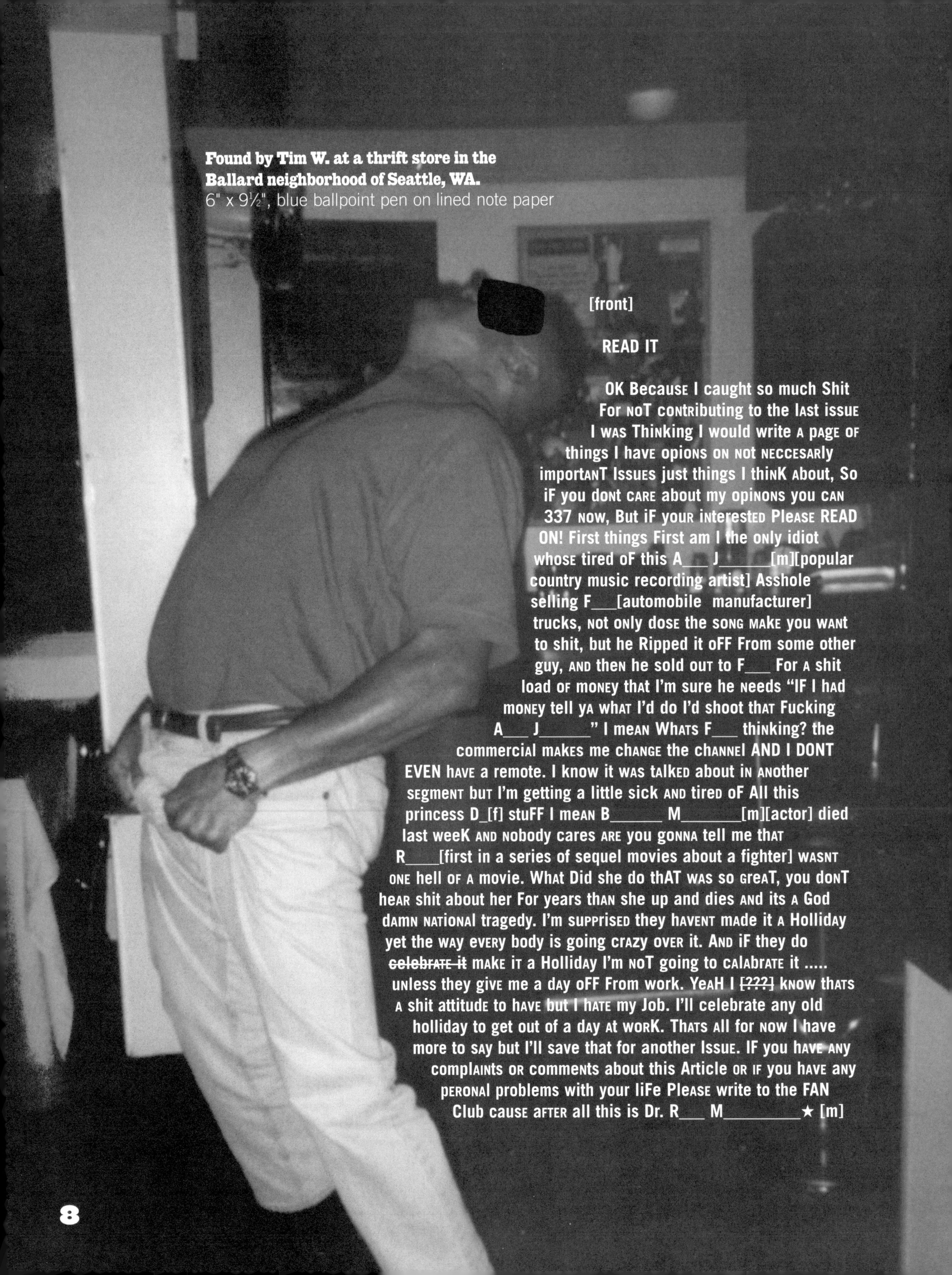

Found by Tim W. at a thrift store in the Ballard neighborhood of Seattle, WA.
6" x 9½", blue ballpoint pen on lined note paper

[front]

READ IT

OK Because I caught so much Shit For noT contRibuting to the last issue I was Thinking I would write a page of things I have opions on not neccesarly importanT Issues just things I thinK about, So iF you dont care about my opinons you can 337 now, But iF your interested Please READ ON! First things First am I the only idiot whose tired oF this A___ J______[m][popular country music recording artist] Asshole selling F___[automobile manufacturer] trucks, not only dose the song make you want to shit, but he Ripped it oFF From some other guy, and then he sold out to F___ For a shit load of money that I'm sure he needs "IF I had money tell ya what I'd do I'd shoot that Fucking A___ J______" I mean Whats F___ thinking? the commercial makes me change the channel AND I DONT EVEN have a remote. I know it was talked about in another segment but I'm getting a little sick and tired oF All this princess D_[f] stuFF I mean B______ M_______[m][actor] died last weeK and nobody cares are you gonna tell me that R____[first in a series of sequel movies about a fighter] wasnt one hell of a movie. What Did she do thAT was so greaT, you donT hear shit about her For years than she up and dies and its a God damn national tragedy. I'm supprised they havent made it a Holliday yet the way every body is going crazy over it. And iF they do ~~celebrate it~~ make it a Holliday I'm noT going to calabrate it ..... unless they give me a day oFF From work. YeaH I ~~[???]~~ know thats a shit attitude to have but I hate my Job. I'll celebrate any old holliday to get out of a day at worK. Thats all for now I have more to say but I'll save that for another Issue. IF you have any complaints or comments about this Article or if you have any peronal problems with your liFe Please write to the FAN Club cause after all this is Dr. R___ M_________★ [m]

READ IT

OK BECAUSE I caught so much shit for not contributing to the last issue I was thinking I would write a page of things I have opions on not neccesarily important issues just things I think about, so if you dont care about my opinons you can 337 now, But if your intrested please read on! First things first am I the only idiot whose tired of this [redacted] Asshole selling [redacted] trucks, not only dose the song make you want to shit, but he ripped it off from some other guy, and then he sold out to [redacted] for a shit load of money that I'm sure he needs "If I had money tell ya what I'd do, I'd shoot that Fucking [redacted] I mean whats [redacted] thinking? the commercial makes me change the channel and I dont even have a remote. I know it was talked about in another segment but I'm getting a little sick and tired of all these princess [redacted]

[redacted]
o nobody cares
ll me that
hell of a
she do that
dont hear
f years than
d its a
ragedy. I'm
t made it a
day every body
it, and if they
ake it a Holliday
elebrate it....
s a day off from
now thats a
e but I hate
any old holliday
at work, thats
mate to say
or another issue
plaints or
article or if
l problems with
ite to the fan
ause after all this is
Dr. [redacted]*

Found in the 2nd floor bathroom of an apartment building on SW Porter in Portland, OR, by Adam K. and Andy G.
7 15/16" x 10 7/16", blue ballpoint pen on lined notebook paper

who ever
IS Putting Bags
of these turds in
the toilet, I ~~[illegible]~~
Guess because (He-She)
is unable or don't
want to use the
toilet You are plugging
it. We all PAY the
price cuz of you.
Don't get caught
~~I'll fuck~~

Or the Price will
Be Paid by You!!

[right] Found by Rick and Eric on some poor fool's bed in a Seattle, WA, youth hostel.
3¾" x 6¾", black rollerball ink on pre-printed-with-green-ink daily planner paper

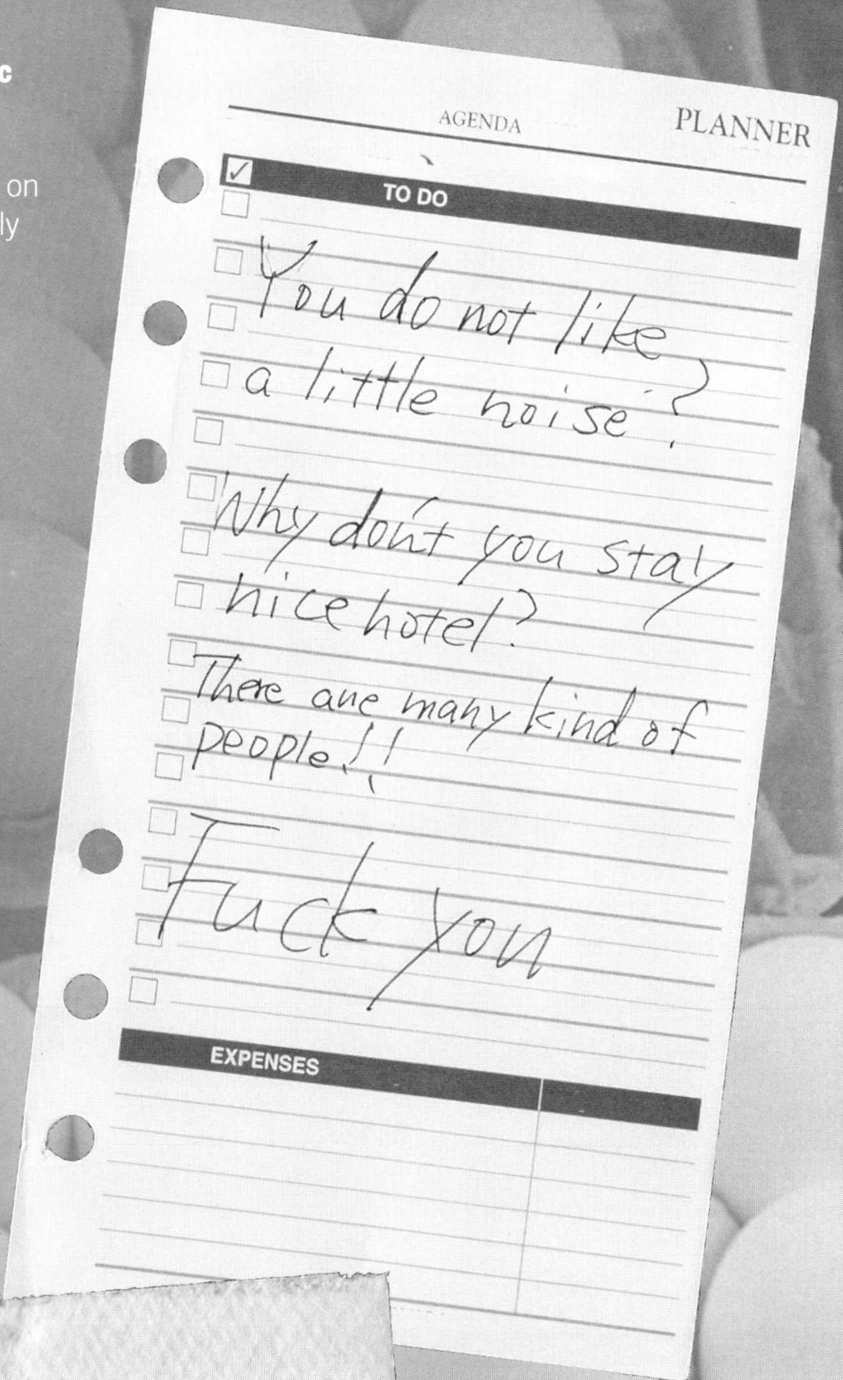
AGENDA PLANNER

TO DO

You do not like
a little noise?

Why don't you stay
nice hotel?
There are many kind of
people!!

Fuck you

EXPENSES

[below]
[front]
Dear: Mom
I want go home Seriously I hate it here! thank you for the heart but dont Send packages anymore every one crowdes around me & goes what is it what is it I hate it! Everything Sucks! Were doing the exact samething as last year

—C______[f]

[back, not shown]
H____ W [f]
4___ 4_th Ave S
Seattle WA
981__

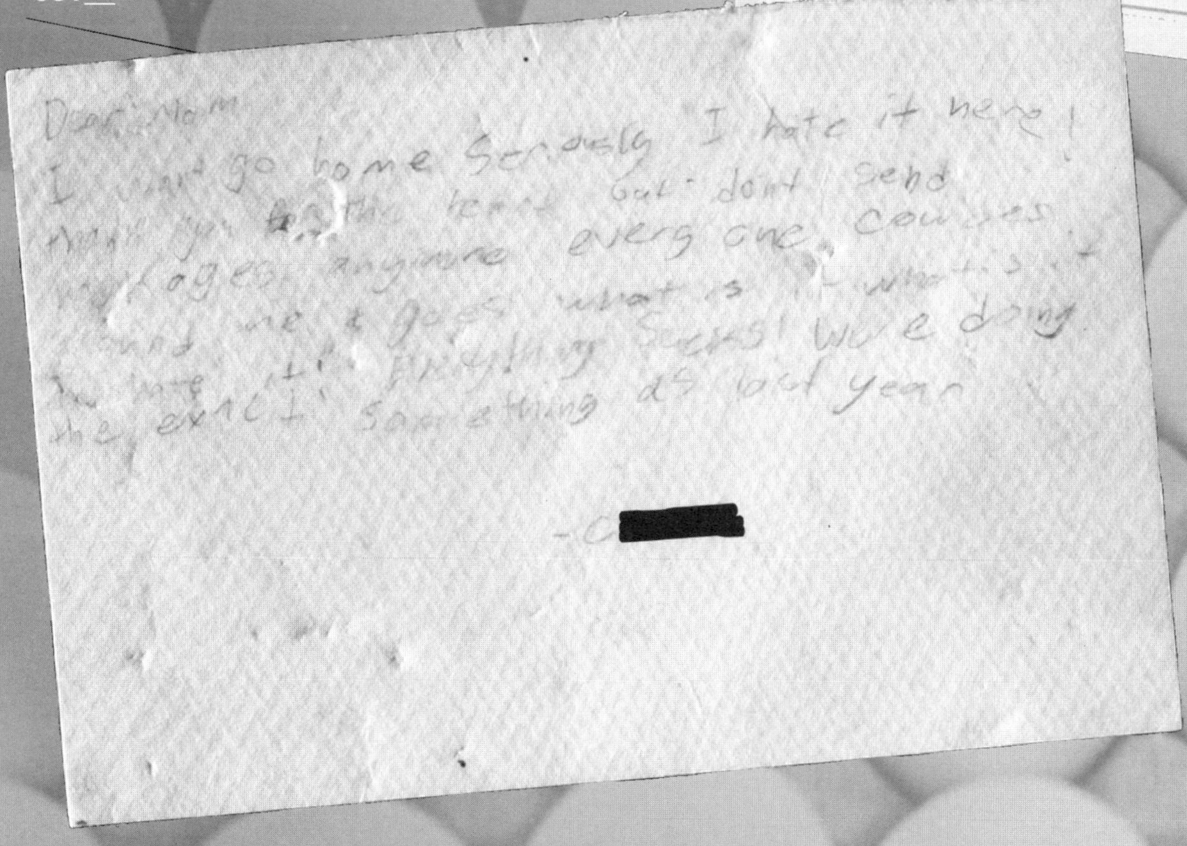
Dear: Mom
I want go home Seriously I hate it here!
thank you for the heart but dont send
packages anymore every one crowdes
around me & goes what is it what is it
I hate it! Everything Sucks! Were doing
the exact samething as last year

—C[redacted]

[left] Found by Meluna W. on the west sound of Orcas Island, WA.
3⅞" x 6", pencil on watercolor paper

LOVE STORY

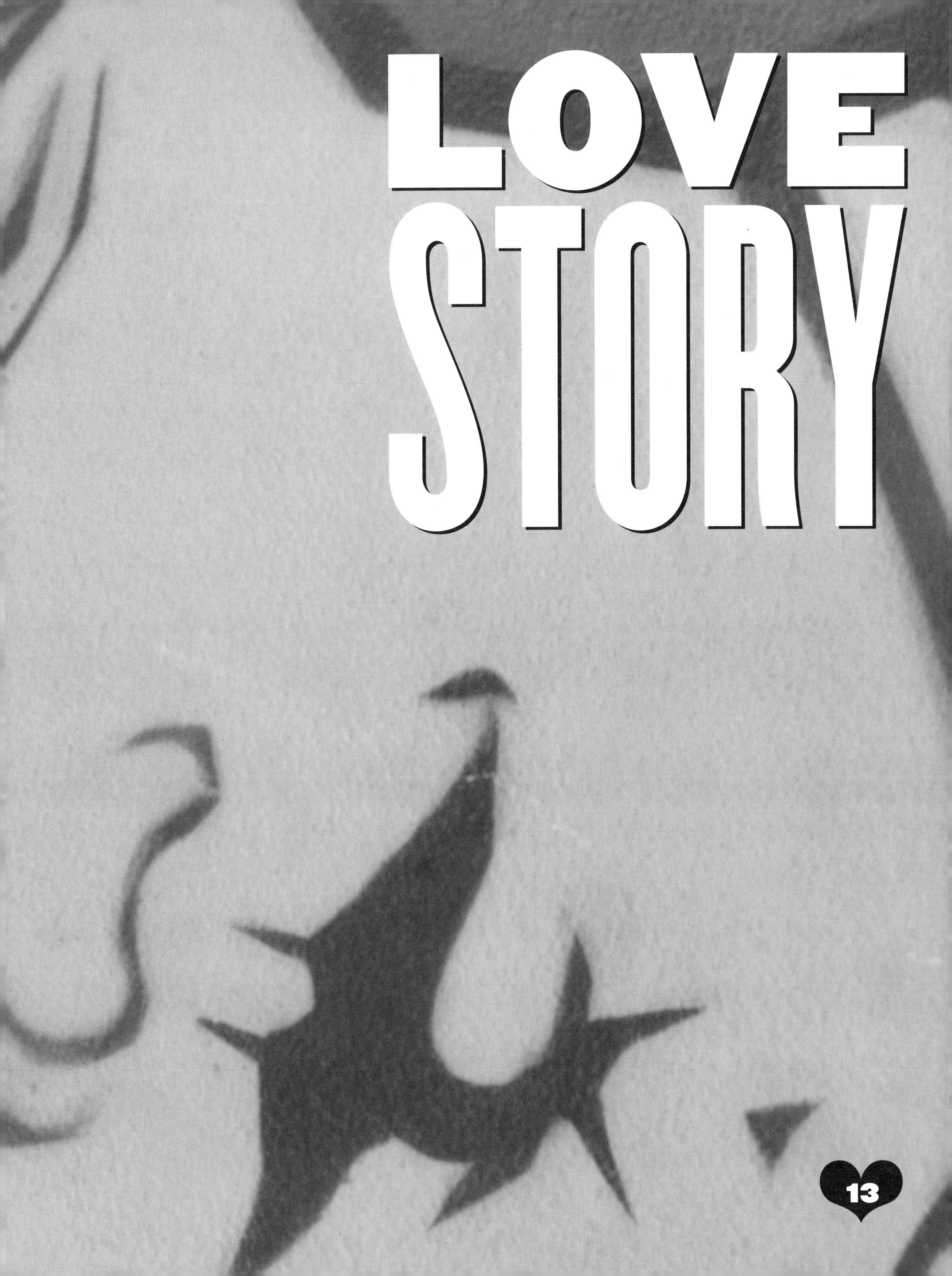

My love,

We're watching a movie called "Birdie" in psychology class and it's really neat so far. I like it quite alot. I love you. I love having you tell me about what the future will be like and how we'll live and how sweet it will be. I can't believe we've been together nearly 3 months. We basically started being together 2 days before your birthday and now it's April. It doesn't seem that long but at the same time I can't remember a time without you, without loving you. I'm trying to improve my handwriting and make it slightly less sprawling. 25 more minutes of class, or maybe 30 minutes. I miss you. Tie me down to your bed, legs spread, thighs trembling. Fuck me whenever you wish, you don't have to ask if I want you, you know I always do. I'm such a good little slave that way, a perfect little slut for you, always wanting, always needy, always loving you. 3 more minutes of class. I need to get in shape, I feel flabby. B[redacted]in my psychology class has decided I'm his little submissive and we joke about him brainwashing me. But it's just joking because we both know I'm yours, all of me. Take me anyway you choose, twist my nipples till I can barely even breathe and I want your hand stroking me between my leg, up to my clit, down inside me and back up again, like Sunday evening and your other hand wrapped around my throat tighter until I come, no breath to moan or make a sound. Then afterwards being wrapped up tight in your arms, safe and sweet gasping for breath my body relaxed, cunt still tingling slightly while you tell me pretty things and I never want to move again. I love you. I really do, very much. My nail polish has all chipped off. Let me be your slave forever.

love,

C[redacted]. or whatever you choose to call me

P.S. I love you humiliating me, shaming me w/ my own actions. Like last night, I'm still ashamed but I loved every second of your power over me.

P.P.S. I need your help on an english paper this weekend, if you have time. I love you.

My Love,
We're watching a movie called "Birdie" in psychology class and it's really neat so far. I like it quite alot. I love you. I love having you tell me about what the future will be like and how we'll live and how sweet it will be. I can't believe we've been together nearly 3 months. We basically started being together 2 days before your birthday and now it's April. It doesn't seem that long but at the same time I can't remember a time without you, without loving you. I'm trying to improve my handwriting and make it slightly less sprawling. 25 more minutes of class, or maybe 30 minutes. I miss you. Tie me down to your bed, legs spread, thighs trembling. Take me whenever you wish, you don't have to ask if I want you, you know I always do. I'm such a good little slave that way, a perfect little slut for you, always wanting, always needy, always loving you. 3 more minutes of class. I need to get in shape, I feel flabby. B__[m] in my psychology class has decided I'm his little submissive and we joke about him brain washing me. But it's just joking because we both know I'm yours, all of me. Take me anyway you choose, twist my nipples till I can barely even breathe and I want your hand stroking me between my leg, up to my clit, down inside me and back up again, like Sunday evening and your other hand wrapped around my throat tighter until I come, no breath to moan or make a sound. Then afterwards being wrapped up tight in your arms, safe and sweet gasping for breath my body relaxed, cunt still tingling slightly while you tell me pretty things and I never want to move again. I love you. I really do, very much. My nail polish has all chipped off. Let me be your slave forever.

love,
C_______ [f], or whatever you choose to call me my love.

P.S. I love you humiliating me, shaming me w/ my own actions. Like last night, I'm still ashamed but I loved every second of your power over me.

P.P.S. I need your help on an english paper this weekend, if you have time. I love you.

Found by an anonymous conspirator in a briefacse left at a store in Portland, OR.
8½" x 11", black rollerball ink on yellow notebook paper

C [redacted]
480
5555 783
I Want You To Know That
I Care About You Alot, And I Don't
Want Us To Break Up. I Will Give You
What You Want With No Strings Attach
-ed And That We Can Work This Out.
If Time + Space Is What You Want, Just
Think Of All The Good Times We Have
Had Talking On The Phone. You Make
Me Laugh When I Need A Good Laugh
And You Make Me Cry When You +
I Have A Difference Of Opinions
And Don't Understand Why. I Don't
Want Us To Break Up Since You
Make me Very Happy, And I Make
You Happy Too. I Need You To Know
That When We Talk About Our
Pasts That We Don't Need To Ruin
The Futures We Can Create With
Each Other's Dreams + Ambitions. Please
Don't Break With Me Since We Both
Have Had Terrible Pasts, And We Can
New Beginnings For You And I. Please
C [redacted] Give Me One Last Chance BC/
U Say Were Thru I Know I Dr U Crzy
Its The Best That I Can Do

Found under the Burnside Bridge in Portland, OR, by Peter N.
3⅝" x 8", blue rollerball ink on back of green spiral notebook cover

480
5555
783

C______[f],

I Want You To Know That I Care About You Alot, And I Don't Want Us To Break Up. I Will Give You What You Want With No Strings Attach-ed And That We Can Work This Out. If Time + Space Is What You Want, Just Think Of All The Good Times We Have Had Talking On The Phone. You Make Me Laugh When I Need A Good Laugh And You Make Me Cry When You + I Have A Difference Of Opinions And Don't Understand Why. I Don't Want Us To Break Up Since You make me very Happy, And I make You Happy Too. I Need You To Know That When We Talk About Our Pasts That We Don't Need To Ruin The Futures We Can Create With Each Other's Dreams + Ambitions. Please Don't Break ↑ With Me Since We Both Have Had Terrible Pasts, And We Can New Beginnings For You And I. Please C______[f], Give Me One Last Chance BC/ U Say Were Thru I Know I Dr U Crzy its The Best That I Can Do

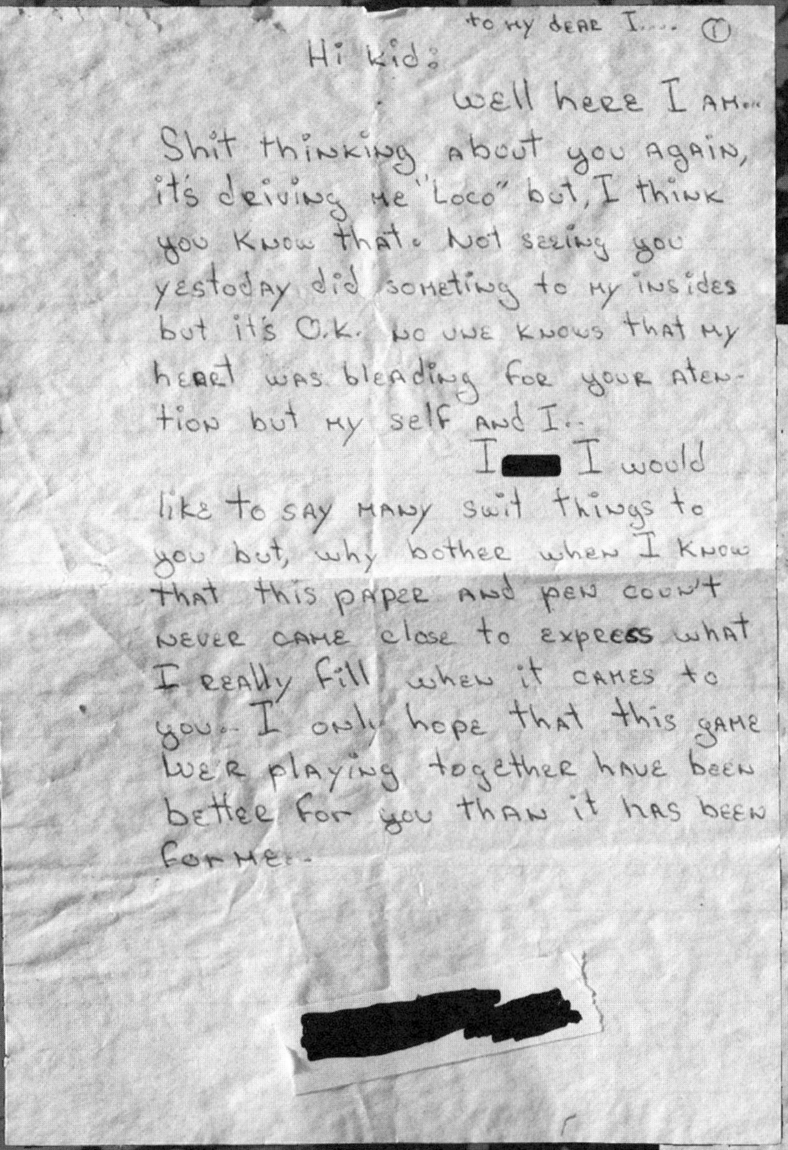
to my dear I.... ①

Hi kid:

well here I am...

Shit thinking about you again, it's driving me "Loco" but, I think you know that. Not seeing you yestoday did someting to my insides but it's O.K. no une knows that my heart was bleading for your aten-tion but my self and I..

I [redacted] I would like to say many swit things to you but, why bothee when I know that this paper and pen coun't never came close to express what I really fill when it cames to you.. I only hope that this game we'r playing together have been bettee for you than it has been for me..

[redacted]

[front]

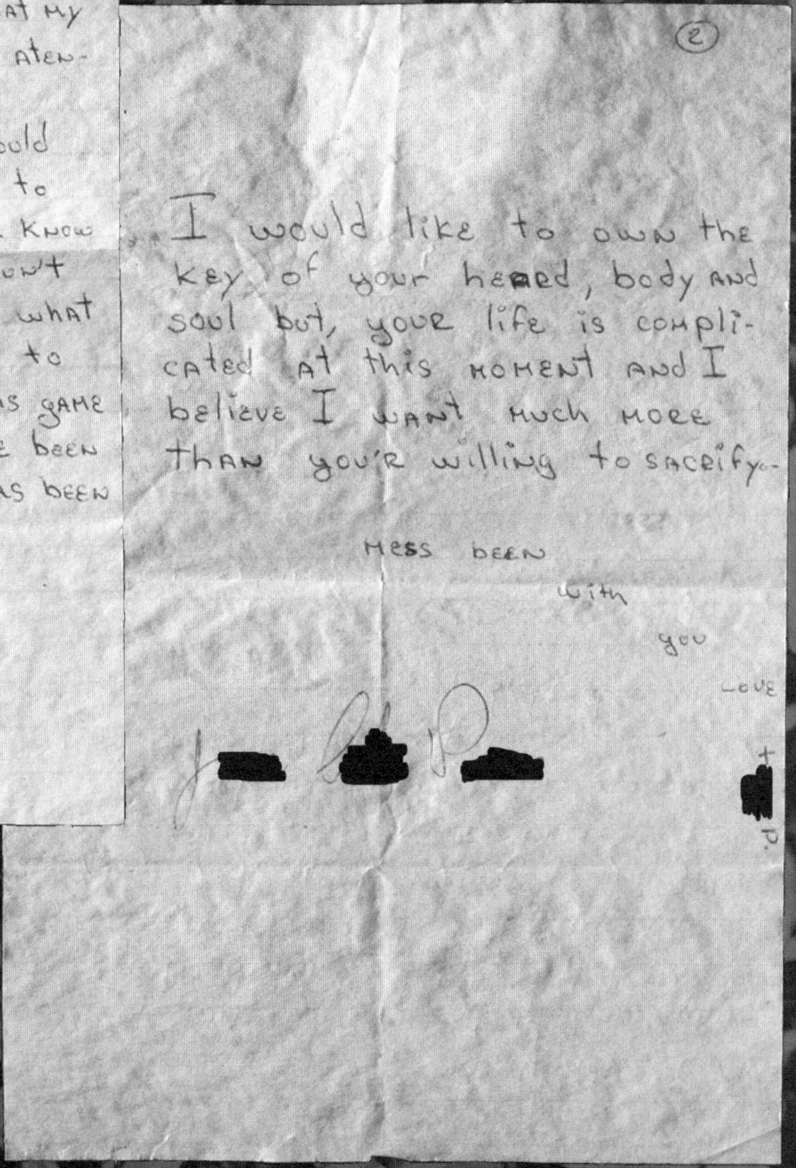
②

I would like to own the key of your heard, body and soul but, your life is compli-cated at this moment and I believe I want much more than you'r willing to sacrify..

mess been with you love

[redacted] P [redacted]

T [redacted] P.

Found by David Anthony in Seattle, WA.
4⅞" x 7⅛", blue ballpoint pen on yellow notepaper

[back]

[front]
to my dear I.... ①
Hi kid: Well here I am...

Shit thinking about you again, it's driving me "Loco" but, I think you Know that. Not seeing you yestoday did someting to my insides but it's O.k. no une knows that my heart was bleading for your aten-tion but my self and I..

I___[m] I would like to say many swit things to you but, why bother when I know that this paper and pen coun't never came close to express what I really fill when it cames to you.. I only hope that this game we'r playing together have been better for you than it has been for me..

[back]
②
I would like to own the key of your heard, body and soul but, your life is compli-cated at this moment and I believe I want much more than you'r willing to sacrify..
mess been with you love T___[m] P.
[illegible signature]

Found by Diana L. in a Mukilteo, WA, high school library.
$7\frac{5}{8}$" x $10\frac{7}{16}$", lime green felt marker on spiral notebook paper

K____[m],
I am sorry that your mad at me. you said that what you did at the game was just a joke. I didn't think it was funny. It hurt me alot. I also don't appreciate your calling me a reject or an idiot all the time. I thought that you were just going through a phase and that it would pass. If you don't want to be my boyfriend can we at least be friends rather than enemies? I don't want to loose you as a friend. Sorry for anything I did wrong

A______[m]

K[redacted],

I am sorry that your mad at me.
You said that what you did at
the game was just a joke. I
didn't think it was funny. It
hurt me alot. I also don't
appreciate you calling me a
reject or an idiot all the time.
I thought that you were just
going through a phase and
I thought it would pass. If you
don't want to be my boyfriend
can we at least be friends rather
than enemies? I don't want to
loose you as a friend.
Sorry for any thing I did wrong

[redacted]

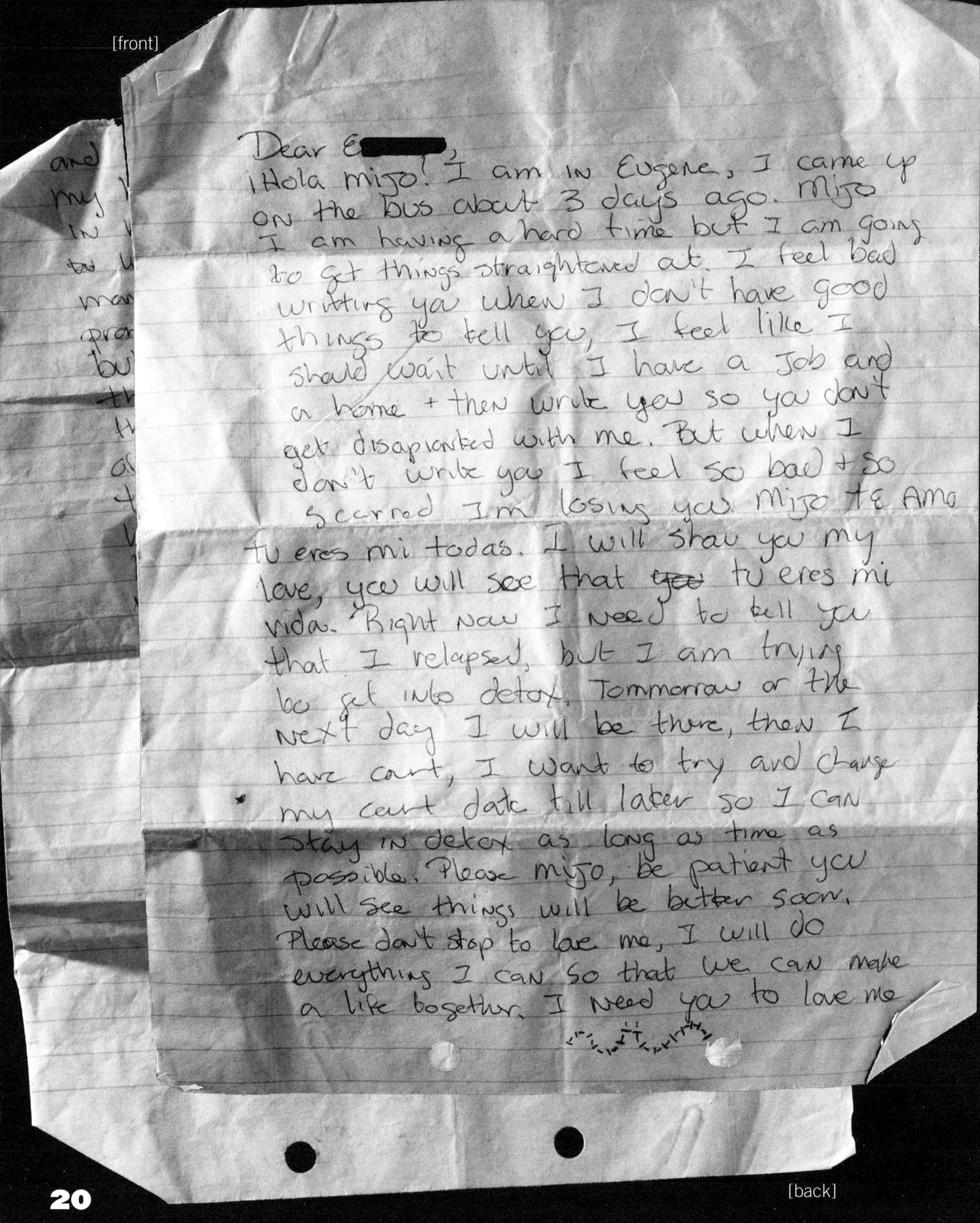

Dear [redacted],
¡Hola mijo! I am in Eugene, I came up on the bus about 3 days ago. Mijo I am having a hard time but I am going to get things straightened out. I feel bad writting you when I don't have good things to tell you, I feel like I should wait until I have a job and a home + then write you so you don't get disapionted with me. But when I don't write you I feel so bad + so scarred I'm losing you. Mijo te amo tu eres mi todas. I will show you my love, you will see that ~~you~~ tu eres mi vida. Right now I need to tell you that I relapsed, but I am trying to get into detox. Tommorrow or the next day I will be there, then I have court, I want to try and change my court date till later so I can stay in detox as long as time as possible. Please mijo, be patient you will see things will be better soon. Please don't stop to love me, I will do everything I can so that we can make a life together. I need you to love me

[back]

[front]
Dear E_____[m],
¡Hola Mijo! I am in Eugene, I came up on the bus about 3 days ago. Mijo I am having a hard time but I am going to get things straightened out. I feel bad writting you when I don't have good things to tell you, I feel like I should wait until I have a Job and a home + then write you so you don't get disapionted with me. But when I don't write you I feel so bad + so scarred Im losing you. Mijo te amo to eres mi todas. I will Show you my love, you will see that ~~you~~ tu eres mi vida. Right now I need to tell you that I relapsed, but I am trying to get into detox. Tommorrow or the next day I will be there, then I have court, I want to try and change my court date till later so I can Stay in detox as long as time as possible. Please mijo, be patient you will See things will be better soon. Please don't stop to love me, I will do everything I can So that we can make a life together. I need you to love me

[back]
and know that I love you with all my heart. + I Need you to have faith in me. In one month I will be ~~w~~ working, sending you money; saving money for our life in Mexico. I promise. I know you are tired of this but life is hard out hear, try to understand that I am trying my best but sometimes things ar to strong times. I ~~will~~ think of you every minut of every day there is NOT a moment that goes but that I dont think of you. I Love you so much, I will Show you. Give me one month to get my life ~~straig~~ put back together, will Will be together soon + make a beautiful family. that is all I want in this life, to be with you.

Love
R______ [f]
Mama
XOX

Found by Andrew C. at a mall in downtown Eugene, OR.
8 3/8" x 10 15/16", blue ballpoint pen on yellow notebook paper

A[redacted]

Hi babe, Just a few lines to
say thanks for everything that you
have been doing B[redacted] and D[redacted] Put
22^{00} on my books but I'm sure
you already know that. I am in the
Middle of Playing cards so I'll be in
and out... :) I'm back.. do ya miss
Dad :)? Well Another day with out the
Hearings officer.. makes 18 days so far.
it Don't Really mater through. I Exsept
to do 30 days bear min anyways...
Hey look at it this way I'll be in
some what good shape and Drug free
and A clean head.

Well baby this is going to be
short but At least I wrote Ha?
Keep telling baby that I love her
and miss her! And Really Keep tell-
ing yourslef that I love you. Well
thats About All for now love.

Keep writing Bitch.

Loving olny you
two! XXX
B

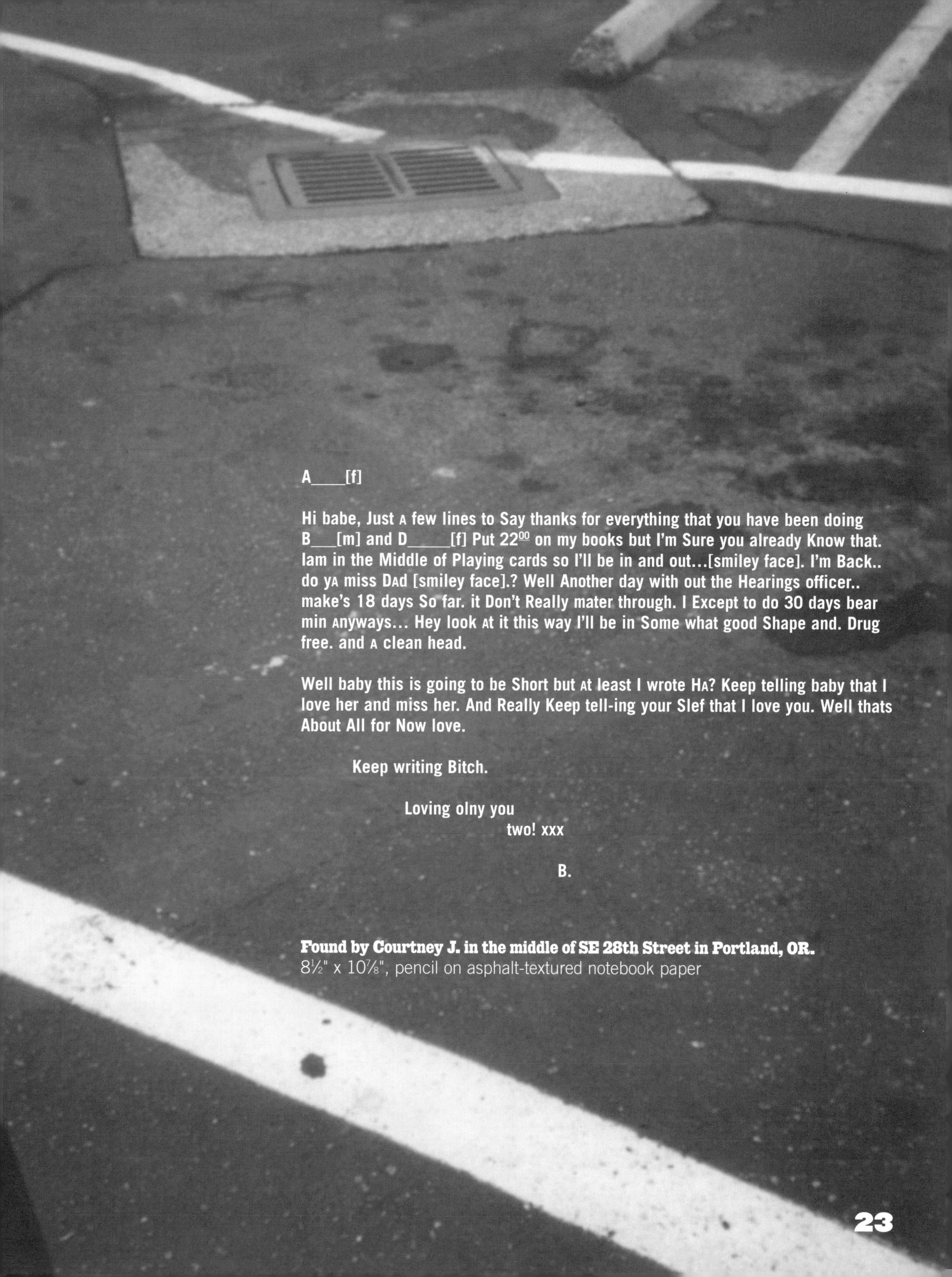

A____[f]

Hi babe, Just A few lines to Say thanks for everything that you have been doing B___[m] and D_____[f] Put 22^{00} on my books but I'm Sure you already Know that. Iam in the Middle of Playing cards so I'll be in and out…[smiley face]. I'm Back.. do yA miss DAd [smiley face].? Well Another day with out the Hearings officer.. make's 18 days So far. it Don't Really mater through. I Except to do 30 days bear min Anyways… Hey look At it this way I'll be in Some what good Shape and. Drug free. and A clean head.

Well baby this is going to be Short but At least I wrote HA? Keep telling baby that I love her and miss her. And Really Keep tell-ing your Slef that I love you. Well thats About All for Now love.

Keep writing Bitch.

Loving olny you
two! xxx

B.

Found by Courtney J. in the middle of SE 28th Street in Portland, OR.
8½" x 10⅞", pencil on asphalt-textured notebook paper

[outside, not shown]
Just ReAD it. Then RiP it up. ImportANT. RiP up After reADING

[inside]
[page 1]
FucK, whAt cAN sAy? Exept I'm truly Sorry. I know you doN't wANt to talk to me. You probaly want to Kill, I Almost wANT to do my self iN. I got so much to sAy.. I wish I could SAy it to your pretty fAce. I wANt to explAiN why whAt hAppeNed, hAppeNed, but it tAke About a million pieces of pAper to write it dowN, And I would get hAND crAmps + thAt would suck. I thiNk you need heAr whAt I got to sAy. It's goNNA be Awhile before you'll tAlk to me AgAiN. I know. I doN't blAme you. ~~¥~~ you didn't deserve WhAt I (+ those girls) did to you. KNow one does, but especially you. You were nothiNg but nice + cAriNg to me, + I cAre About you so much, too much I love you ~~for~~ for christ's sAke, And Not in thAt J.D. Sort of wAy. I don't Know, I just felt u~~m~~nwANted by you, undeserAble. You sAid yourself thAt you Still got the hots for T___[m] + we didn't hAve an intimAte reAlAtionship iN our future. ThAt hurt. It Also hurt that you sAid you wANted to hANg out w/ me 2 nights iN a Row but totAlly strAight up dissed me both nights. If you didn't wANt hANG out with me, you could of At voiced mAiled

[back of page 1]
me sAying so, So After you hurt me, I did I stupid, immAture thiNg, I told you about thAt Shit to get you bAck I guess. Stupid C____[m], FuckiNg stupid. I'm so mAD @ my Self. WhAt I did to you hAs hAppened to me on numerous occAssioNs. So I Know how your feeling, reAlly. ThAt's why I'm mADe @ myself. your so perfect + beutiful, considerAte, just plAiN fuckiNg Sweet. Why I did to you of All people, I'll never Know. I lost oNe of my fAvorite people in my life. I prAy we cAn be frieNDs AgAiN (I doN't eveN belive iN god) It won't be for A loNg time. unfortunAtly. Why the fuck did I do this to us. Fuck. Fuck. Fuck. Remember, It wAsN't All ~~be~~ me. their were ~~A~~other "pArties-" iNvolved. M___[m] to, I ~~did~~ don't wANt to crush his world to. you got to Atleast let me Know if he knows. Fuck. I wish I Could mAke you hAppy + vice versA. ~~yo~~ We both deserve it. I wish I would hAve to you how much i liked (now love) you when it mAttered. I wish I could be w/ you + ~~wh~~ I wish thAt stupid shit nevered hAppened. There's nothiNg I cAN do except hope thAt you cAN, somewhere, deep down inside, forgive me. SomedAy will never come soon enough.

[page 2]
I'm reAlly fuckiNg hurt to. pissed off @ my imAture jeAlousy. I never felt for ANYONE truly, ANyoNe the way I feel for you. I'll quit cAlliNg + pAgiNg you from ~~k~~now oN. I Know its to sooN to tAlk. Sorry I'm so ANNoyiNg Just remember I'm hurt, seriously wouNDED Also. I will AlwAys love + rember you. I promise.

Νew tune
— S o r r y —
–How do SAy you'Re Sorry
How do you Apologize
How do you run bAck iN the Arm
you never should have Left lAst night
How cAN I mAke this go AwAy?
How could I give myself AwAy
How could I've been with some one
who's not you?
How Do you ~~Apologize~~ you sAy you're sorry
How Do you Apologiz
How could i tAke Someone so precious
AND Hurt her, this druNkeN guy
AND everything else wAs true
AND I'd do AnythiNg to prove it to you
ThAt I wAs drunk or Sober
I Still wANted you
So how do you SAy your sorry
To some oNe who better off
findiN ANother guy
AND everything else I sAiD wAs true
AND I'd do AnthiNg to prove to you
If I was druuk or sober It still would hAve bee you
♥–C____[m]

[reply]
Dearest C____[m] + your pack of Whores. . .
FUCK OFF
AND DIE.
Jesus hates you,
L___[f]

Found by someone too afraid to come forward.
Pages 1 and 2: 7⅞" x 10½", blue ballpoint ink and permanent black marker on spiral notebook paper
Reply: 3½" x 3½", orange felt-tip marker on offwhite notepaper

Fuck, what can I say? Except
I'm truly sorry. I know you
don't want to talk to me. You
probably want to kill. I almost
want to do myself in. I got
so much to say. I wish I could
say it to your pretty face. I want
to explain why what happened, happened
but it take about a million pieces of
paper to write it down, and I would
get hand cramps & that would suck.
I think you need hear what I got
to say. It's gonna be awhile before
you'll talk to me again. I know. &
don't blame you. You didn't deserve
what I (& those girls) did to you. Know
one does, but especially you. You were
nothing but nice & caring to me, &
I care about you so much. too much
I love you for christ's sake. And
not in that J.D. sort
Know. I just felt unwant
undiserable. You said you
you still got the hots f
we didn't have an intim
in our future. that h
hurt that you said you w
hang out w/ me 2 nigh
but totally straight up
nights. If you didn't wa
with me, you could of

ne,
I
you
cking
hat
how
sed
utiful,
ny
ter
ple
s
n't
"
eart
h

d o
it
way
&
its
own
woul
you

Dearest C[redacted]
& your pack of
whores...
FUCK OFF
AND DIE.
Jesus hates you,
L[redacted]

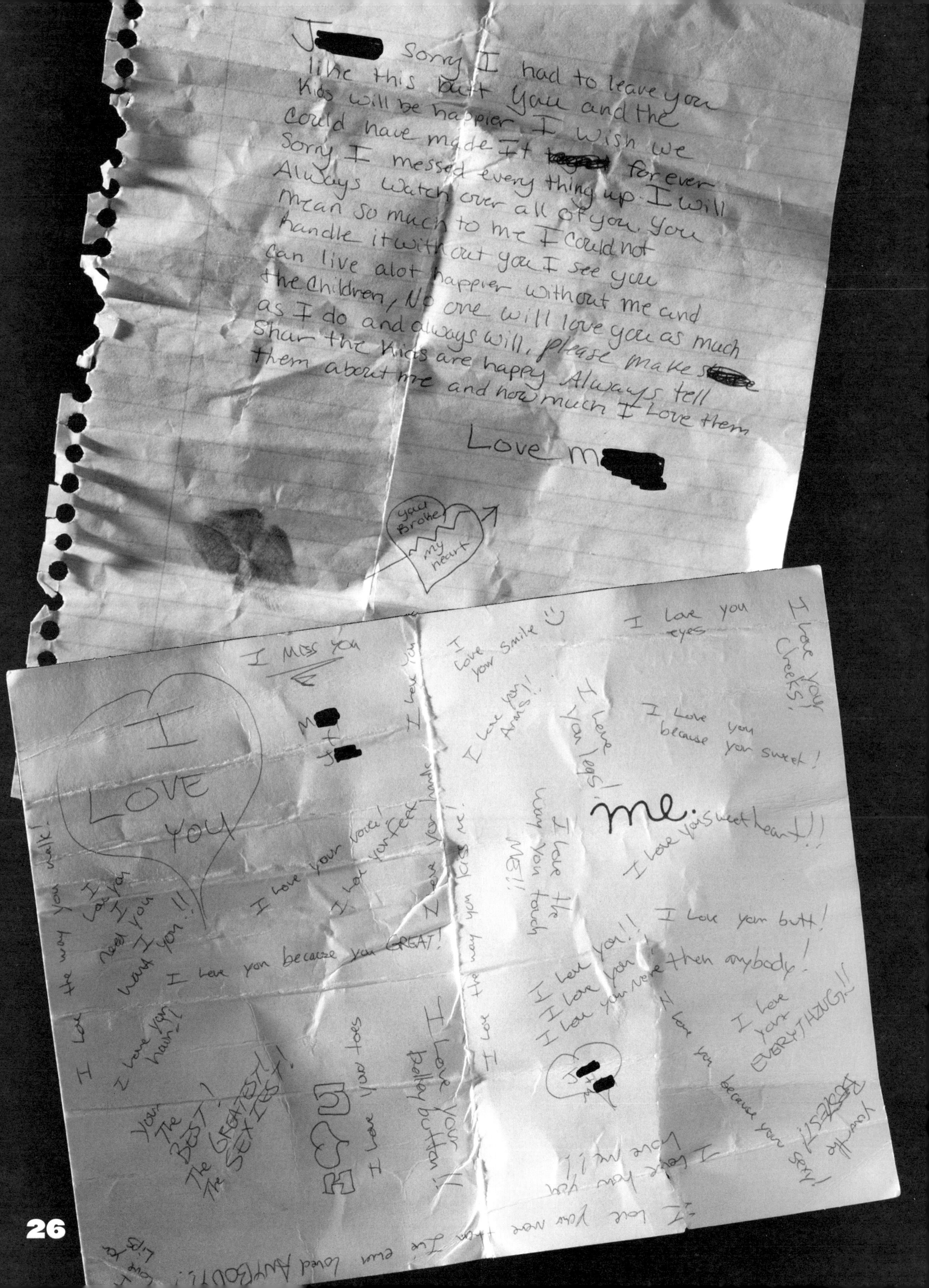

J[redacted] Sorry I had to leave you
like this but you and the
kids will be happier I wish we
could have made it [redacted] forever
Sorry I messed every thing up I will
Always watch over all of you. You
mean so much to me I could not
handle it without you I see you
can live alot happier without me and
the children, No one will love you as much
as I do and always will, please make s[redacted]
Shur the kids are happy Always tell
them about me and how much I Love them

Love M[redacted]

[Greeting card message]
What do you call someone who loves you?
me.

[handwritten messages inside card]
I LOVE YOU [inside a heart]...I MISS YOU...M____[f] + J____[m][written twice, each time within a heart]...I Love the way you walk!...I Love you I need you I want you!!...I Love your hair!!...I Love your voice!...I Love your feet...I Love you because you GREAT!...Your The BEST! The GREATEST! The SEXIEST!...I Love your Lips...I♥U...I Love your toes... I Love your belley button!!...I Love your smile [smiley face]...I Love you Arms!!...I Love you eyes...I Love your Cheeks!...I Love you legs!...I Love you because you sweet!... I Love the way you touch ME!!...I Love the way you Kiss me!...I Love you Sweetheart!!... I Love your butt!...I Love you!! I Love you!! I Love you more than anybody!...I Love your EVERYTHING!!...I Love you because your sexy!...Your the BESTEST!...I Love how you Love me!!...I Love you more than I've ever Loved ANYBODY!!

[letter]
J____[m] Sorry I had to leave you like this butt You and the Kids will be happier I wish we could have made It ~~toget~~ for ever Sorry I messed every thing up. I will Always Watch over all of you. You mean so much to me I Could not handle it without you I see you can live alot happier without me and the Children, No one will love you as much as I do and always will. Please make ~~shure~~ Shur the Kids are happy Always tell them about me and how much I Love them

Love M____[f]

[inside heart with zig zag arrow through it] you Broke my heart

[lipstick kiss]

Please tell my dad my Sisters my grandmas and everyone Else I love them

Tell j____[m] Im sorry I will miss him also

Found by Dug in Puyallup, WA.
Greeting card: $10\frac{11}{16}$" x $8\frac{1}{8}$", blue ballpoint pen on torn and folded greeting card
Letter: 8" x $10\frac{1}{4}$", black ballpoint pen and lipstick on spiral notebook paper

If Words Could Express
What you mean To ME or How
~~I~~You make me feel it Would be
as A poor man with 2 million-Dollars
or A chose between a Ford Station Wagon
aNd a Meceeds Benz

When You Were born people looked
at You and Said OH Shes so beautiful
they OOH and AAHED AS they Stared
At you at your Birth

Found by S. Solomon on Monday, August 25, 1997, at 6:00 a.m. near a bank on First Avenue South in Seattle, WA.
8½" x 10⅞", blue ballpoint pen on rainsoaked, white notebook paper

Nice meeting you! I took
this before I left
❤Call me!

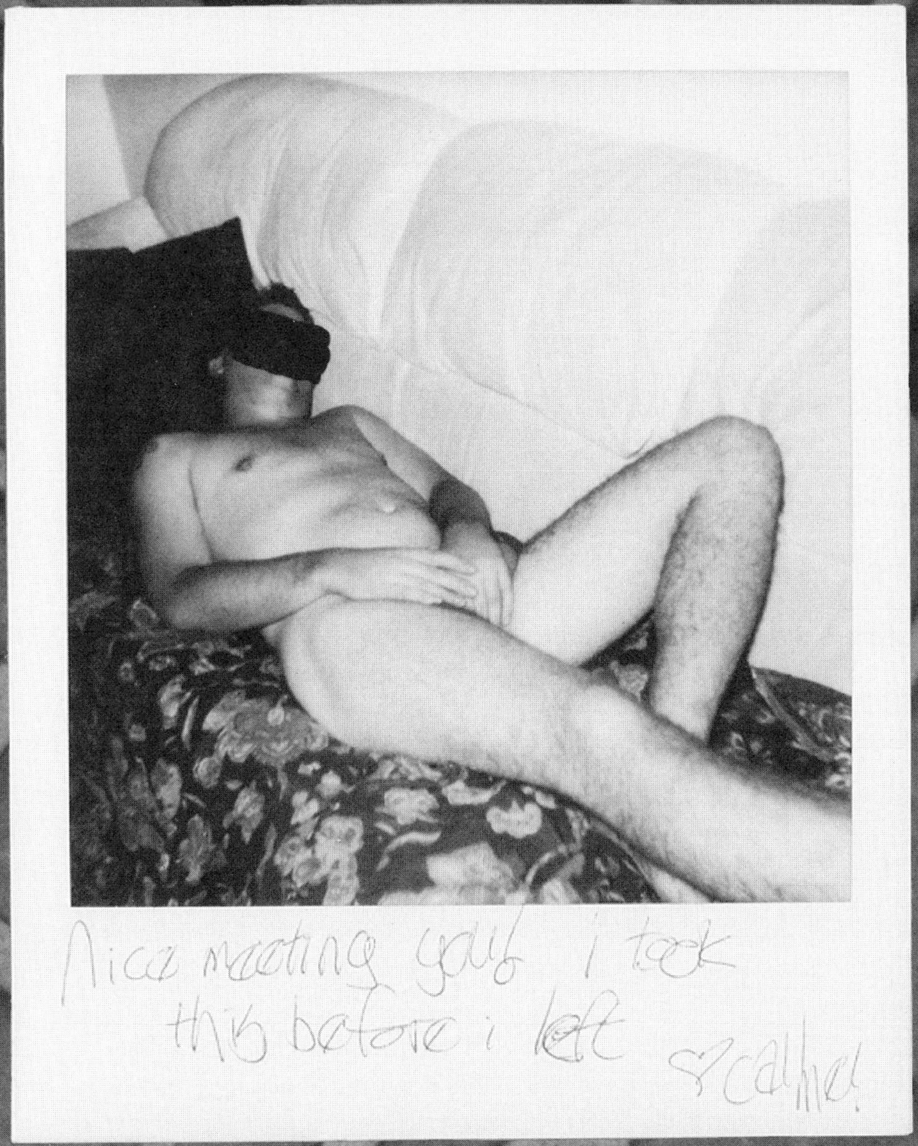

Found by Slap Pappy of Phoenix, AZ, in a paperback book he bought at a yard sale.
3½" x 4¼", color instant photo with writing in blue ballpoint pen

[front]
I
To: M____[f] 10:43.c.m. NiNE~SEVEN7⁰⁰
Saturday EVENiNG........

[First 14 words scribbled out] What's GoinG ON BabY~GirL? Ain't Shit GoinG ON MY waY. I didn't write You bac reaL QuiC. Cuz I had to ~~hu~~ HustlE UP ME a CouPLe "SheLL"s. Don't worry ~~th~~ thouGh. I Got Enouf to Last me till I hit the Yard. I don't liKe this Lil "whatever=Fuc it" attitude. but You aldedY → aPPoLiGized. so I won'T tRiP. Just don't Come ~~at~~ at me LiKE that no more. You Know what I meant bY "FLYin." You ain't Going nowhere well for a Second I Couldn't tell what the fuc was GoinG ON. WhY would You say there is another Reason behind all this? Shit just look how You have been Comin' at me LateLY. I ain't tRYin' to triP. Well be able to talk lil less than a month.What Kind of bull-shit has same MY waY? Just the Same as allwayz. I ain't ~~not~~ tRYin a ~~talk~~ SPeaK on it riGht now. So if I seem UPtiGht. don't thinK it → is Cuz of You. ALRiGHt. but I do Know that I'm not tryin'a arGue with You RiGht now. ~~You were mad~~ AlriGht?....... You were mad. so You maKe some wild ass coments. M____[f], all that does is uPset me even further. so I can say some → ← thinG that will Get You mad aGain. It's a NeVer EndinG CYcLe. You see what I'm sayin'? HEY, I see You ain't Put "Mrs. M____ S. D____[f]. but I Guess that's cuzz I didn't. When ~~I~~ we Get married and I Get uPset at You what am I Gonna do? Well I hoPE You don't do some shit liKE that aGain. [begin yellow highlighter] You tell me what's GoinG oN. we Can deal with it and move on. but when You attemPt to hide ~~from~~ Shit from me. it onLY multiPY's mY aNGeR. that ain't Good! Do You understand me, M____[f]? You told me everYthang in Your Last Letter huh? ALRiGht. droP it alriGht. Yes, that's fuced uP about that abortion shit. but as hard as it sounds. droP that. It's over No. I ~~wouldn't~~ wouldn't asK <u>MY</u> bitch to do that. or aNY bitch for that matter. So "I Shouldn't be ~~a~~ asKin' that of anY ~~bith~~ bitch Sides →

[back]
II
You that Shit" Damn. YouR a Possesive ~~lil~~ LiL thanG ain't You. [smiley face] Calm. down M____[f]. ain't nothinG to worry about. I don't Remember what I meant bY "I feel You. LooK at me." I 'member Sayin' it. Let me Know what I was sPeaKin' ON, alriGhts. Wow. Wow. hold on a second. ~~w~~Let's Get SomethinG straiGht. I don't Got "mY bitchez". I Got mY bitch. and that's You. Your mY Mutha-fucin' bitch. if You Got a Problem with it You Let me Know and You won't neveR have to woRRY about me Callin' MY bitch aGain in Your life. Is that understood? Fuc M____[f]. I don't LiKe fliPin' on You. but Shit You is Kicin' a dead horse. I done exPlaned this to You. You hurtin' YoursELf. Let that be for I fuccin-fliiP the fuc out. This is a dumb subject who, did I asK to maRRY? And ~~LooK~~ LooK who is trYina triP on me. [end yellow highlighter] but sinCE I can See You done worKed YouRself uP over nuthin'. I'ma do liKe I alwaYz do and exPLane Shit to You. Listen, and if You Got a broble with it, save it till I Get out for ouR best intrest Cuz I'm not in the mood for this ~~aG~~ ~~arGue~~ ~~argu~~ arGue in' sh throu a letter shit. AlriGht. Look I Could've just Lie and wouldn't be GoinG thru this Shit, but I ain't lied to You Yet so whY would. I've told You everY.thinG haven't I. Do You honestLY thinK that I would let Some bitch come between ~~me & me & m~~ me & You? ReGuardless of how Good the taLK was. M____[f], we've had some deeP conversations, and everYthinG I say to You is on the Serious tiP. Let me asK You a serious Question. I Know the answeR, ~~but~~ but do You? Do You have a lac of con → ← fidence with me M____[f]? You shouldn't worRY. If I told You not to write or talK or fuc with anY one, it would mean that I have a lac of confidence. that I was afraid that theY would taKe you away from me. If that haPPended it would onLY mean You were never mine. Do You under → ← stand what I'm saYin'. It's hard for me to taLK when I →

Found by Rick R. all crumpled up at a bus stop on Division Street in Portland, OR.
8⅜" x 10¾", black ballpoint pen, pencil and yellow highlighter on notebook paper

To: M[redacted] 10:43 p.m. Nine~Seven 7oo

Saturday Evening.......

[redacted] What's going on Baby~Girl? Ain't shit going on my way. I didn't write you for real doe cuz I had to [illegible] hustle wit me a couple shell's. Don't worry [illegible] though. I got enough to last me till I hit the yard. I don't like this lil "whatever~fuc it" attitude. But you already → [illegible] at me like that no more. You know what I meant by "Flip'in" you ain't going nowhere. But for a second I couldn't tell what the fuc was going on. Why would you say there is another reason behind all this? Shit just look how you have been comin' at me lately. I ain't tryin to trip. We'll be able to talk in less than a month. What kind of bull-shit has came my way? Just the same as allwayz. I ain't ~~not~~ tryina [illegible] speak on it right now. So if I seem uptight, don't think it is cuz of you. Alright. But I do know that I'm not tryina argue with you right now. ~~[illegible]~~ Alright?......

You were mad, so you make some wild ass comments. M[redacted] all that does is upset me even further so I can say some→ ←thing that will get you mad again. It's a never ending cycle. You see what I'm sayin? Yep I see you ain't put "Mrs. M[redacted] S.[redacted]. But I guess that's cuzz I didn't. When we get married and I get upset at you what am I gonna do? Well I hope you don't do some shit like that again. If you tell me what's going on. We can deal with it ~~[illegible]~~ and work out. But when you attempt to hide ~~[illegible]~~ shit from me it only makes it's my [illegible] that ain't good! Do you understand me M[redacted]? You told me everything in your last letter huh? Alright. [illegible] deal it alright. Yes. [illegible] fed up about that abortion shit. But as hard as it sounds. Drop that. It's over. No I ~~[illegible]~~ wouldn't ask my bitch to do that, or any bitch for that matter. So I shouldn't be askin' that of any ~~[illegible]~~ bitch sides Em→

←stand what I'm sayin'. It's hard for me to talk when I

HAVE I MARKED THIS UP ENOUGH

IN THIS [redacted]

[redacted], Darling, Lover,

you are the greatest friend I've ever had my [redacted] and grade you've made school for me so [redacted] in the spare time we have, your great as a [redacted] round person. We have to get together as mu[ch as we] can. THIS IS ANNOYING These past years have been really fu[n] by knowing you. As each year goes by the mo[re] ing it is. I wonder what our Senior year will [be] EVILE ☺ Even though we have had fights this year we always made up being instant be[st] friends. Well (changing the subject again) in the 6th grade we had [redacted] [redacted] & [redacted] [redacted] and in the 7th [redacted] now Bubba (just [redacted]) think Bubba [redacted]

THE "V" DICK JANE SPOT

SCHOOL DAYS

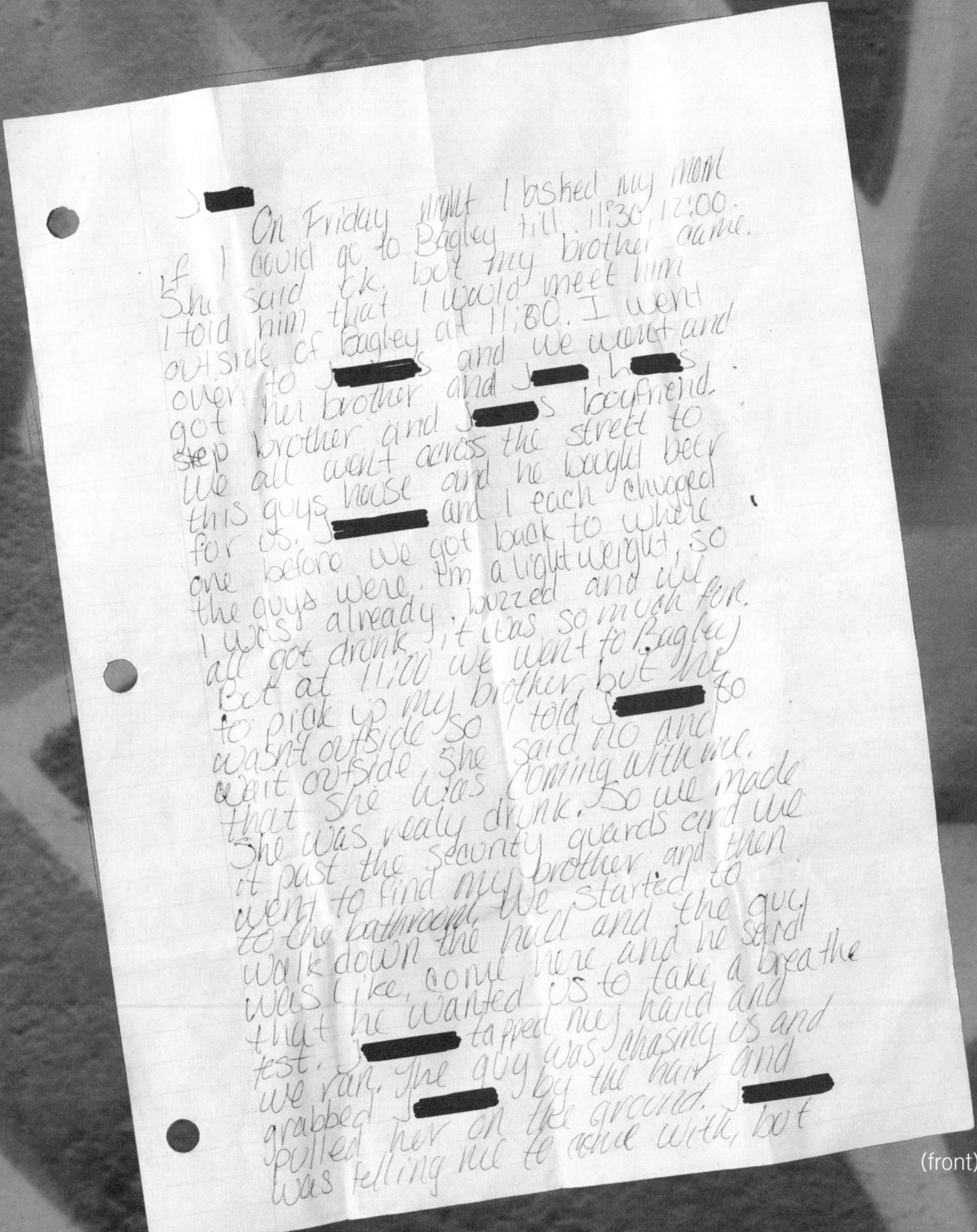

J[redacted]
On Friday night I asked my mom if I could go to Bagley till 11:30,12:00. She said ok. but my brother came. I told him that I would meet him outside of Bagley at 11:00. I went over to J[redacted]s and we went and got her brother and J[redacted], L[redacted]s step brother and J[redacted]s boyfriend. We all went across the street to this guys house and he bought beer for us. J[redacted] and I each chugged one before we got back to where the guys were. I'm a light weight, so I was already buzzed and we all got drunk, it was so much fun. But at 11:00 we went to Bagley to pick up my brother but he wasn't outside so I told J[redacted] to wait outside, she said no and that she was coming with me. She was realy drunk. So we made it past the security guards and we went to find my brother and then to the bathroom. We started to walk down the hall and the guy was Like, come here and he said that he wanted us to take a breathe test. J[redacted] tapped my hand and we ran. The guy was chasing us and grabbed J[redacted] by the hair and pulled her on the ground. J[redacted] was telling me to come with, but

(front)

J_____[f]

On Friday night I asked my mom if I could go to Bagley till 11:30,12:00. She said ok. but my brother came. I told him that I would meet him outside of Bagley at 11:00. I went over to J______'s[f] and we went and got her brother and J_____[m], L___'s[m] step brother and J______'s[f] boyfriend. We all went across the street to this guys house and he bought beer for us. J______[f] and I each chugged one before we got back to where the guys were. I'm a light weight, so I was already buzzed and we all got drunk it was so much fun. But at 11:00 we went to Bagley to pick up my brother but he wasn't outside so I told J______[f] to wait outside, she said no and that she was coming with me. She was realy drunk. So we made it past the security guards and we went to find my brother and then to the bathroom. We started to walk down the hall and the guy was Like, come here and he said that he wanted us to take a breathe test. J______[f] tapped my hand and we ran. The guy was chasing us and grabbed J______[f] by the hair and pulled her on the ground. J______[f] was telling me to come with, but

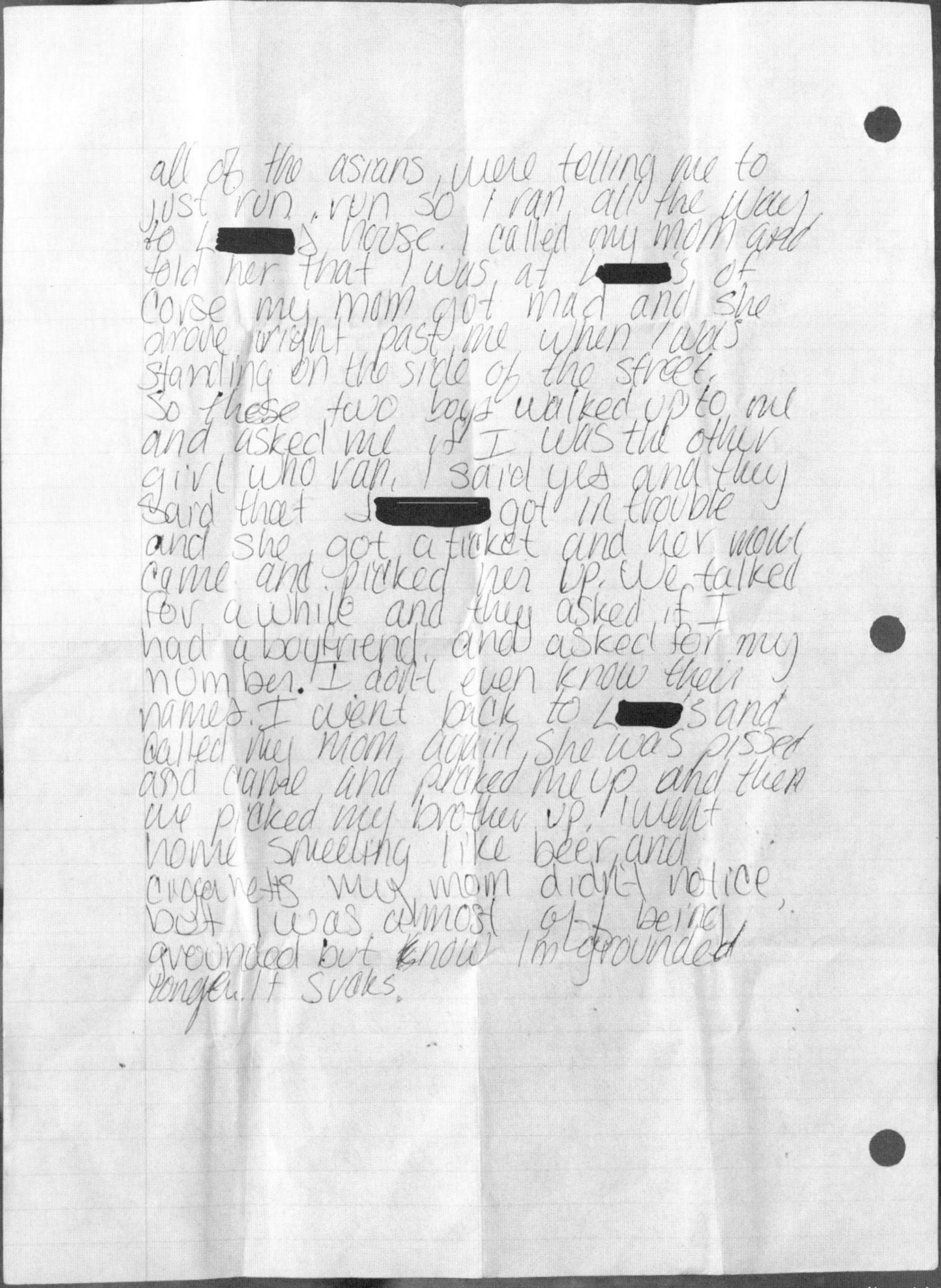
all of the asians, were telling me to
just run, run so I ran all the way
to [redacted]'s house. I called my mom and
told her that I was at [redacted]'s of
corse my mom got mad and she
drove wright past me when I was
standing on the side of the street.
So these two boys walked up to me
and asked me if I was the other
girl who ran. I said yes and they
said that [redacted] got in trouble
and she got a ticket and her mom
came and picked her up. We talked
for a while and they asked if I
had a boyfriend, and asked for my
number. I don't even know their
names. I went back to [redacted]'s and
called my mom again, she was pissed
and came and picked me up and then
we picked my brother up. I went
home smelling like beer and
cigaretts my mom didn't notice,
but I was almost off being
grounded but know I'm grounded
longer. It sucks.

(back)

all of the asians, were telling me just run, run so I ran all the way to L____'s[f] house. I called my mom and told her I was at L____'s[f] of corse my mom got mad and she drove right past me when I was standing on the side of the street. So these two boys walked up to me and asked me if I was the other girl who ran. I said yes and they said that J______[f] got in trouble and she got a ticket and her mom came and picked her up. We talked for a while and they asked if I had a boyfriend, and asked for my phone number. I don't even know their names. I went back to L____'s[f] and called my mom again she was pissed and came and picked me up and then we picked my brother up. I went home smelling like beer, and cigaretts my mom didn't notice, but I was almost off being grounded but know I'm grounded longer. It sucks.

Found by Joel S. at 2 a.m. on November 17, 1997, outside the front doors of a high school in Vancouver, WA.
8⅜" x 10¾", blue ballpoint pen on notebook paper

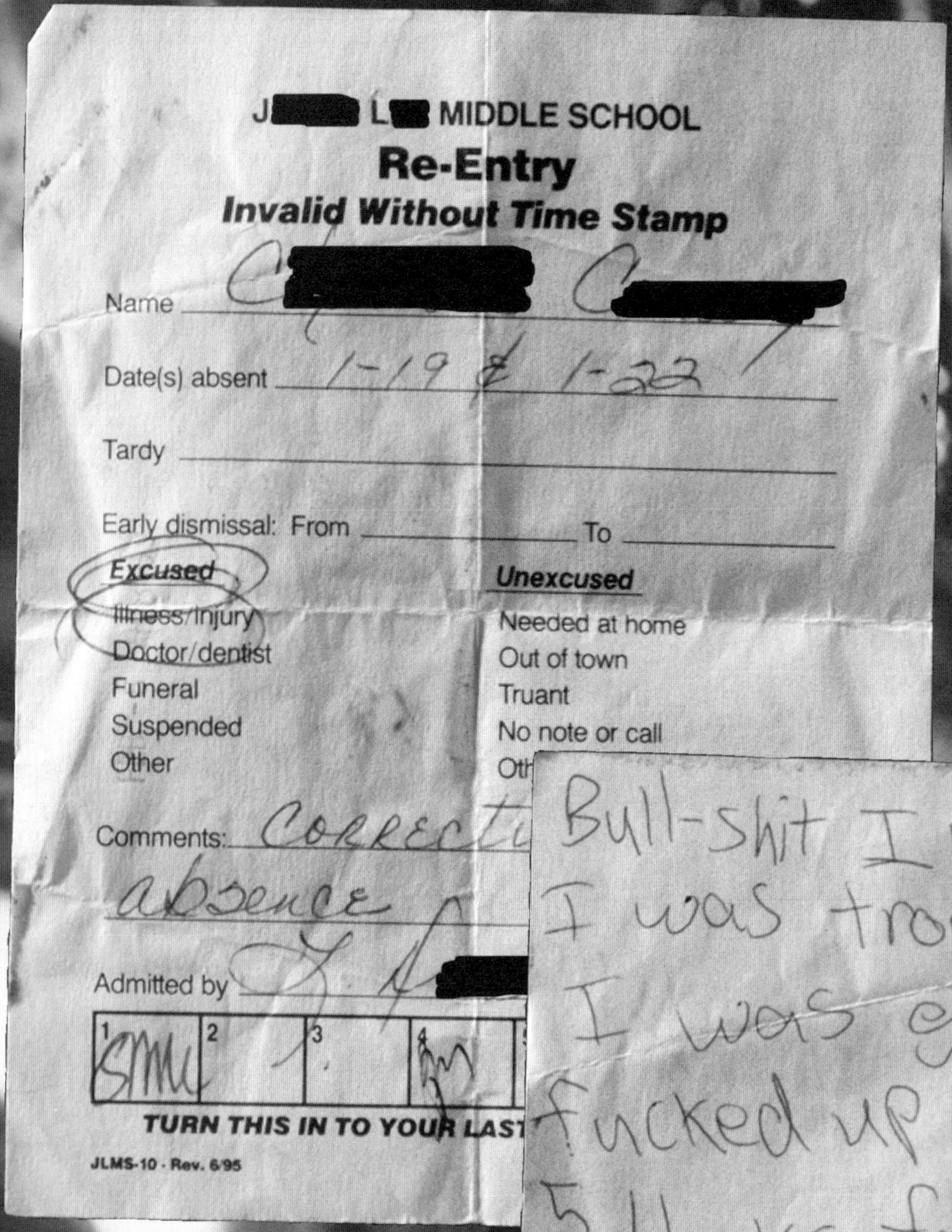

J[redacted] L[redacted] MIDDLE SCHOOL

Re-Entry

Invalid Without Time Stamp

Name C[redacted] C[redacted]

Date(s) absent 1-19 & 1-22

Tardy

Early dismissal: From ______ To ______

Excused	***Unexcused***
Illness/injury	Needed at home
Doctor/dentist	Out of town
Funeral	Truant
Suspended	No note or call
Other	Oth

Comments: CORRECTI… absence …

Admitted by [redacted]

1 SMW	2	3	4	

TURN THIS IN TO YOUR LAST

JLMS-10 - Rev. 6/95

(front)

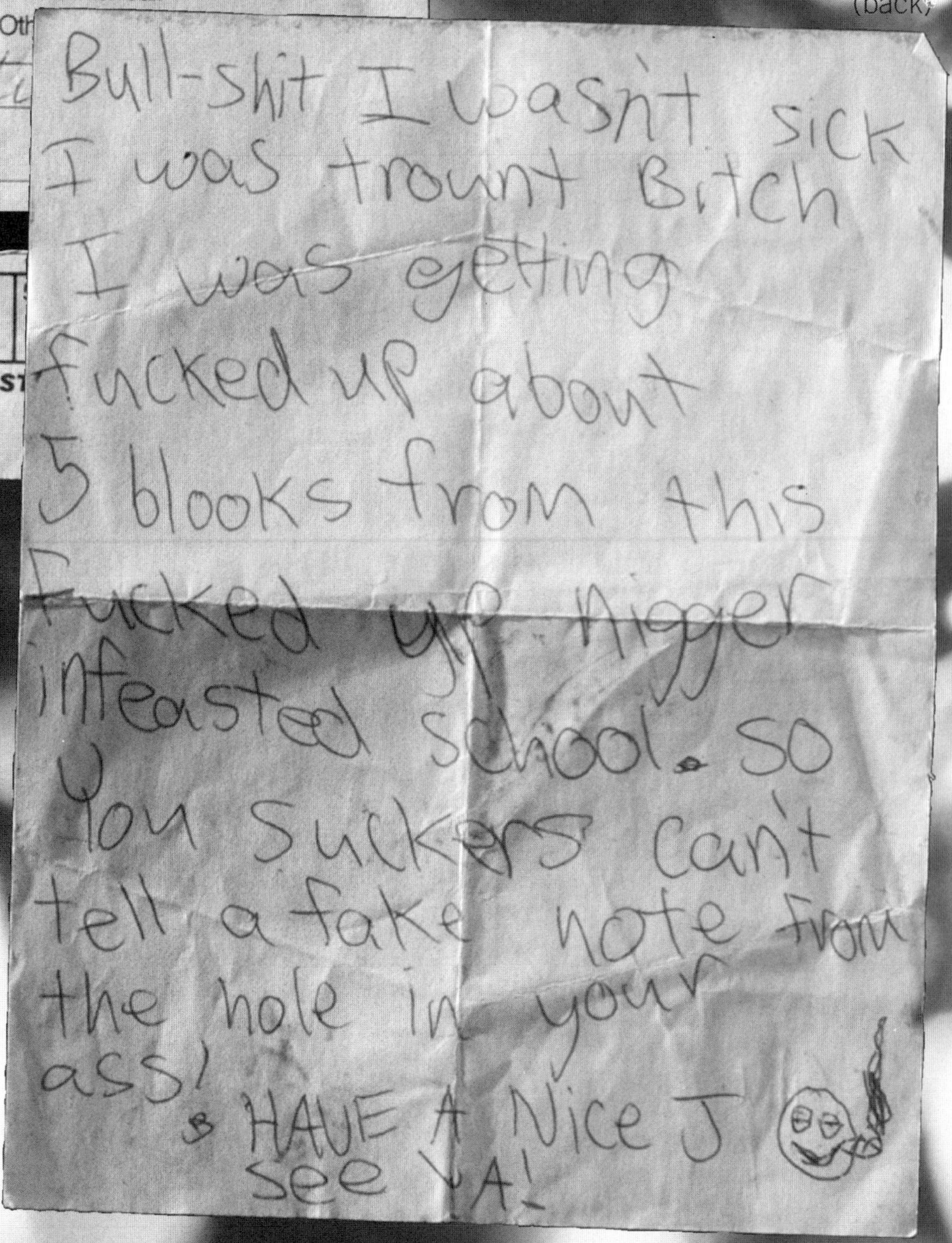

(back)

Bull-shit I wasn't sick
I was trount Bitch
I was getting
fucked up about
5 blooks from this
fucked up nigger
infeasted school. So
You suckers can't
tell a fake note from
the hole in your
ass!
HAVE A Nice J
see YA!

Found by Tony M. in the bathroom of an abandoned house in Tacoma, WA.
4¼" x 5½", black rollerball ink; blue, black and green ballpoint pen; and red-ink time stamp on preprinted white paper

hey sup? Nothin here. I love you, and I hope you don't break up with me. Do you want me to kiss you? yes or NO I'm doing silent reading
you are really fine [redacted] said you were cute but not fine and so I kicked her and got grounded. I love you so much and I can't tell you how much. I want to see you in the summer and talk to you on the phone. bye

I ♥ you

[redacted]
+
[redacted] forever

Love
[redacted]

Found by Linda A. on June 11, 1997, outside a fifth grade room at an elementary school in Toledo, WA.
8⅜" x 10¾", pencil on notebook paper

Sep. 30

Hey [redacted]

Sup Bitch! Not much w/ me, but I called [redacted] from lunch and told him about when you where getting mad cuz [redacted] and shit. He thinks you have feelings for him. I think he's cute, but once he talks, it ruins the whole thing! Don't cha agree? So your mom made you come to school today? Ha Ha! The play this morning was so stupid! So ya wanna get fucked up this weekend, and Tuesday? If we have to choose, I'd rather do it this weekend, but I don't know if [redacted] does. Well he still wants [redacted]s #, what a fag! If he talked to her, I would <u>never</u> talk to him again! I know you wouldn't either! [redacted]'s hair looks fucked up today! Laugh at him when ya see him! My brother said he would tell if I wore the Nikes, yeah and what am I wearing? That's what I thought, so Buck You [redacted]! Anywayz W/B soon!

♡ ya Alwayz

W/D

[redacted]

P.S. [redacted] said "Why did you call me a fucker"? I'm like sorry, I was just playin w/ you!

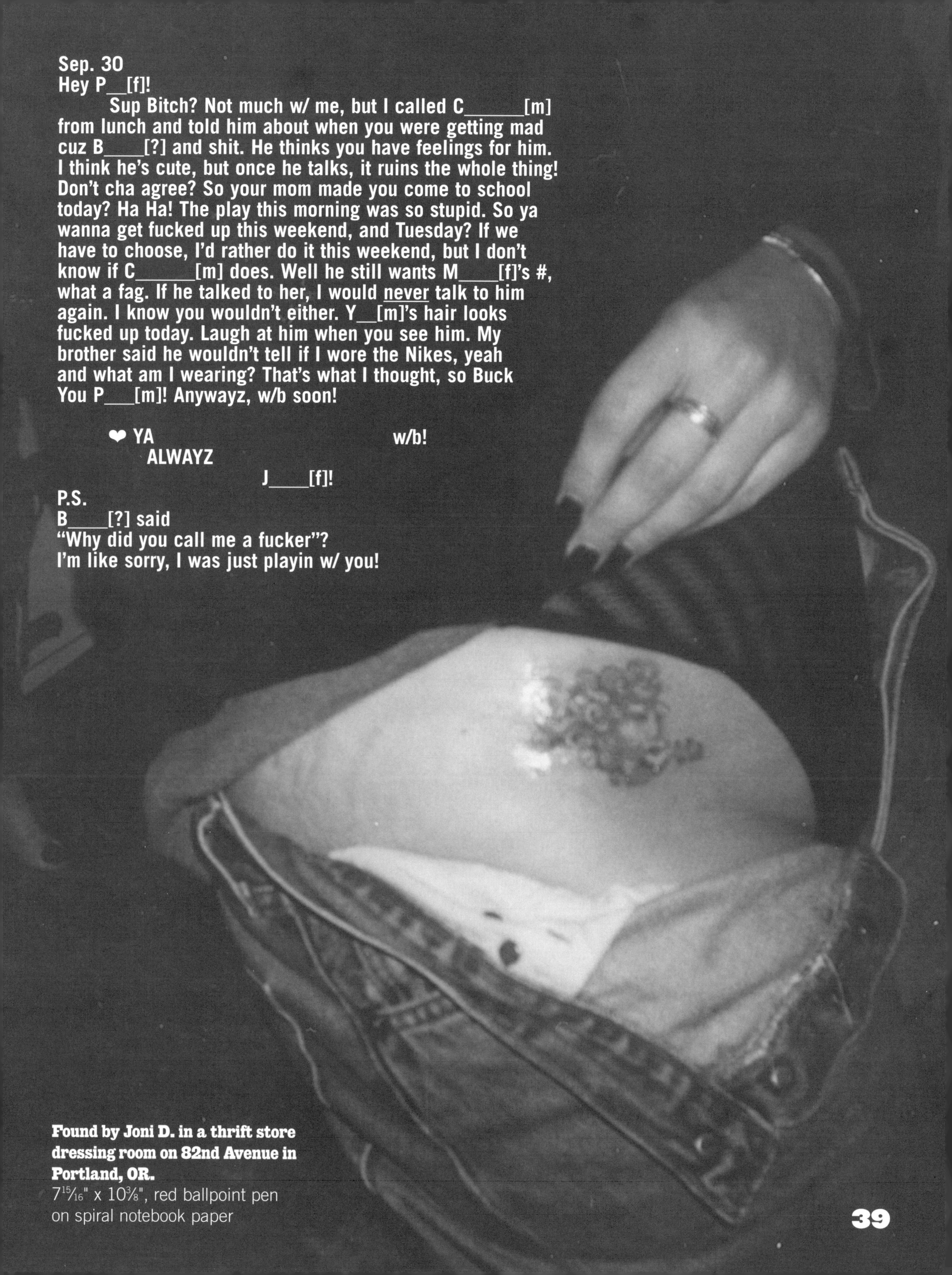

Sep. 30
Hey P__[f]!

Sup Bitch? Not much w/ me, but I called C______[m] from lunch and told him about when you were getting mad cuz B____[?] and shit. He thinks you have feelings for him. I think he's cute, but once he talks, it ruins the whole thing! Don't cha agree? So your mom made you come to school today? Ha Ha! The play this morning was so stupid. So ya wanna get fucked up this weekend, and Tuesday? If we have to choose, I'd rather do it this weekend, but I don't know if C______[m] does. Well he still wants M____[f]'s #, what a fag. If he talked to her, I would never talk to him again. I know you wouldn't either. Y__[m]'s hair looks fucked up today. Laugh at him when you see him. My brother said he wouldn't tell if I wore the Nikes, yeah and what am I wearing? That's what I thought, so Buck You P___[m]! Anywayz, w/b soon!

❤ YA ALWAYZ
w/b!
J____[f]!

P.S.
B____[?] said
"Why did you call me a fucker"?
I'm like sorry, I was just playin w/ you!

Found by Joni D. in a thrift store dressing room on 82nd Avenue in Portland, OR.
7 15/16" x 10 3/8", red ballpoint pen on spiral notebook paper

Found by BJ in Portland, OR.
8½" x 10⅞", pencil on notebook paper

Dear, J[redacted]

I exept your apology but what I don't exept is that you Kicked us out of the group and with out us it is not a group it is Sopose to be me t[redacted] and you but if you do want to Kick us out thats fine but its wrong but the reson i was mad at you yesterday is because you made me drop my purse and everything came out and I had to pick it all up and some things broke when it fell and then you had your nerve to ask me what happend and that is why I Said forget about me and you but i guess you did not hear me and I hate when you act stuped I like when your Sweet to me but you havent been for a while but I gots to go.

Love
A[redacted]

Dear, J_____[m]

I exept your apology but what I don't exept is that you Kicked us out of the group and with out us it is not a group it is Sopose to be me t___[?] and you but if you do want to Kick us out thats fine but its wrong but the reson i was mad at you yesterday is because you made me drop my purse and everything came out and I had to pick it all up and some things broke when it fell and then you had your nerve to ask me what happend and that is why I Said forget about me and you but i guess you did not hear me and I hate when you act stuped I like when your Sweet to me but you havent been for a while but I gots to go.

Love
A_____[f]

Hi J[redacted]
I am el loco I am gowing Insane.
I like the cats. Pepole around me
suck this hole class sucks. I am depressing
arint I. I Love you I go by by now.
Love A[redacted]

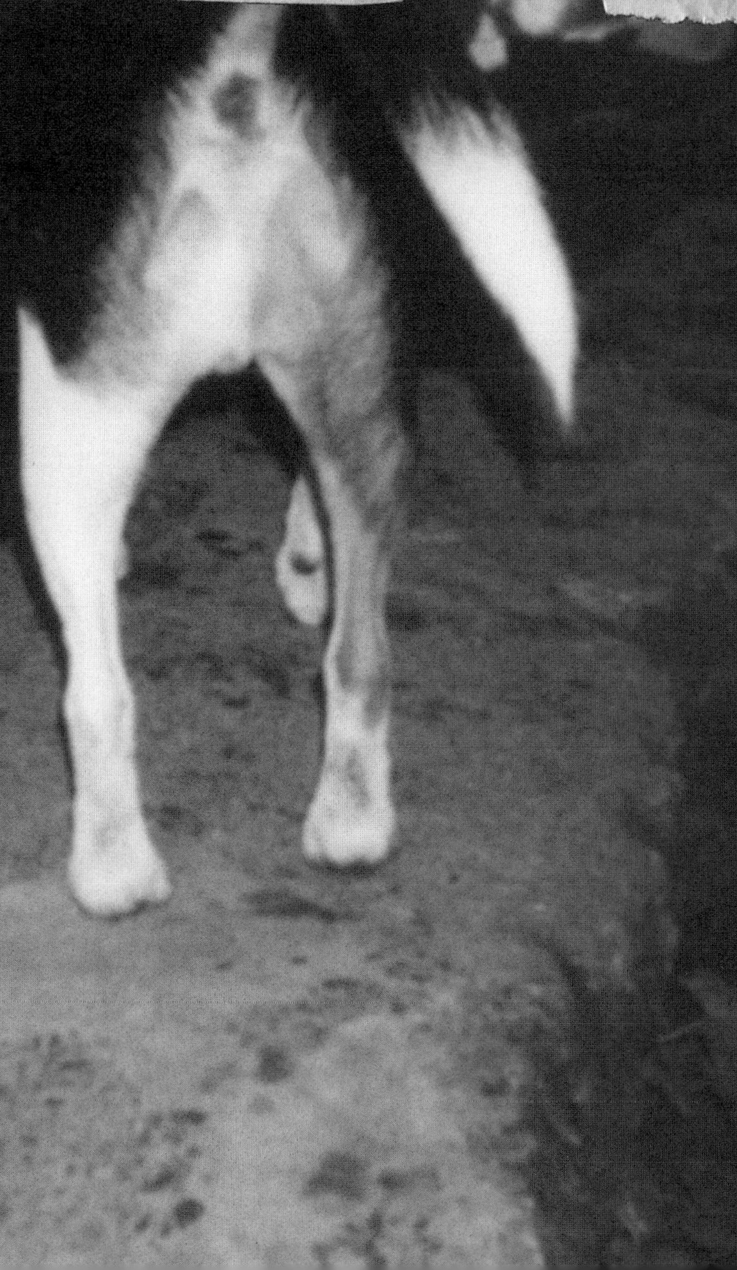

Hi J____[f]:
I am el loco I am gowing Insane. I like the cats. Pepole around me suck theis hole class sucks. I am depressing arint I. I Love you, I go by by now.

Love A____[m]

Found by Walker wedged in the door of a locker at a high school in Spokane, WA.
Approximately 8" x 5½", pencil on torn notebook paper

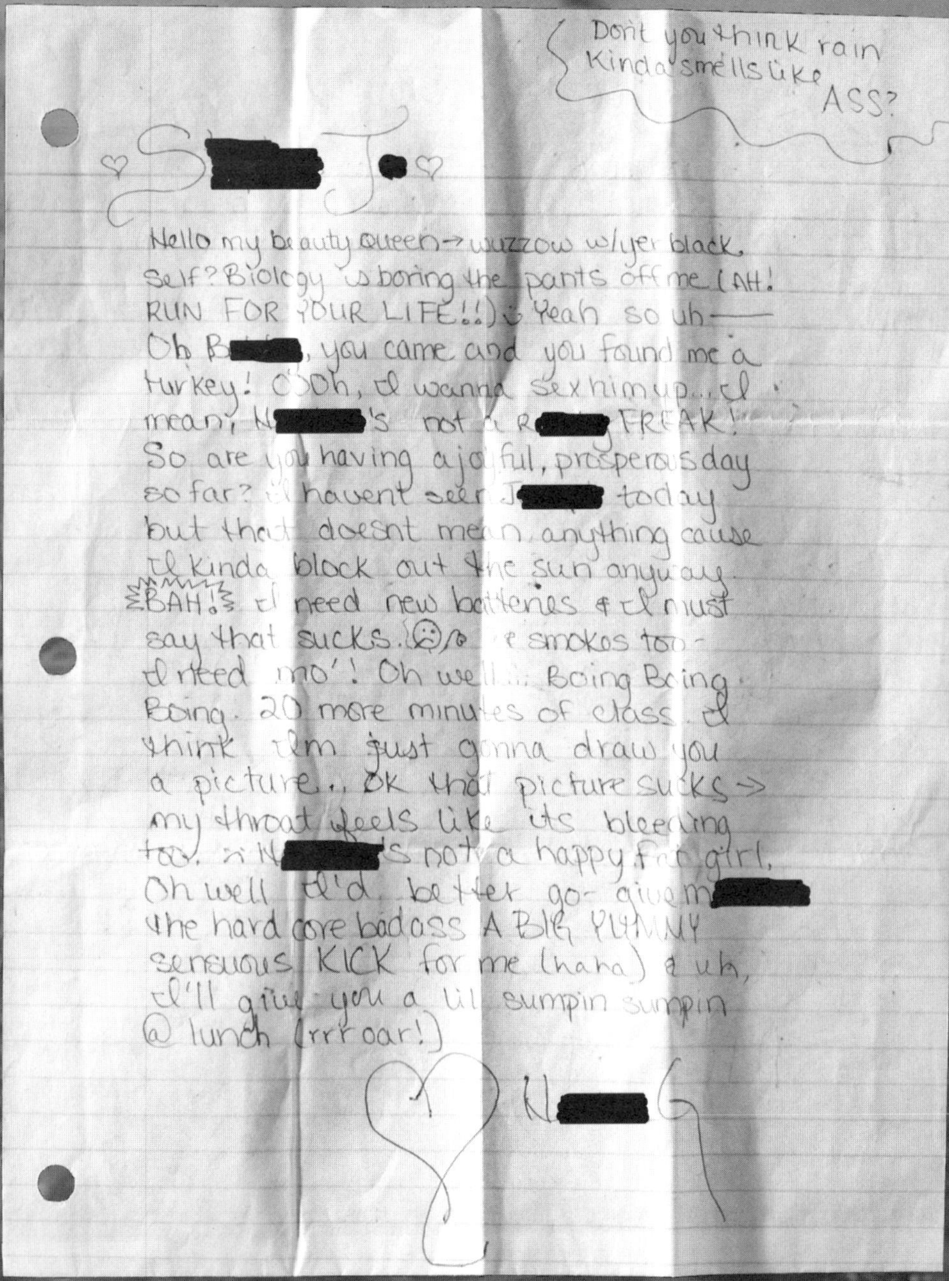

Don't you think rain Kinda smells like ASS?

♡ S[redacted] J[redacted] ♡

Hello my beauty queen → wuzzow w/yer black Self? Biology is boring the pants off me (AH! RUN FOR YOUR LIFE!!) ☺ Yeah so uh—— Oh B[redacted], you came and you found me a turkey! OOh, I wanna sex him up... I mean, H[redacted]'s not a R[redacted] FREAK! So are you having a joyful, prosperous day so far? I havent seen J[redacted] today but that doesnt mean anything cause I Kinda block out the sun anyway. BAH! I need new batteries & I must say that sucks. ☹ & smokes too - I need mo'! Oh well... Boing Boing Boing. 20 more minutes of class. I think Im just gonna draw you a picture.. OK that picture sucks → my throat feels like its bleeding too. ☹ H[redacted]'s not a happy fat girl. Oh well I'd better go- give M[redacted] the hard core badass A BIG YUMMY sensuous KICK for me (haha) & uh, I'll give you a lil sumpin sumpin @ lunch (rrroar!)

♡ H[redacted] G

(front)

[front]
Don't you think rain Kinda smells like ASS?
♥ S______ J_[f] ♥
Hello my beauty queen → wuzzow w/yer black Self? Biology is boring the pants off me (AH! RUN FOR YOUR LIFE!!)[smiley face] Yeah so uh——Oh B____[m], you came and you found me a turkey! OOOh, I wanna sex him up…I mean, H______[f]'s not a R____[m] FREAK! So are you having a joyful, prosperous day so far? I haven't seen J_____[m] today but that doesn't mean anything cause I Kinda block out the sun anyway. BAH! I need new batteries & I must say that sucks. [smoking smiley face with a hand gesturing 'thumbs down'] & smokes too - I need mo'! Oh well…. Boing Boing Boing. 20 more minutes of class. I think Im just gonna draw you a picture… OK that picture sucks → my throat feels like its bleeding too. [sad face] H______[f]'s not a happy fat girl. Oh well I'd better go- give M______[m] the hard core badass A BIG YUMMY sensuous KICK for me (ha ha) & uh, I'll give you a lil sumpin sumpin @ lunch (rrroar!)

♥ H______ G [f]

[back]
HaHa A_______[m][smiley face] shaved his head (moan, bone, groan) Sheesh he's fuckin hot!

[profile drawing of person from chest down with flames coming from his/her behind]
Guess Who! Blazed
Man, All I did was hit her Lightly on the arm!

[drawing of fat girl falling] Ahhhhh! jiggle jiggle
FUCK IT, I AINT GONNA LIE - IM FAT (NOT BIG BONED)

[drawing of lake and swimming fish with labels pointing to fish]
Smells Like ASS!
Lake of Hilhi Punk Rock Fish T_____ H_______[m][brand name] Hat Preppie Fish Goth Fish

I ♥ My S______ J_[f]!

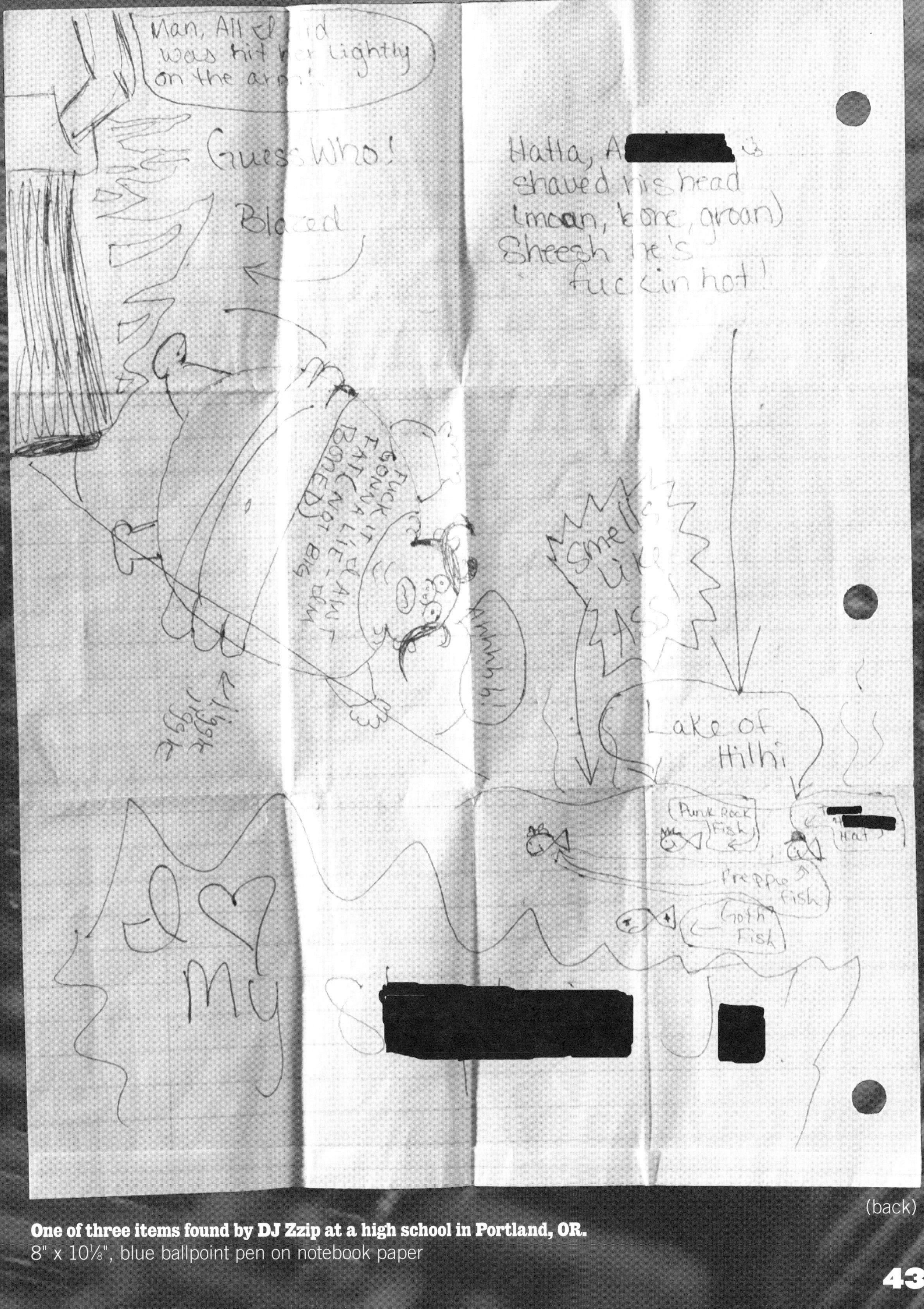

(back)

One of three items found by DJ Zzip at a high school in Portland, OR.
8" x 10⅛", blue ballpoint pen on notebook paper

YOU SUCK!

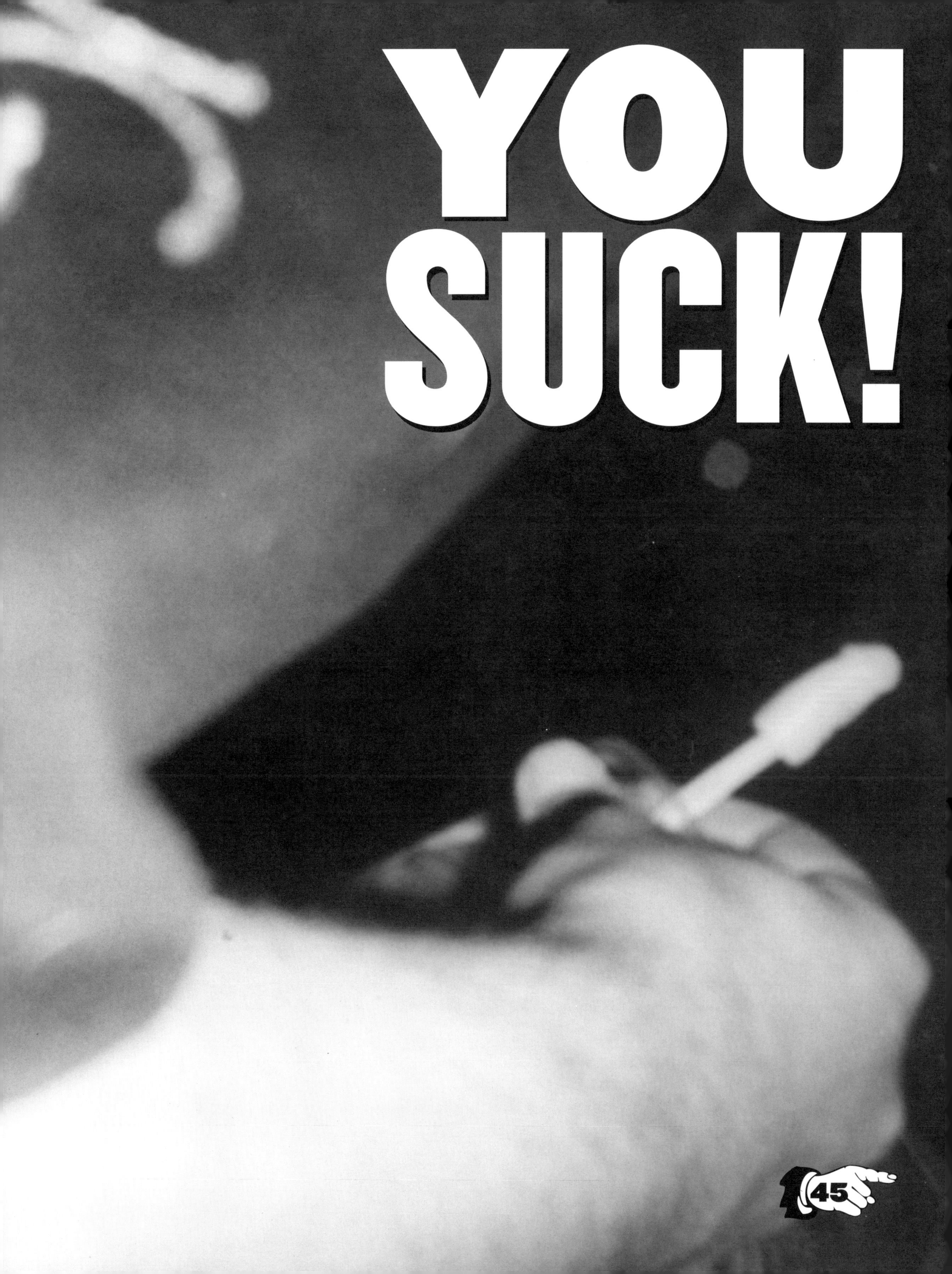

(front)

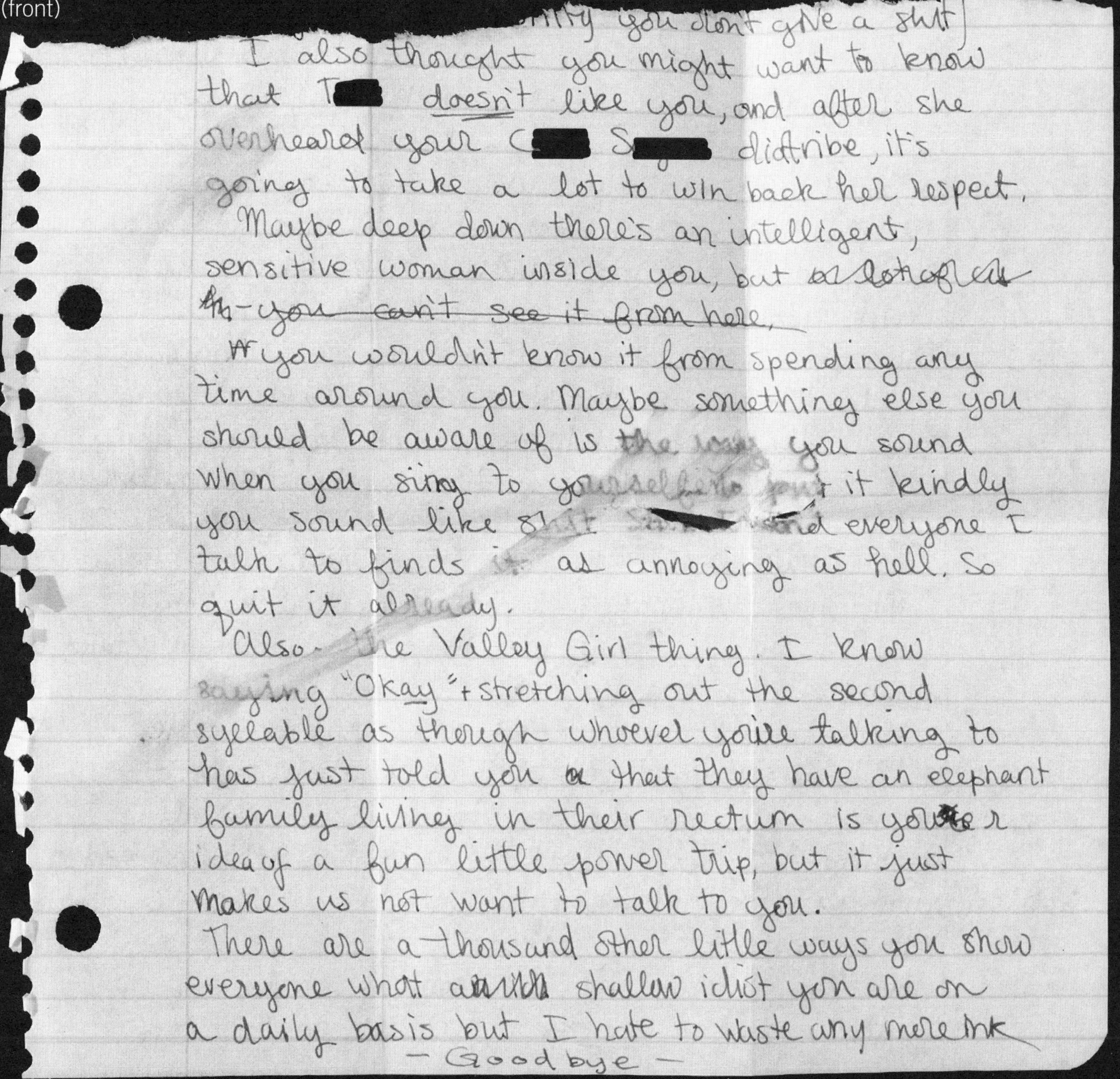

…ity you don't give a shit)
I also thought you might want to know that T[redacted] doesn't like you, and after she overheard your C[redacted] S[redacted] diatribe, it's going to take a lot to win back her respect.
Maybe deep down there's an intelligent, sensitive woman inside you, but ~~a lot of us th- you can't see it from here.~~
~~If~~ you wouldn't know it from spending any time around you. Maybe something else you should be aware of is the way you sound when you sing to yourself. To put it kindly you sound like shit [redacted] and everyone I talk to finds it as annoying as hell. So quit it already.
Also - the Valley Girl thing. I know saying "Okay" + stretching out the second syllable as though whoever you're talking to has just told you ~~a~~ that they have an elephant family living in their rectum is your idea of a fun little power trip, but it just makes us not want to talk to you.
There are a thousand other little ways you show everyone what ~~an idi~~ shallow idiot you are on a daily basis but I hate to waste any more ink
– Goodbye –

[front]
ity you don't give a shit) I also thought you might want to know that T___[f] <u>doesn't</u> like you, and after she overheard your C___ S____[m][well-known, now-deceased astronomer] diatribe, it's going to take a lot to win back her respect. Maybe deep down there's an intelligent, sensitive woman inside you, but ~~a lot of us th-you can't see it from here~~. you wouldn't know it from spending any time around you. Maybe something else you should be aware of is the way you sound when you sing to yourself. To put it ou sound like <u>shit</u> [illegible] and everyone I talk to finds it as annoying as hell. So quit it already.

Also - the Valley Girl thing. I know saying "Ok<u>ay</u>" + stretching out the second syllable as though whoever you're talking to has just told you ~~a~~ that they have an elephant family living in their rectum is you~~'re~~ r idea of a fun little power trip, but it just makes us not want to talk to you.

There are a thousand other little ways you show everyone what ~~an idi~~ shallow idiot you are on a daily basis but I hate to waste any more ink

– Good bye –

(back)

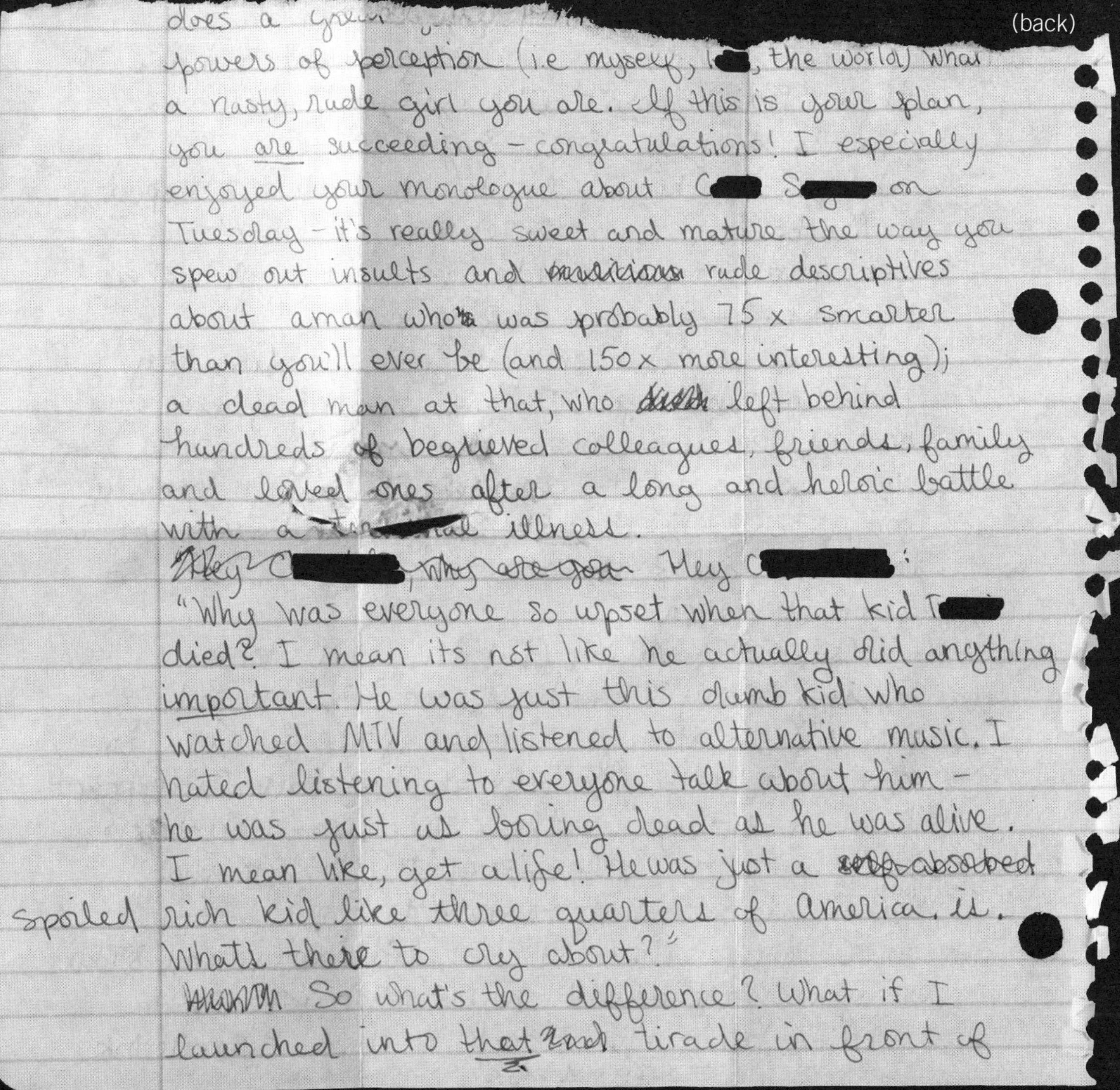
does a gr[illegible]
powers of perception (i.e myself, [redacted], the world) what a nasty, rude girl you are. If this is your plan, you <u>are</u> succeeding – congratulations! I especially enjoyed your monologue about C[redacted] S[redacted] on Tuesday – it's really sweet and mature the way you spew out insults and ~~malicious~~ rude descriptives about aman who~~'s~~ was probably 75x smarter than you'll ever be (and 150x more interesting); a dead man at that, who ~~died~~ left behind hundreds of begrieved colleagues, friends, family and loved ones after a long and heroic battle with a [redacted] illness.
~~Hey C~~[redacted]~~, why are you~~ Hey C[redacted]:
"Why was everyone so upset when that kid T[redacted] died? I mean its not like he actually did anything <u>important</u>. He was just this dumb kid who watched MTV and listened to alternative music. I hated listening to everyone talk about him – he was just as boring dead as he was alive. I mean like, get a life! He was just a ~~self-absorbed~~ spoiled rich kid like three quarters of America is. What's the~~ir~~re to cry about?"
~~Huh~~ So what's the difference? What if I launched into <u>that</u> ~~2nd~~ tirade in front of

[back]
powers of perception (i.e myself, T___[f], the world) what a nasty, rude girl you are. If this is your plan, you <u>are</u> succeeding – congratulations! I especially enjoyed your monologue about C___ S____ [astronomer mentioned before] on Tuesday – it's really sweet and mature the way you spew out insults and ~~malicious~~ rude descriptives about aman who~~'s~~ was probably 75x smarter than you'll ever be (and 150x more interesting); a dead man at that, who ~~died~~ left behind hundreds of begrieved colleagues, friends, family and loved ones after a long and heroic battle with a terminal illness.
~~"Hey C______[f], why are you~~ Hey C______[f]:
"Why was everyone so upset when that kid T_____[m] died? I mean its not like he actually did anything <u>important</u>. He was just this dumb kid who watched MTV and listened to alternative music. I hated listening to everyone talk about him – he was just as boring dead as he was alive. I mean like, get a life! He was just a ~~self-absorbed~~ spolied rich kid like three quarters of America is. What's the~~ir~~re to cry about?"
~~Huh?~~ So what's the difference? What if I launched into <u>that</u> ~~2nd~~ tirade in front of

Found by the Pussy Power Posse on November 5, 1997, in the freshman hall at a high school in Everett, WA.
Approximately 8" x 7⅛", blue rollerball ink on notebook paper

A[redacted],

I don't know what to say I have tried to call you... page you. I recieved no response from you.
I know I told you after my doctor's appt. I would call you. And I did that was March 23rd, ... I haven't heard a peep.

Now, I'm moving, I am trying to be nice to let you know, but again, when I page you, I get no response. My Ultrasound is coming up Monday 6th....

If you want me to let you in this baby's life, you need to act a little differently...

If you are going to act stupid go ahead. It doesn't matter to me, but to let you know I did give the State your name, last address, etc, ... for child support. I refuse to not have you financially responsible.... Emotionally responsible, I could care less... but I need you to be in some way responsible!... I hope you have a child w/ whats-her face - because it ain't working with me. I found some little well, a lot juicy facts about your wife.... All I can say is yuck! I am glad I got that AIDS test too!.... shoot..... Yes I believe my source...

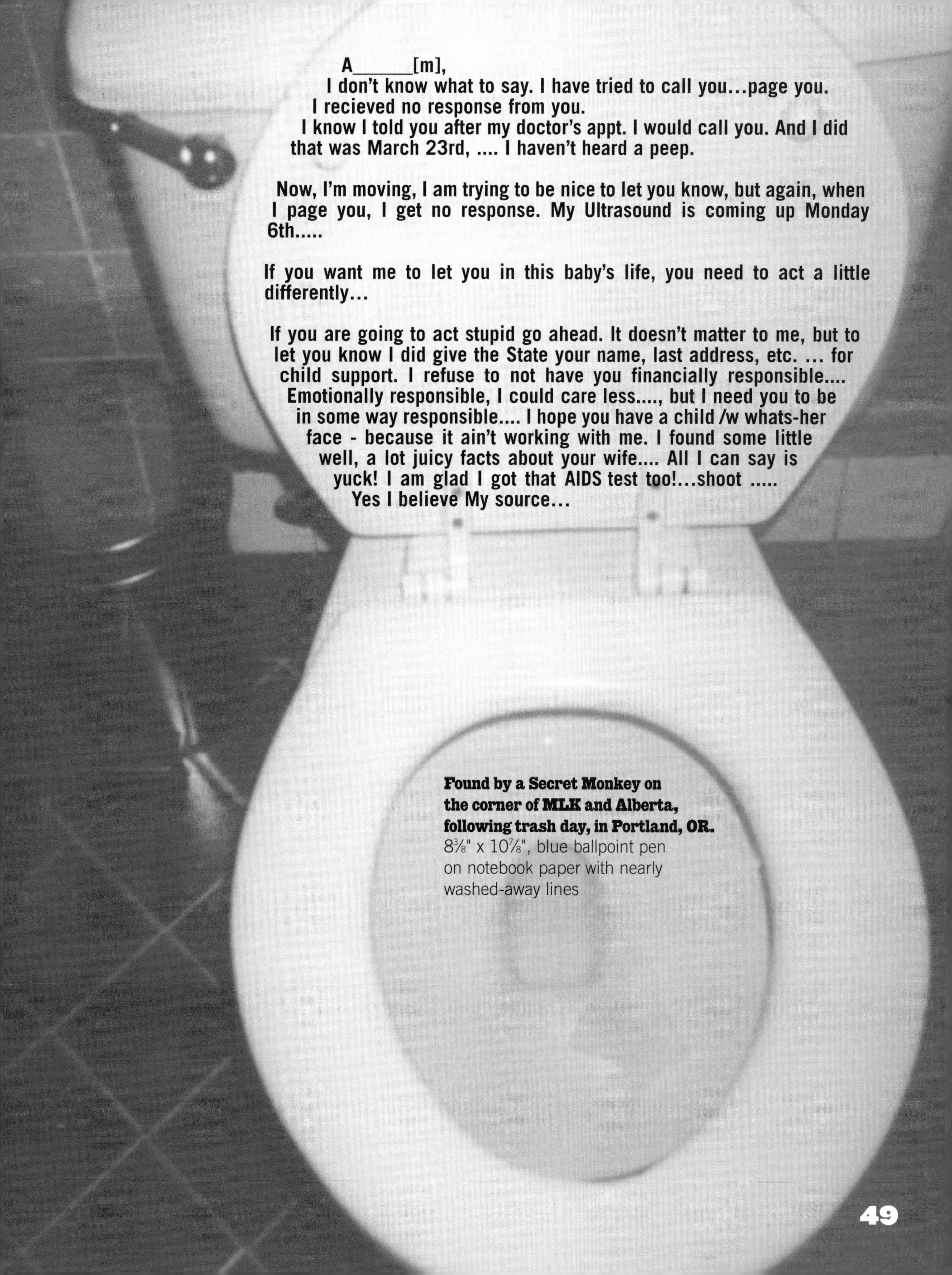

A______[m],

I don't know what to say. I have tried to call you...page you. I recieved no response from you.

I know I told you after my doctor's appt. I would call you. And I did that was March 23rd, ... I haven't heard a peep.

Now, I'm moving, I am trying to be nice to let you know, but again, when I page you, I get no response. My Ultrasound is coming up Monday 6th.....

If you want me to let you in this baby's life, you need to act a little differently...

If you are going to act stupid go ahead. It doesn't matter to me, but to let you know I did give the State your name, last address, etc. ... for child support. I refuse to not have you financially responsible.... Emotionally responsible, I could care less...., but I need you to be in some way responsible.... I hope you have a child /w whats-her face - because it ain't working with me. I found some little well, a lot juicy facts about your wife.... All I can say is yuck! I am glad I got that AIDS test too!...shoot .....
Yes I believe My source...

Found by a Secret Monkey on the corner of MLK and Alberta, following trash day, in Portland, OR.
8⅜" x 10⅞", blue ballpoint pen on notebook paper with nearly washed-away lines

K____[m] YOU OWE
ME FuCKiN MONEY
YOU LITTLE FUCKER
YOU KNOW WHO
the FUCK this is
you /mFuckeR

Found by Murray S. on University Avenue near NE 53rd Street in Seattle, WA.
Approximately 8⅝" x 5⅞", pencil on light green spiral notepaper

[redacted] You owe
me Fuckin money
you little Fucker!
You know who
the Fuck this is
you MFucker

M[redacted] A[redacted] L[redacted] B[redacted], Also KNOW AS M[redacted], L[redacted] B[redacted] Born ON JANUARY 20, 1953. Also NOTE MRS L[redacted] B[redacted], is Addicted to COCAINE AND SOME OTHER DRUGS. MRS L[redacted] B[redacted] HAS Also BEEN KEEPING COMPANY with CONVICTED Child Molesters. SHE HAS BEEN SEEN socializing with SEVERAL OTHER SEX OFFENDERS TOO. MRS L[redacted] B[redacted], HAS BEEN KNOW to EXCHANGES SEXS for DRUGS. SHE Also HAS BEEN Knowm to SCAM MONEY FROM PEOPLE.

MRS. L[redacted] B[redacted], is VERY DANGEROUS TO THE Public. SHE HAS BEEN KNOW to SEll CRACK TO MINORS. CHILDREN ETC. M[redacted] L[redacted] B[redacted] - is A VERY Sick WOMAN. SHE is SO FAR GONE THAT SHE is DANGERSOUS TO HER SEIF THE Public. Please REALIZE THE officals CANNT Do ANYTHING to Protect you FROM Mrs L[redacted] B[redacted].

Found by Stengar on the corner of 2nd Avenue and Wall Street in downtown Seattle, WA.
8½" x 11", photocopy on white paper

J_____[m] likes to Suck penises
he licks them up + down.
first he takes off their pants
and then he goes to town

Found by Dumpster Diving at a private middle school/high school in Corvallis, OR.
8" x 10½", folded, black ballpoint pen on notebook paper

PILLOW TALK

I think you should
step out for a minute
+ pick up some condoms
at O____'s [store].
Any Kind.

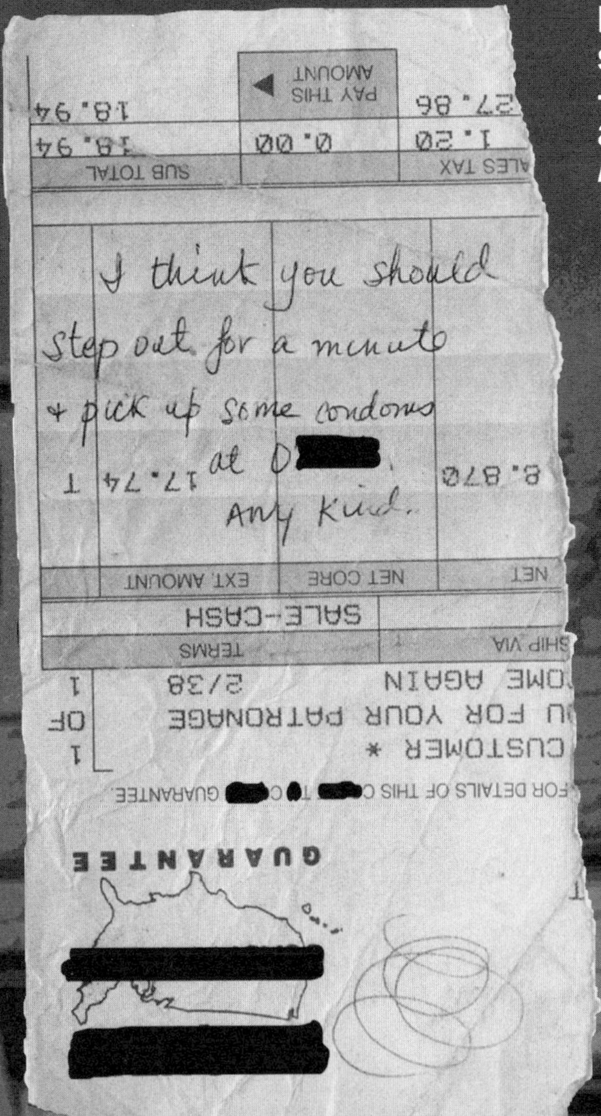

Found on a sunny morning in October, 1997, by Simers & Fried at a bus stop on the corner of Stark and 12th in southeast Portland, OR.
Approximately 2⅞" x 5½",
black ballpoint pen
on auto repair receipt

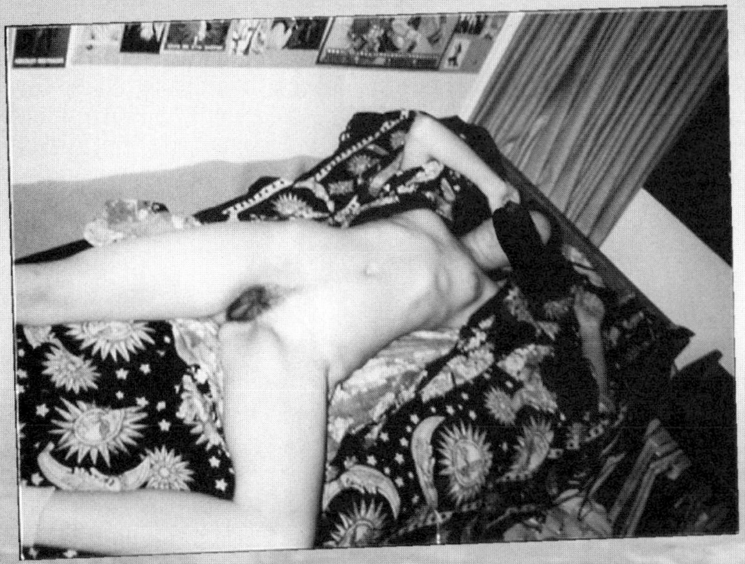

Found by an intern of "The Rocket".
Four 3" x 5", color photographs
Photo directly above is approximately
2⅜" x 4", black-and-white

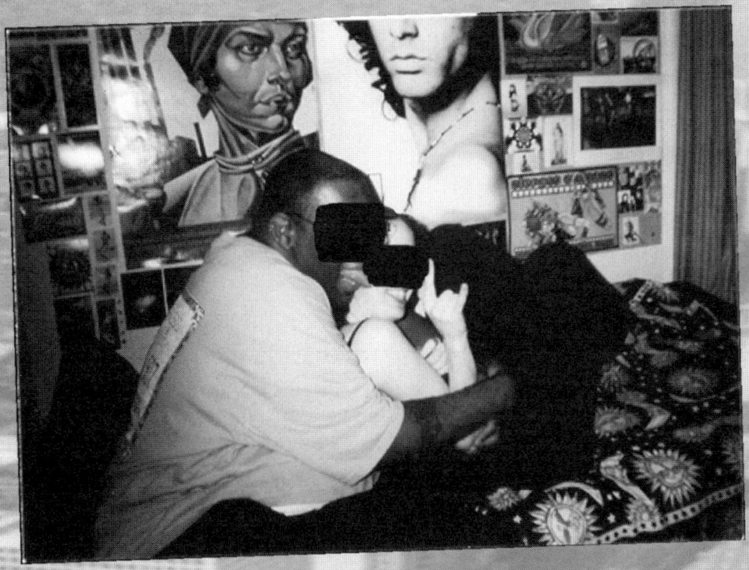

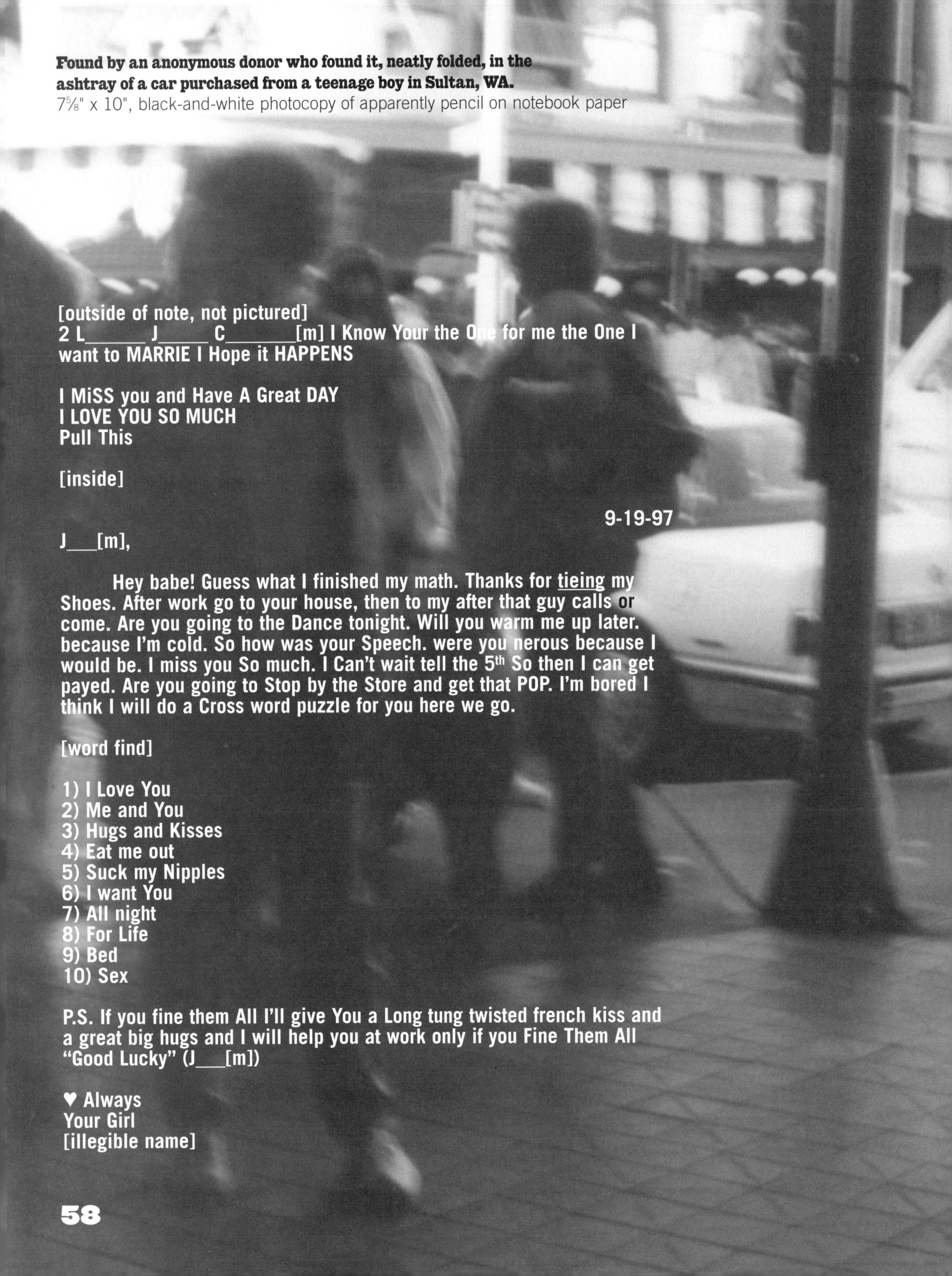

Found by an anonymous donor who found it, neatly folded, in the ashtray of a car purchased from a teenage boy in Sultan, WA.
$7\frac{5}{8}$" x 10", black-and-white photocopy of apparently pencil on notebook paper

[outside of note, not pictured]
2 L_____ J_____ C_______[m] I Know Your the One for me the One I want to MARRIE I Hope it HAPPENS

I MiSS you and Have A Great DAY
I LOVE YOU SO MUCH
Pull This

[inside]

9-19-97

J___[m],

Hey babe! Guess what I finished my math. Thanks for tieing my Shoes. After work go to your house, then to my after that guy calls or come. Are you going to the Dance tonight. Will you warm me up later. because I'm cold. So how was your Speech. were you nerous because I would be. I miss you So much. I Can't wait tell the 5th So then I can get payed. Are you going to Stop by the Store and get that POP. I'm bored I think I will do a Cross word puzzle for you here we go.

[word find]

1) I Love You
2) Me and You
3) Hugs and Kisses
4) Eat me out
5) Suck my Nipples
6) I want You
7) All night
8) For Life
9) Bed
10) Sex

P.S. If you fine them All I'll give You a Long tung twisted french kiss and a great big hugs and I will help you at work only if you Fine Them All "Good Lucky" (J___[m])

♥ Always
Your Girl
[illegible name]

9-19-97

J[redacted],

Hey babe! Guess what I finished my math. Thanks for tieing my shoes, After work go to your house, then to my after that guy calls or come, Are you going to the Dance tonight. will you warm me up later, because I'm cold. So how was your speech. were you nervous because I would be. I miss you so much. I can't wait tell the 5th so then I can get payed. Are you going to stop by the store and get that POP. I'm bored I think I will do a cross word puzzle for you here we go.

I	L	O	V	E	Y	O	U	A	B	C	D	E	M	F	G
W	I	H	U	G	S	A	N	D	K	I	S	S	E	S	H
A	Z	L	X	D	C	Y	T	C	O	M	E	I	A	L	B
N	J	O	E	Y	L	U	C	D	Y	R	O	U	N	E	E
T	O	R	L	F	O	R	L	I	F	E	E	X	D	E	D
Y	J	I	A	E	C	O	N	D	O	M	S	V	Y	R	T
O	O	U	M	A	L	L	N	I	G	H	T	D	O	H	G
U	X	T	F	U	C	K	M	E	N	O	W	L	U	L	X
Y	A	B	C	D	A	L	W	A	Y	S	Z	B	A	Y	E
E	F	G	S	E	L	P	P	I	N	Y	M	K	C	U	S

1) I Love You
2) Me and You
3) Hugs and Kisse
4) Eat me out
5) Suck my Nippl
6) I want You
7) All night
8) For Life
9) Bed
10) Sex

P.S. If you fine them All I'll give You a Long tung twisted french kiss and a great big hugs and I will help you out work only if you Fine Them All "Good Lucky" (J[redacted])

Always Your [redacted]

S[redacted],

OMIGOD, LAST NIGHT B[redacted] CAME OVER! WE WERE GETTING IT ON AND WELL, LETS JUST SAY, HE CURED MY CONSTIPATION! I COULDN'T BELIEVE THAT HE MISSED! IT HURT SO BAD, I HEARD IT RIP! I DIDN'T SAY ANYTHING BECASE I WAS IN SHOCK. WHAT SHOULD I DO? SHOULD I DUMP HIM BECAUSE HE IS A BAD FUCK? YOU DUMPD M[redacted] WHEN HE MADE THAT MISTAKE. I CAN HARDLY SIT DOWN!

WRITE BACK PLEASE!

- ME

S____[f],

OMIGOD, LAST NIGHT B____[m] CAME OVER! WE WERE GETTING IT ON AND WELL, LETS JUST SAY, HE CURED MY CONSTIPATION! I COULDN'T BELIEVE HE MISSED! IT HURT SO BAD, I HEARD IT RIP! I DIDN'T SAY ANYTHING BECASE I WAS IN SHOCK. WHAT SHOULD I DO? SHOULD I DUMP HIM BECAUSE HE IS A BAD FUCK? YOU DUMPD M___[m] WHEN HE MADE THAT MISTAKE. I CAN HARDLY SIT DOWN!

WRITE BACK PLEASE!

—ME

[inside heart] LOVE ALWAYS

Found by Allison H. in a Salem, OR, high school commons.
8" x 10⅜", pencil on notebook paper

Photos on this and the following three pages found by Anonymous in an envelope from a bank in Seattle, WA.
3½" x 4¼", instant color photographs with dirt and coffee stains

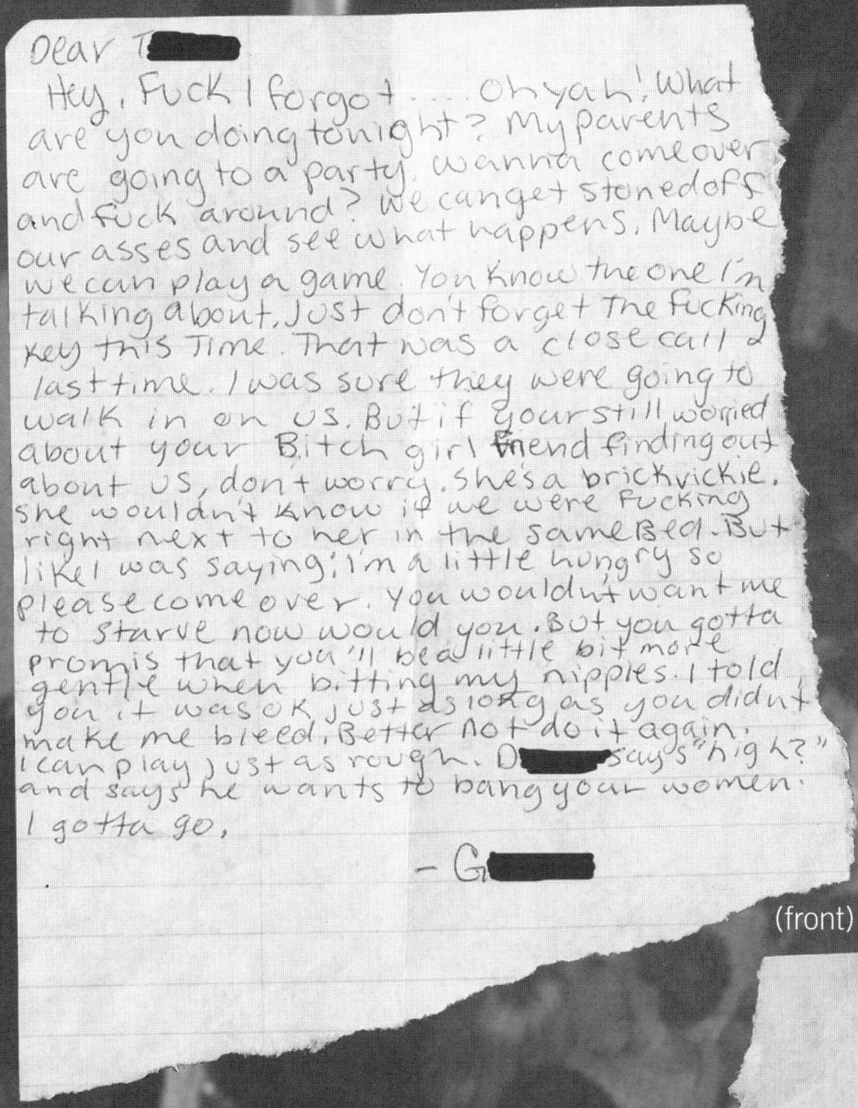

Dear T____[m],
Hey, Fuck I forgot....Oh yah! What are you doing tonight? My parents are going to a party. wanna come over and Fuck around? we can get stoned off our asses and see what happens. Maybe we can play a game. You Know the one I'm talking about. Just don't forget the Fucking key this Time. That was a close call last time. I was sure they were going to walk in on us. But if your still worried about your Bitch girl Friend finding out about us, don't worry. She's a brickvickie. She wouldn't know if we were Fucking right next to her in the same Bed. But like I was saying: I'm a little hungry so Please come over. You wouldn't want me to Starve now would you. But you gotta promis that you'll be a little bit more gentle when bitting my nipples. I told you it was OK just as long as you didn't make me bleed. Better not do it again. I can play just as rough. D____[m] says "High?" and says he wants to bang your women.
I gotta go.
—G___[f]

(front)

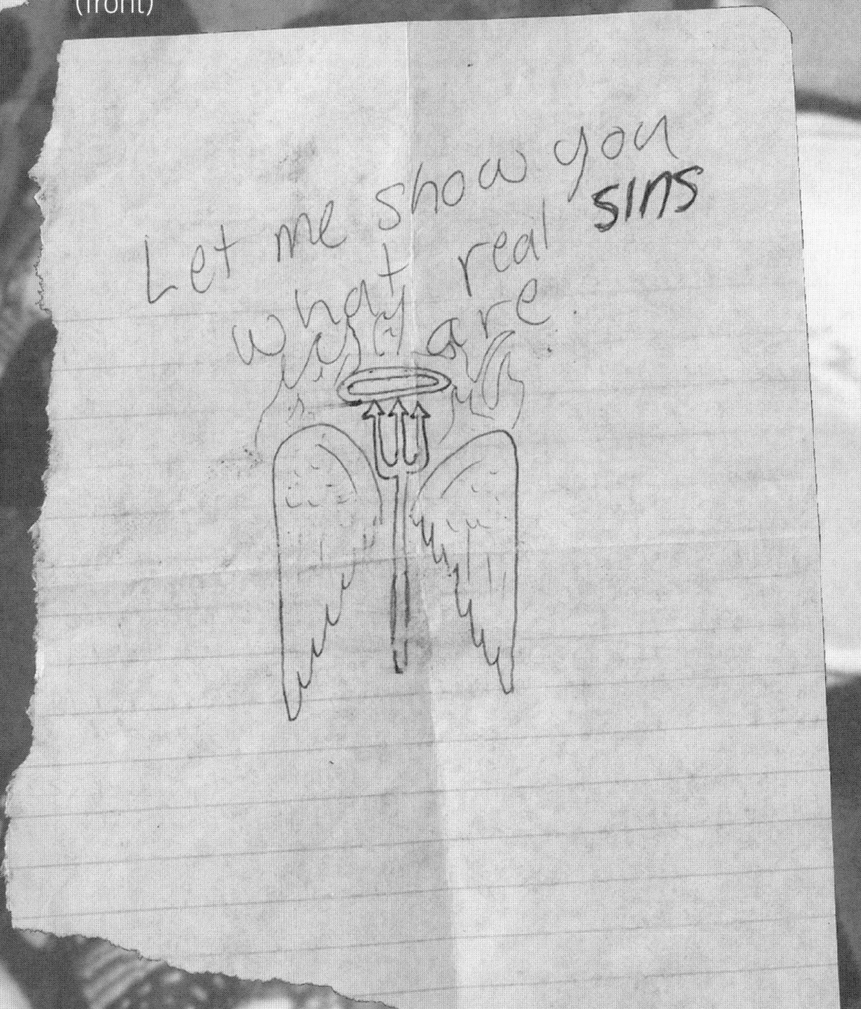

(back)

Found by The Gang outside a record store in Smokey Point, WA.
Approximately 5" x 6", blue ballpoint pen on notebook paper

OU CAN REACH ME WEEKDAY
Y MOBILE #, 7[redacted]-1[redacted]. I
MBER WHERE I COULD CALL YO
OTRACTED CONVERSATION TO

GIVE ME SOME THOUGHT, &
THE CASE MAYBE!

HOPE TO HEAR FROM YO

J[redacted]

Found by Matt, in a downtown Portland, OR, hotel, in an envelope with two other letters (one of which is pictured on pages 68–69) responding to a personal ad asking for a man to join a ménage à trois.
8½" x 11", blue rollerball ink and color dot-matrix print on white paper

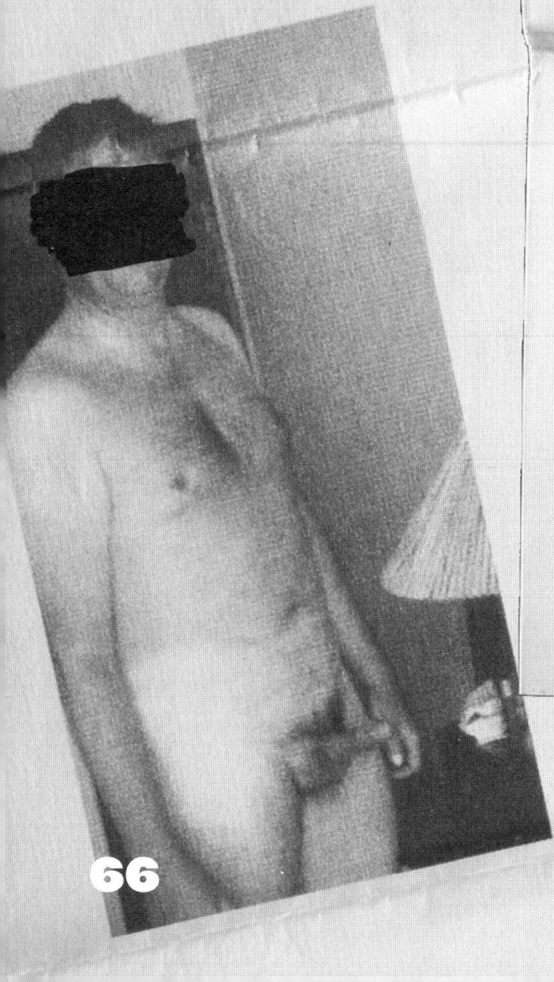

HI COACH!

MAY I JOIN YOUR TEAM? I REALLY DO ENJOY THE GA
I COULD BECOME A WINNING SWITCH-HITTER. JOINING TH
BAT COULD BE THE OPPORTUNITY TO AGAIN APPRECIATE THE
OF SEXUAL GRATIFICATION AVAILABLE BETWEEN A WOMAN &

YOUR AD CONTAINS NO SPECIFICS AS TO AGE, SO I COUL
THIS WITH A 0-2 COUNT & A TIPPED BALL HEADING DIREC
MITT. THIS FROM THE FACT THAT YOU 2 ARE IN YOUR 20
INTO MY 40S. AGE IS OF NO CONCERN TO ME, BUT IF YOU A
PARTNER CLOSER TO YOUR OWN AGE BRACKET, THAT'S UND

IN THE EVENT THIS DIDN'T RESULT IN MY POPPING OUT
WITH SOME STATS TO SEE IF I QUALIFY TO JOIN THE ROSTE

I'M A MWM, & THIS IS ONE REASON AN EROTIC INNING WITH
THRUST OF MY SEARCH. THAT THE 2 OF YOU SHARE AN EMOTIO
PRECLUDES ONE DEVELOPING BETWEEN US, MINIMIZING THE T
PRESENT TO EITHER MARRIAGE.

MY HEIGHT IS 6', WEIGHT IS 185#, & I HAVE BROWN H
I DON'T CONSIDER MYSELF MODEL MATERIAL, BUT I THINK M
ME REASONABLY ATTRACTIVE. THOUGH NO ONE WOULD CON
"HARD BODY" WORKOUT ENTHUSIAST, I AM FAIRLY FIT. AND
IS SOME INTEREST IN WHAT BAT I SWING. WHILE I'LL NEVE
OF 'OH MY GOD!' WHEN I DROP MY BRIEFS, 'OLE DICKY' S
BEYOND 6", & HAS ALWAYS PROVEN QUITE EFFECTIVE.

I HAVE LIMITED EXPERIENCE WITH BATTING FROM THE OT
I WOULD ~~CATEGORIZE~~ CATEGORIZE MYSELF AS CURIOUS AS O
BI. IN MY LATE TEENS I BECAME INVOLED WITH A MID
THE BALL ROOM DANCE SCHOOL I ATTENDED. SHORTLY INTO TH
HUSBAND JOINED IN THE ACTION, & SOON AFTER I BECAME T
BOTH THEIR ATTENTION. THIS EXPERIENCE WAS PRIMARI
MANUAL & ORAL STIMULATION, THOUGH I DID PROVIDE MY S
STIMULATION TO HIM. I REGRET NOT TAKING THE NEXT
SAMPLING THE TASTE OF HIS BAT. I GUESS THIS IS ST
OF MY CURIOSITY.

I DID ENJOY MANIPULATING HIS BAT & HAVING H
I WOULD HOPE AN AT BAT WITH THE 2 OF YOU WOULD T
TO THE NEXT PLANE & SEE HOW WELL I WOULD ENJO
ACTIVE END & HOW GOOD I MIGHT BE AT IT.

SHOULD YOU LIKE TO CHAT WITH ME TO FURTHER A
TO BECOME A MEMBER OF YOUR TEAM, I WOULD BE PL

[front]

Hi Coach!

May I join your team? I really do enjoy the game & I believe I could become a winning switch-hitter. Joining the 2 of you at bat could be the opportunity to again appreciate the multiple avenues of sexual gratification available between a woman & 2 men.

Your ad contains no specifics as to age, so I could be approaching this with a 0-2 count & a tipped ball heading directly to the catcher's mitt. This from the fact that you 2 are in your 20s, while I'm well into my 40s. Age is of no concern to me, but if you are seeking a Partner closer to your own age bracket, that's understandable.

In the event this didn't result in my Popping out, I'll continue with some stats to see if I qualify to join the roster.

I'm a MWM, & this is one reason an erotic inning with a couple is the thrust of my search. That the 2 of you share an emotional attachment precludes one developing between us, minimizing the threat such would present to either marriage.

My height is 6', weight is 185#, & I have brown hair & blue eyes. I don't consider myself model material, but I think most would judge me reasonably attractive. Though no one would confuse me with a "HARD BODY" workout enthusiast, I am fairly fit. And I suppose there is some interest in what bat I swing. While I'll never hear the gasp of 'OH MY GOD!' when I drop my briefs, 'ole dicky' stands at slightly beyond 6", & has always proven quite effective.

I have limited experience with batting from the opposite side, so I would ~~catorize~~ categorize myself as curious as opposed to actively Bi. In my late teens I became involed with a mid 30s gal who taught the ball room dance school I attended. Shortly into the relationship her husband joined in the action, & soon after I became the object of both their attention. This experience was primarily passive, receiving manual & oral stimulation, though I did provide my share of manual stimulation to him. I regret not taking the next step & not sampling the taste of his Bat. I guess this is still the source of my curiosity.

I did enjoy manipulating his bat & having him suck mine. I would hope an at bat with the 2 of you would allow me to move to the next plane & see how well I would enjoy being on the active end & how good I might be at it.

Should you like to chat with me to further assess my ~~apitit~~ aptitude to become a member of your team, I would be pleased to do so

[back]

You can reach me weekdays, except Wednesdays, between 8 am & 4 pm via my mobile #, 7__-1___. I would prefer it if you could call from a number where I could call you back, so as to not have to explain a Protracted converstaion to a strange incoming number.

Give me some thought, & let me know if I can suit up, or down as the case maybe!

Hope to hear from you soon. Until then, Have Fun!

J___[m]

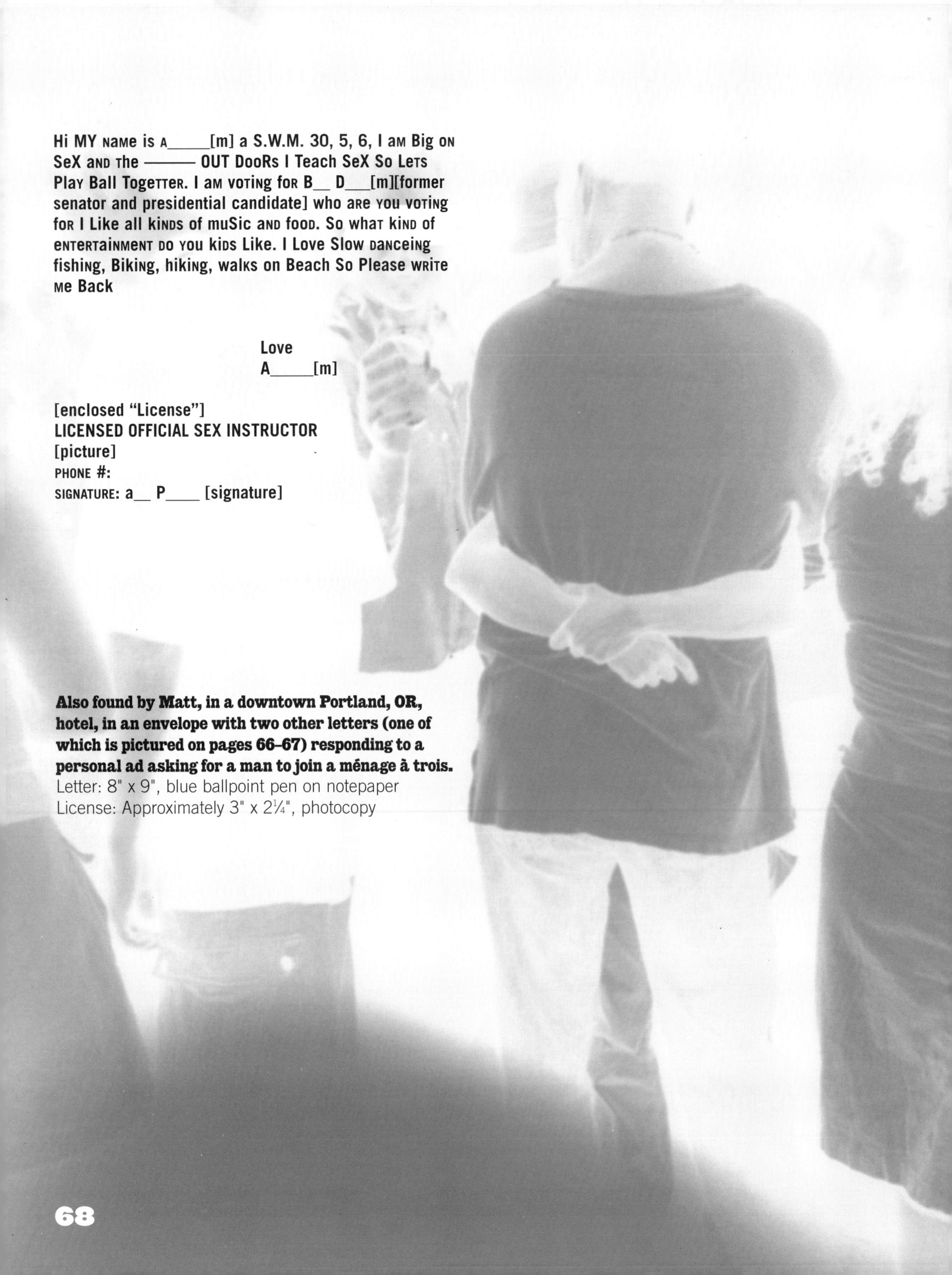

Hi MY NAME is A_____[m] a S.W.M. 30, 5, 6, I AM Big ON SeX AND The ——— OUT DooRs I Teach SeX So LeTs PlaY Ball TogeTTeR. I AM VOTINg FOR B__ D___[m][former senator and presidential candidate] who ARE YOU VOTINg FOR I Like all KINDS of muSic AND FOOD. So WHAT KIND of ENTERTAINMENT DO YOU kiDS Like. I Love Slow DANCEING fishiNg, BikiNg, hikiNg, walKs on Beach So Please WRITE ME Back

Love
A_____[m]

[enclosed "License"]
LICENSED OFFICIAL SEX INSTRUCTOR
[picture]
PHONE #:
SIGNATURE: a__ P____ [signature]

Also found by Matt, in a downtown Portland, OR, hotel, in an envelope with two other letters (one of which is pictured on pages 66–67) responding to a personal ad asking for a man to join a ménage à trois.
Letter: 8" x 9", blue ballpoint pen on notepaper
License: Approximately 3" x 2¼", photocopy

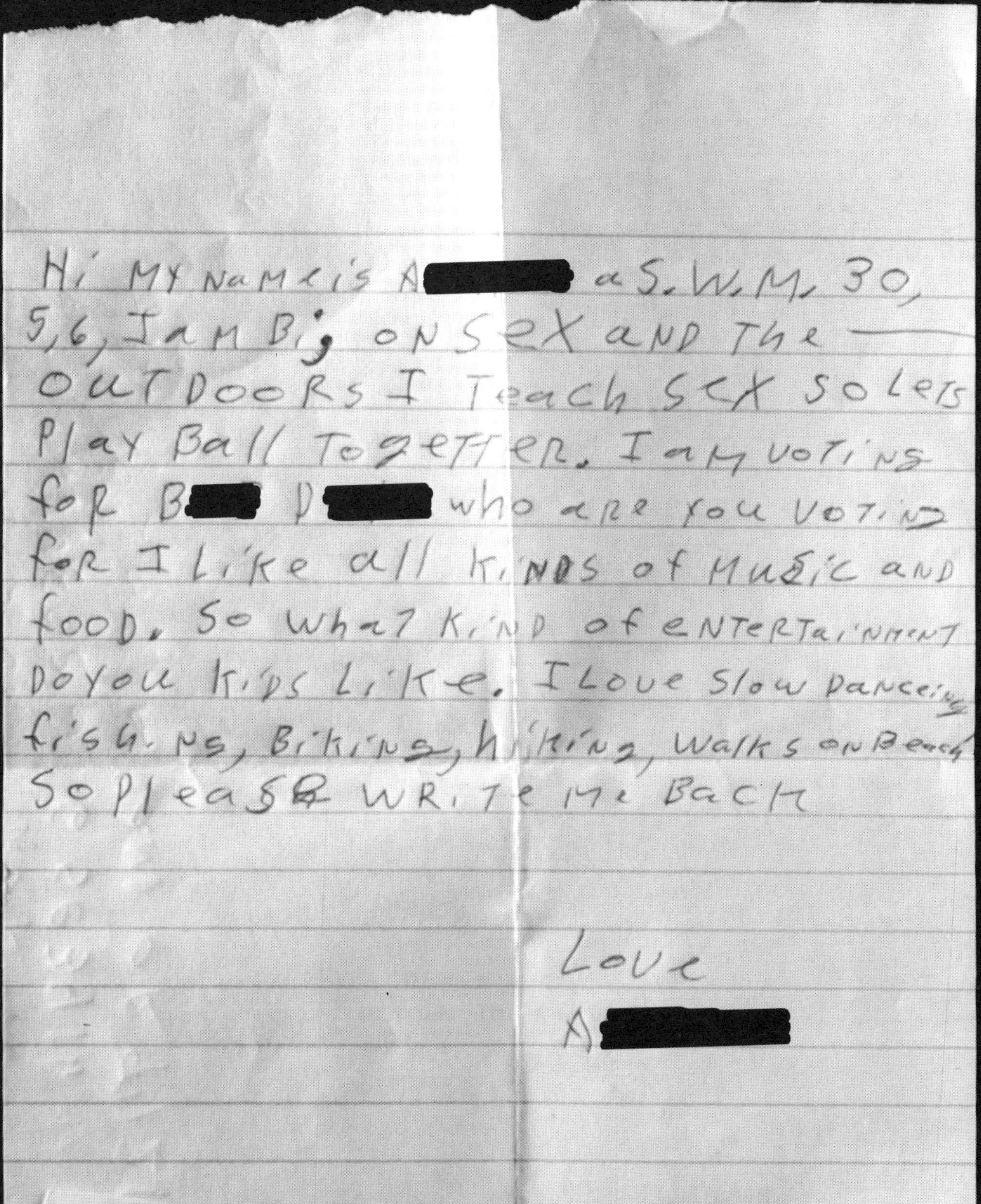

Hi My Name is A[redacted] a S.W.M. 30,
5,6, I am Big on Sex and the —
Outdoors I Teach Sex so lets
Play Ball Togetter. I am voting
for B[redacted] D[redacted] who are you voting
for I like all kinds of music and
food. So what kind of entertainment
do you kids like. I Love slow danceing
fishing, Biking, hiking, walks on Beach
So please write me back

Love
A[redacted]

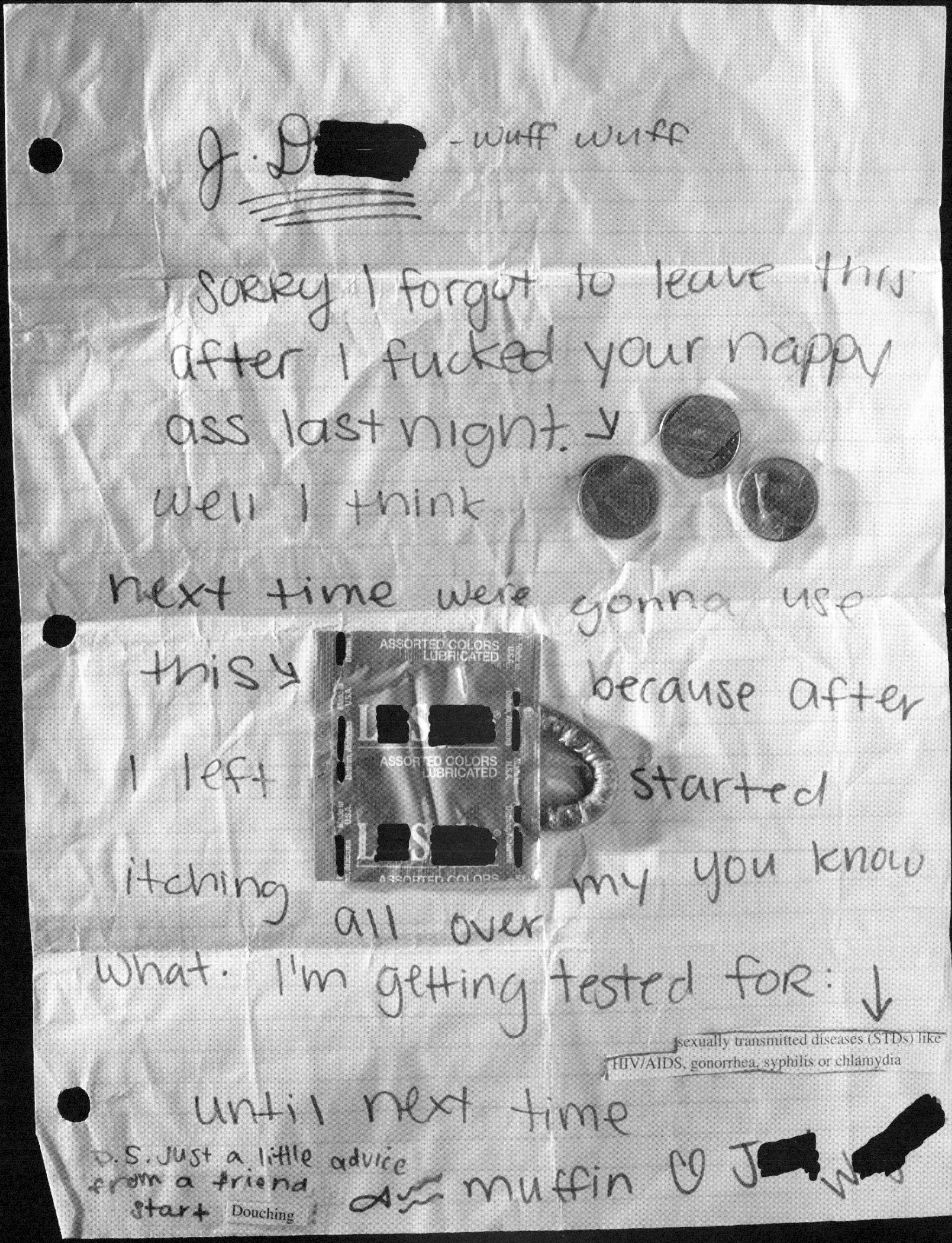

J. D[redacted] - wuff wuff

Sorry I forgot to leave this after I fucked your nappy ass last night. ↘

Well I think

next time were gonna use this ↘

because after I left [redacted] started itching all over my you know what. I'm getting tested for: ↓

sexually transmitted diseases (STDs) like HIV/AIDS, gonorrhea, syphilis or chlamydia

Until next time

muffin ♡ J[redacted]

P.S. Just a little advice from a friend, start Douching!

[opposite]

J. D__[m] - wuff wuff

SORRY I forgot to leave this after I fucked your nappy ass last night. [arrow pointing to pennies] Well I think next time were gonna use this [arrow pointing to condom] because after I left started itching all over my you know What. I'm getting tested foR: [arrow to clipping which says: sexually transmitted diseases (STDs) like HIV/AIDS, gonorrhea, syphilis or chlamydia]
until next time muffin ♥ J__ W_____[m]

P.S. Just a little advice from a friend, Start [clipping] Douching!

Found by someone who does not want to be caught.
8½" x 11", purple felt-tip marker; pennies; green lubricated condom and wrapper; various photocopy clippings on pink paper; and transparent tape on notebook paper

← this is apiture of [redacted] at the beach. [redacted] took the picture.

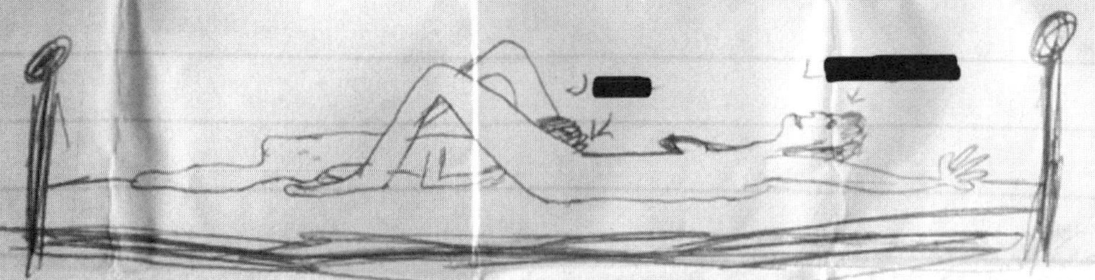

[redacted]'s intentions were innocent, he just came to pick up [redacted] for lunch. [redacted] was out of money so it was off to his house for lunch. Or was it dessert? He made her a microwave pizza. And She ate it. They began kissing and touching. He started to rub her down generously. When the time was right he slipped off her skirt and then her panties. [redacted] believed firmly in equality so she ripped off his clothes and felt his warm, smooth body. She pulled him close to tell him that she loved him. Then he ate her out until she screamed excitedly with orgasmic pleasure. Then they lived happily ever after

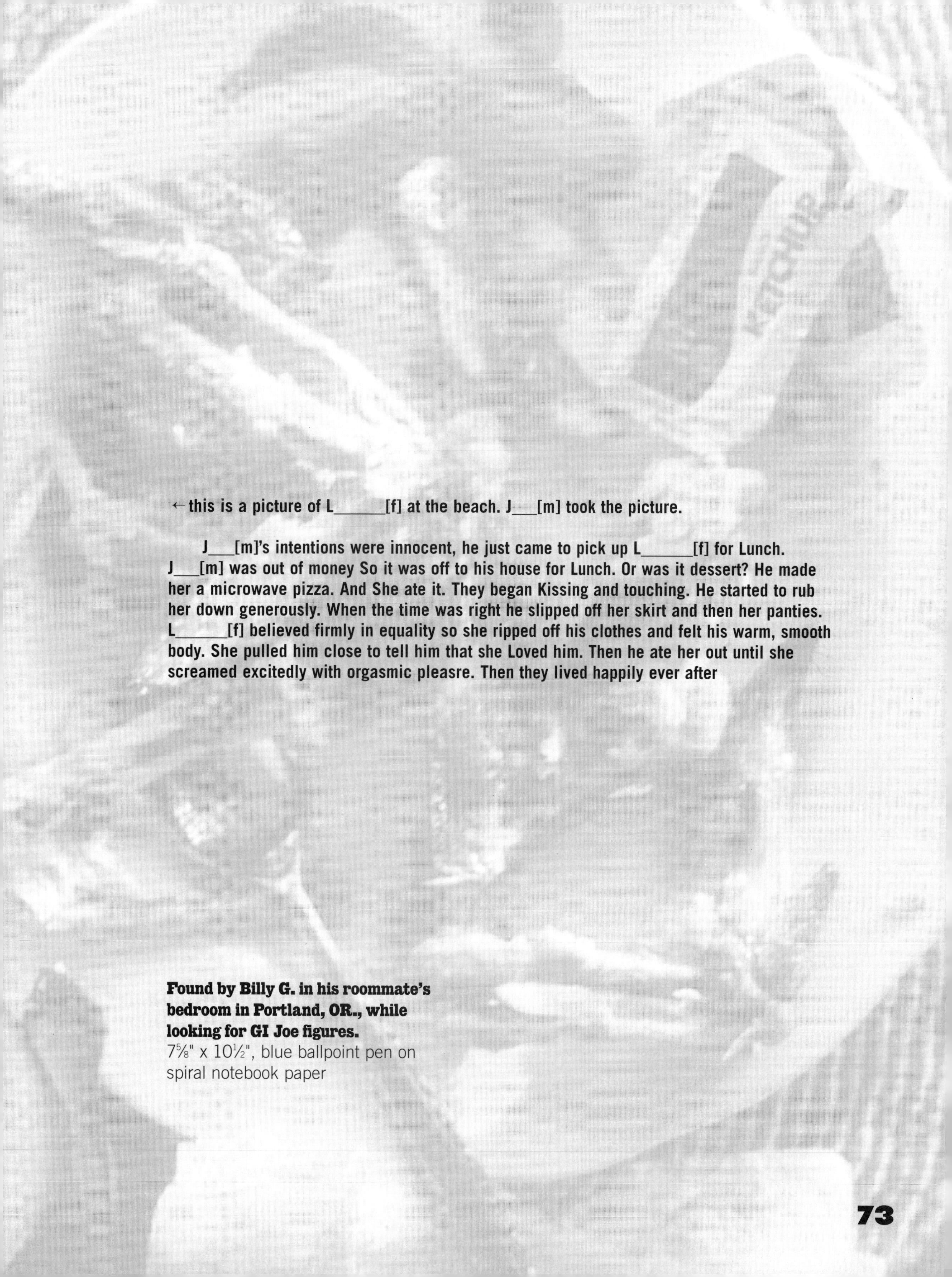

←this is a picture of L______[f] at the beach. J___[m] took the picture.

J___[m]'s intentions were innocent, he just came to pick up L______[f] for Lunch. J___[m] was out of money So it was off to his house for Lunch. Or was it dessert? He made her a microwave pizza. And She ate it. They began Kissing and touching. He started to rub her down generously. When the time was right he slipped off her skirt and then her panties. L______[f] believed firmly in equality so she ripped off his clothes and felt his warm, smooth body. She pulled him close to tell him that she Loved him. Then he ate her out until she screamed excitedly with orgasmic pleasre. Then they lived happily ever after

Found by Billy G. in his roommate's bedroom in Portland, OR., while looking for GI Joe figures.
7⅝" x 10½", blue ballpoint pen on spiral notebook paper

Found by Christine, stuck to a bus stop bench at Second and Fir in Vancouver, BC .
3½" x 4¼", instant color photograph

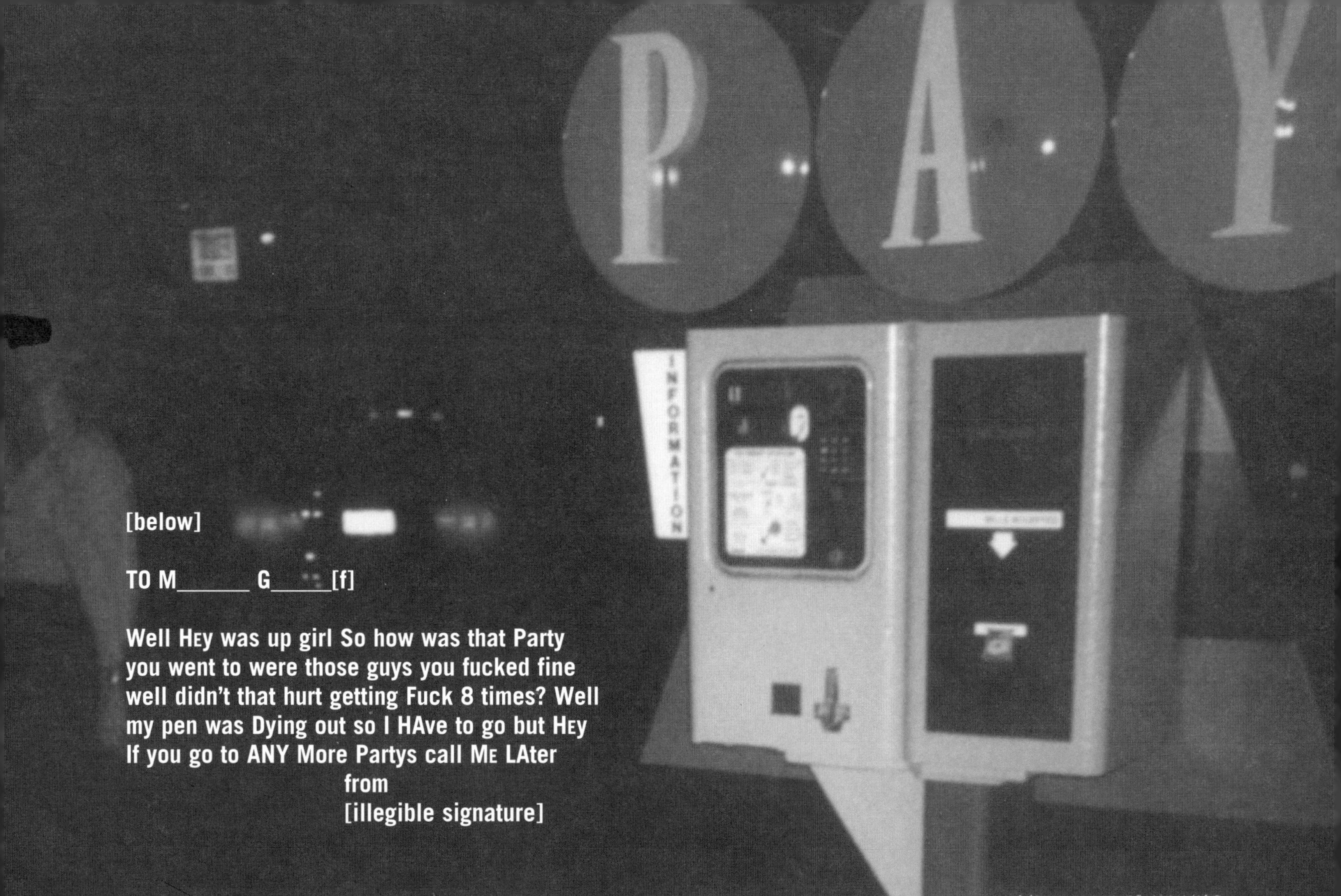

[below]

TO M______ G______ [f]

Well HEY was up girl So how was that Party you went to were those guys you fucked fine well didn't that hurt getting Fuck 8 times? Well my pen was Dying out so I HAve to go but HEY If you go to ANY More Partys call ME LAter
from
[illegible signature]

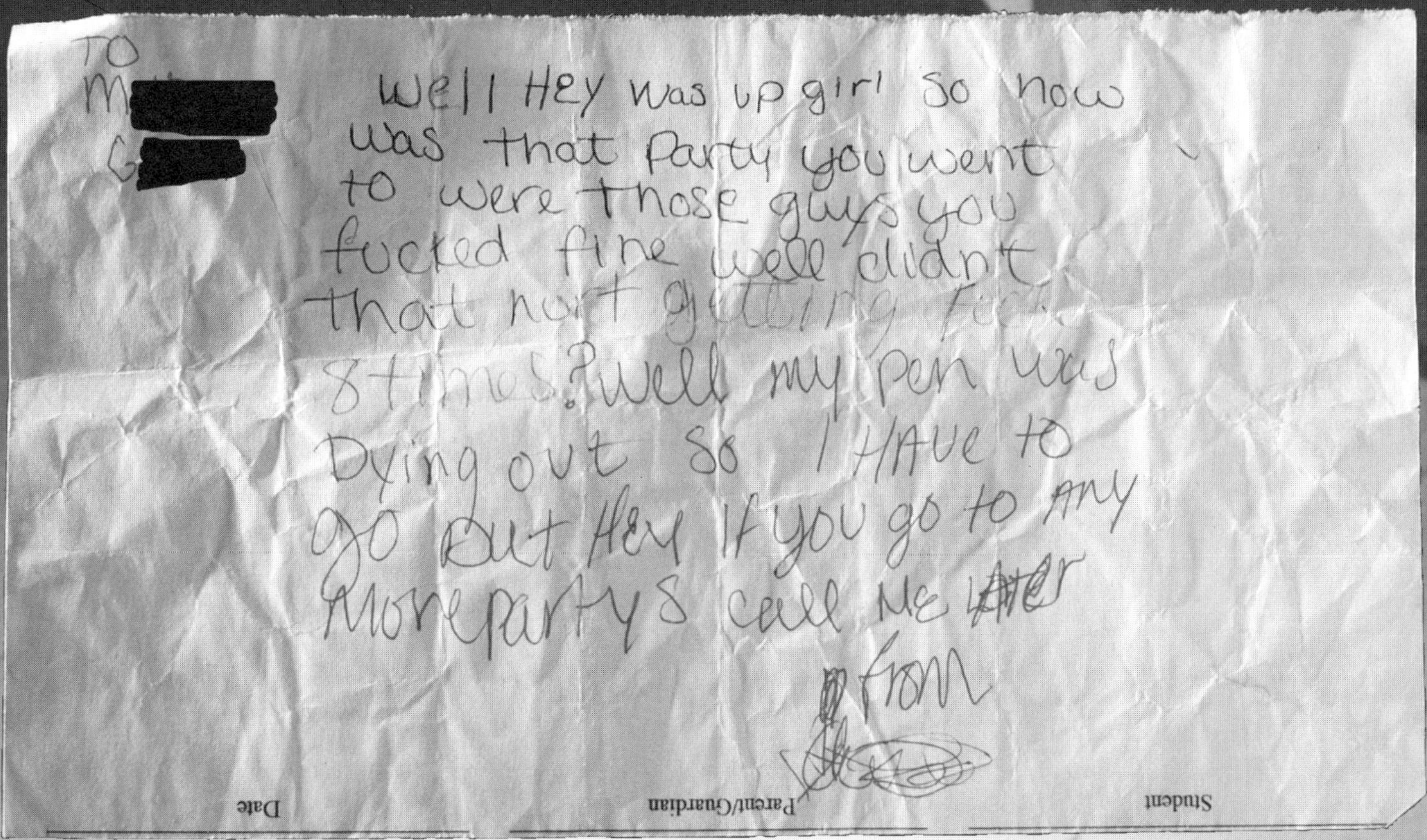
TO
M[redacted]
G[redacted]
Well HEY was up girl So how was that Party you went to were those guys you fucked fine well didnt that hurt getting Fuck 8 times? Well my pen was Dying out So I HAve to go but Hey If you go to Any More partys call Me LAter
from
[illegible signature]

Date
Parent/Guardian
Student

Found by Ryan on a toilet in a boys' restroom of a Forest Grove, OR., high school.
8½" x 4¾", black and red ballpoint pen on the bottom of a photocopied permission slip

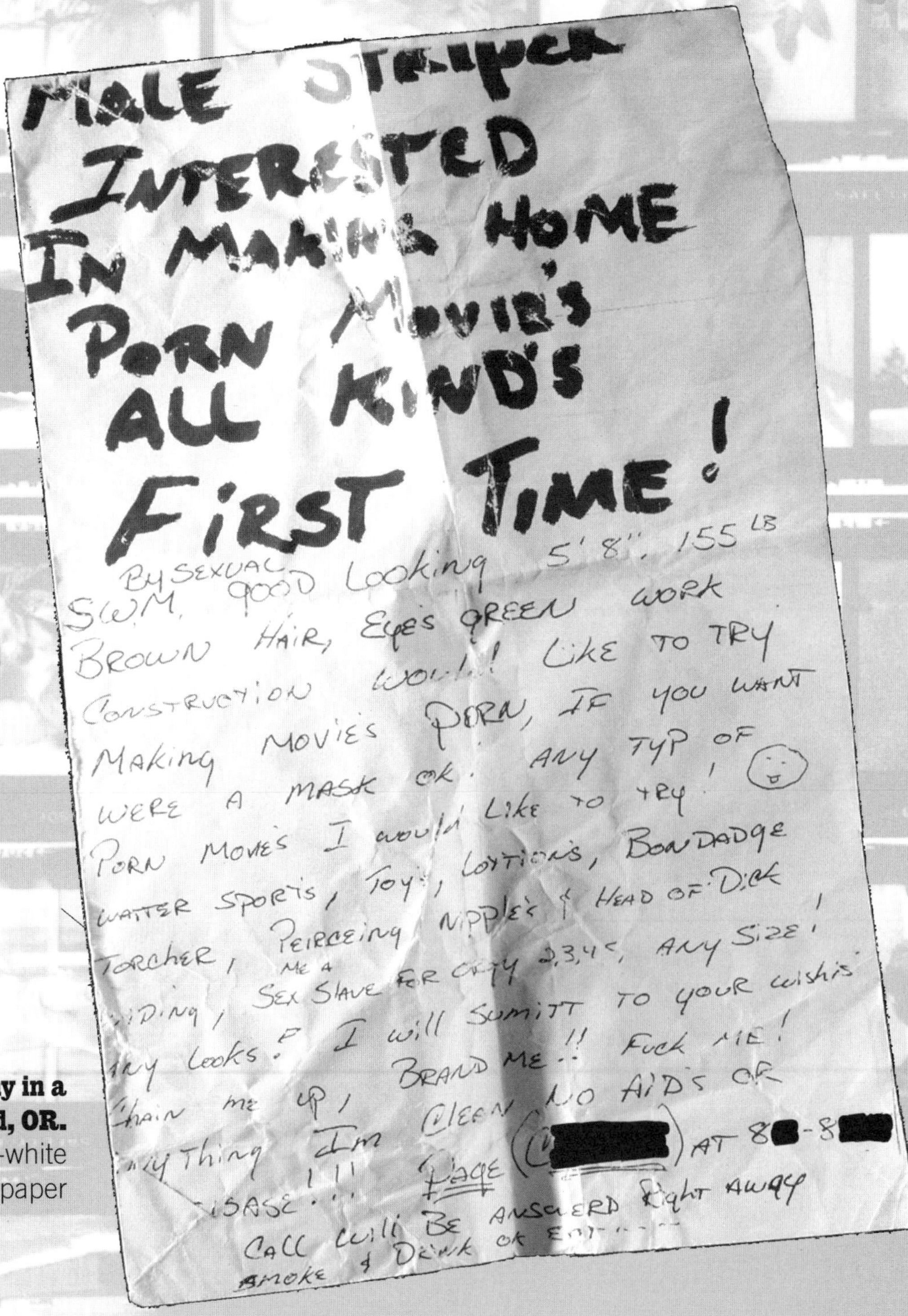
MALE STRIPER
INTERESTED
IN MAKING HOME
PORN MOVIE'S
ALL KIND'S
FIRST TIME!
BY SEXUAL S.W.M. good Looking 5'8" 155 LB
BROWN HAIR, Eyes GREEN work
CONSTRUCTION would LIKE TO TRY
MAKING MOVIES PORN, IF YOU WANT
WERE A MASK OK. ANY TYP OF
PORN MOVIE'S I would LIKE TO TRY!
WATTER SPORT'S, TOY'S, LOYTION'S, BONDADGE
TORCHER, PEIRCEING NIPPLE'S & HEAD OF DICK
WIPING, ME A SEX SLAVE FOR ORGY 2,3,4,5, ANY SIZE!
ANY LOOKS? I will SUMITT TO YOUR WISHIS
CHAIN ME UP, BRAND ME!! FUCK ME!
ANYTHING IM CLEAN NO AID'S OR
DISASE!!! PAGE ([redacted]) AT 8[redacted]-8[redacted]
CALL will BE ANSWERD Right AWAY
SMOKE & DRINK OK E[illegible]

Found by Kate and Anthony in a bank in downtown Portland, OR.
5½" x 8½", black-and-white photocopy on white paper

MALE STRIPER INTERESTED IN MAKING HOME PORN MOVIE'S ALL KIND'S FIRST TIME!
By Sexual S,W,M, good Looking 5'8", 155LB Brown Hair, Eyes green work Construction would Like to try Making movie's porn, if you want were a mask ok. any typ of Porn Movie's I would Like to try! [smiley face] watter sport's, Toy's, Loytion's, Bondadge Torcher, Peirceing nipple's & Head of Dick wiping, Me a Sex Slave for orgy 2,3,4,5, any Size! any Looks? I will Sumitt to your wishis Chain me up, Brand Me!! Fuck me! AnyThing Im Clean No AiD's or disase!!! Page (C______[m]) at 8__-8___ CaLL will Be answerd Right away smoke & Drink ok e[illegible]

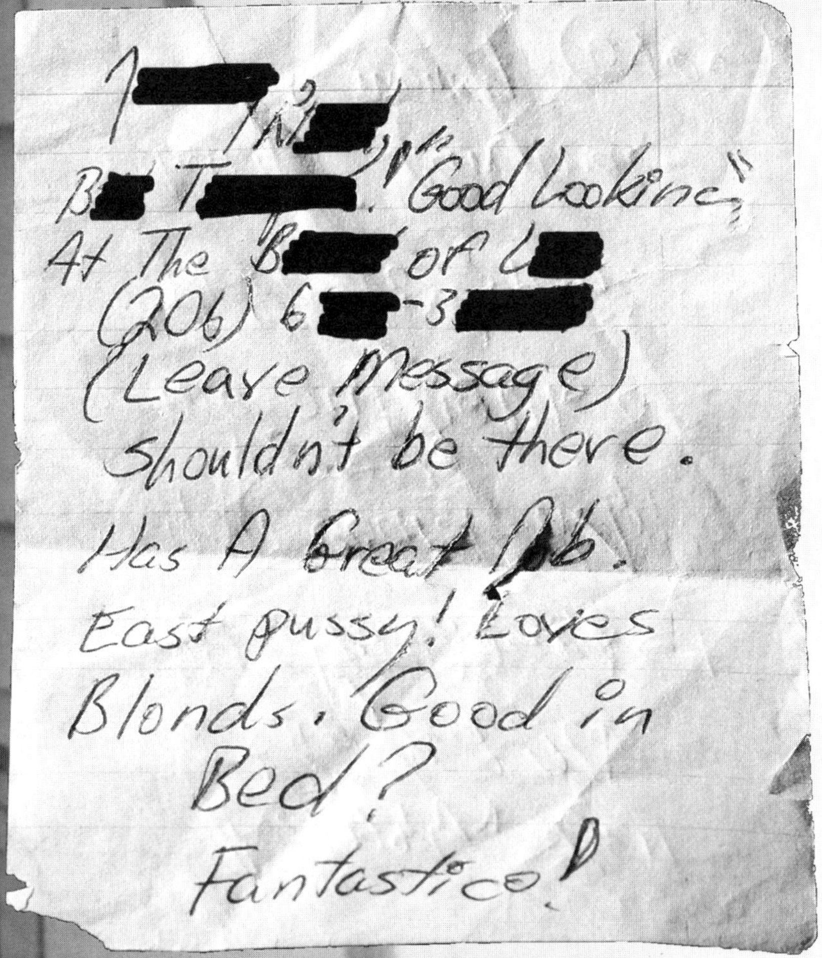

J____[f], N____[f],
B___ T_______[m]! "Good Looking"
At The B____ of L___[mission]
(206) 6__-3___
(Leave Message)
Shouldn't be there.
Has A Great Job.
East pussy! Loves
Blonds. Good in
Bed?
Fantastico!

Found by David R. on the corner of 5th Avenue and Seneca in Seattle, WA., on his way to work.
3¼" x 4⅛", black ballpoint pen on notepaper

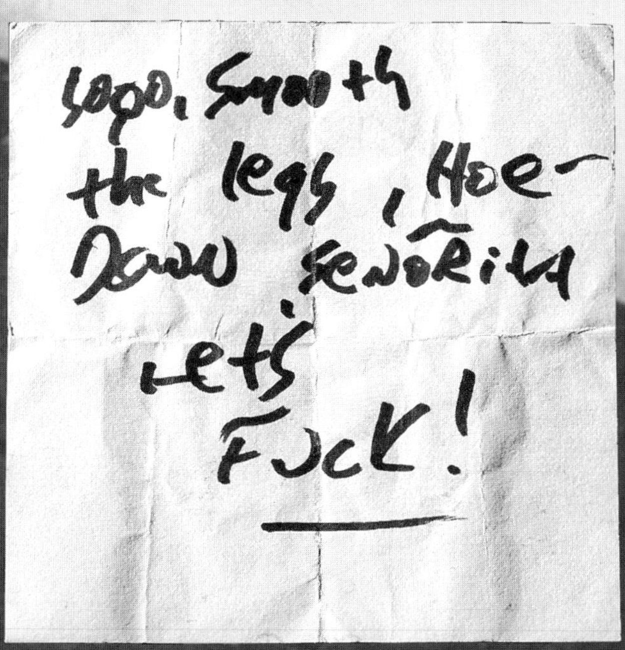

Sooo, Smooth
the legs, Hoe–
Down Señorita
Let'S
FUCK!

Found by Jaki C. on a couch during a party in Portland, OR. She thinks the note may have been meant for her.
3⅜" x 3⅜", black permanent marker on notepaper

PERSONAL THOUGHTS

No read ↓ No read ↓

14425

tuesday
09/16/97 I am really negative this morning because I am really fucking tired and I'm coming down with a cold. This weekend ended too quickly, and today started to slowly. The days recently drag on, but, for the first time in my completly [illegible] up-tight life, I want to start school-work. I'm tired of doing these "bonding" exercises. It is good for the community and all, but after a while, its a pain in the ass. My son of a bitch step-dad is coming back today, and it seems as if every body is totally bummed out. I can go off with a drop of a hat today, so nobody better piss me off.

-A[redacted] a7

wednesday
09/17/97

I am really tired as will I be for the entire school year. I am curious about A[redacted] P[redacted] (A[redacted] B[redacted]) and C[redacted] C[redacted] (C[redacted] B[redacted]), because yesterday on "Days" when they were kissing, I saw a little more tounge action than a acted out kiss. Her ~~toug~~ tounge was in his mouth, and vise versa. A little more than acting, if you ask me...

-A[redacted] -a7

I am getting better all the time. Hopefully I can succesfully join a guild on "quake" and be able to change the name already on "quake".

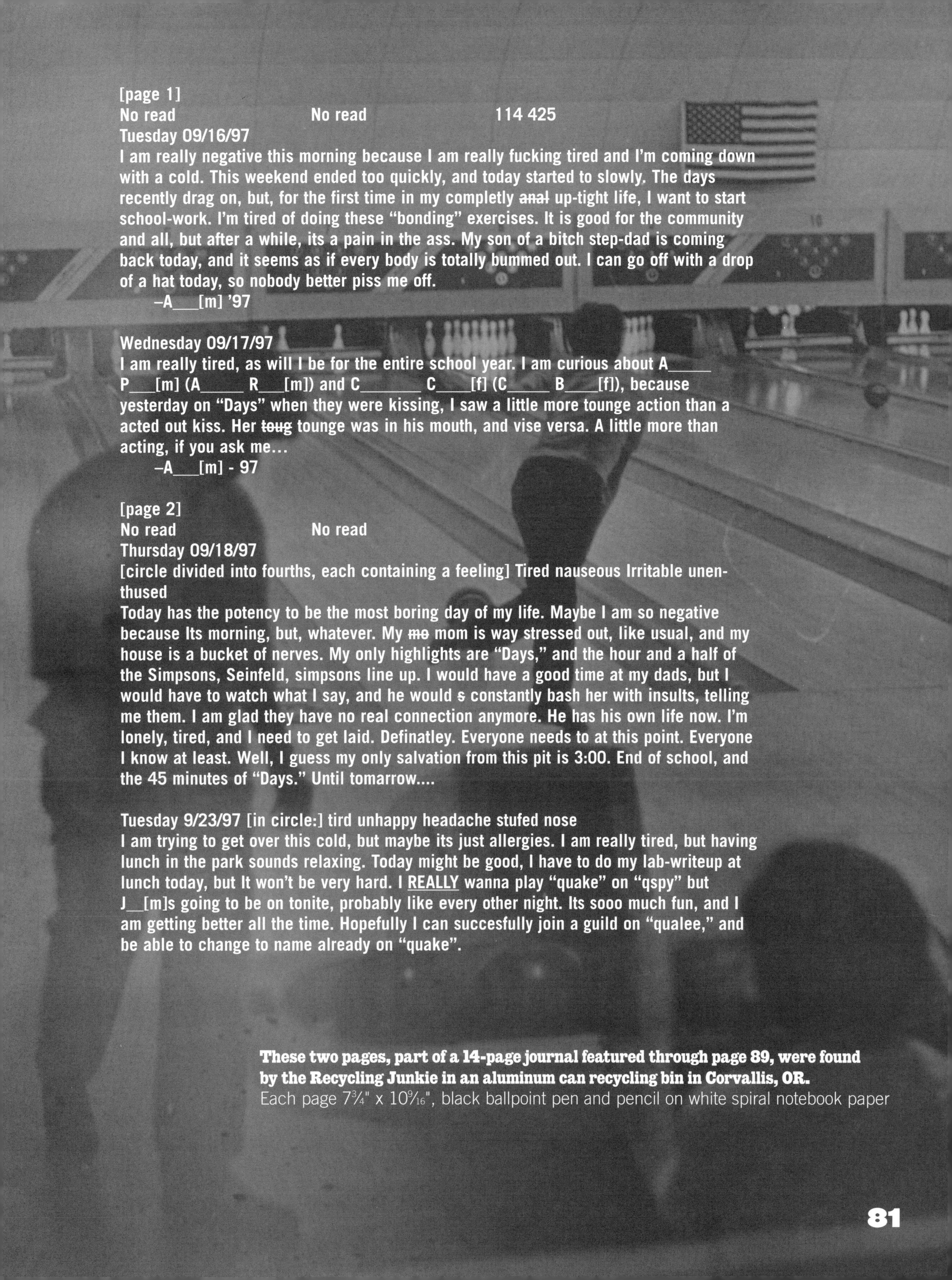

[page 1]
No read No read 114 425
Tuesday 09/16/97
I am really negative this morning because I am really fucking tired and I'm coming down with a cold. This weekend ended too quickly, and today started to slowly. The days recently drag on, but, for the first time in my completly ~~anal~~ up-tight life, I want to start school-work. I'm tired of doing these "bonding" exercises. It is good for the community and all, but after a while, its a pain in the ass. My son of a bitch step-dad is coming back today, and it seems as if every body is totally bummed out. I can go off with a drop of a hat today, so nobody better piss me off.
–A___[m] '97

Wednesday 09/17/97
I am really tired, as will I be for the entire school year. I am curious about A_____ P___[m] (A_____ R___[m]) and C_______ C____[f] (C_____ B____[f]), because yesterday on "Days" when they were kissing, I saw a little more tounge action than a acted out kiss. Her ~~toug~~ tounge was in his mouth, and vise versa. A little more than acting, if you ask me...
–A___[m] - 97

[page 2]
No read No read
Thursday 09/18/97
[circle divided into fourths, each containing a feeling] Tired nauseous Irritable unenthused
Today has the potency to be the most boring day of my life. Maybe I am so negative because Its morning, but, whatever. My ~~mo~~ mom is way stressed out, like usual, and my house is a bucket of nerves. My only highlights are "Days," and the hour and a half of the Simpsons, Seinfeld, simpsons line up. I would have a good time at my dads, but I would have to watch what I say, and he would ~~s~~ constantly bash her with insults, telling me them. I am glad they have no real connection anymore. He has his own life now. I'm lonely, tired, and I need to get laid. Definatley. Everyone needs to at this point. Everyone I know at least. Well, I guess my only salvation from this pit is 3:00. End of school, and the 45 minutes of "Days." Until tomarrow....

Tuesday 9/23/97 [in circle:] tird unhappy headache stufed nose
I am trying to get over this cold, but maybe its just allergies. I am really tired, but having lunch in the park sounds relaxing. Today might be good, I have to do my lab-writeup at lunch today, but It won't be very hard. I REALLY wanna play "quake" on "qspy" but J__[m]s going to be on tonite, probably like every other night. Its sooo much fun, and I am getting better all the time. Hopefully I can succesfully join a guild on "qualee," and be able to change to name already on "quake".

These two pages, part of a 14-page journal featured through page 89, were found by the Recycling Junkie in an aluminum can recycling bin in Corvallis, OR.
Each page 7¾" x 10⁹⁄₁₆", black ballpoint pen and pencil on white spiral notebook paper

[page 3]
Wednesday 9/24/97 [in circle:] negative Tired Itch eyes Nauseus
As you see, I am not a morning person. We're trying a new way of getting ready for school today, because we're always the first ones here. The extra 5 minutes of sleep will do me good...and I might actually get in breakfast ~~in~~ now!! Today I can just barely keep my eyes open, and my allergies are hitting me big-time. My eyes itch like crazy, and I all stuffed-up. Today definatley isn't my day.

Thursday 9/25/97 [in circle:] tird tired tired tired
I am really tired today. I was awake till 3:15 am due to what sounded like a mouse clawing the wall. It was the most annoying sound in the world. I'm in a good mood today, which is really surprising. Science and mythology are today, and I am anxious to tell the myths I read earlier. Mythology is my favorite class, and then comes Science. I think this year, math has the potential to be a good, fun class, just as long as I ask for help if I don't understand Something

Mondy 9/29/97 [in circle:] Sick Sick Sick Sick
Ugh. I have gotten my sisters cold. She had to come back home on friday because she is so sick. She has a real bad immune system, so I doubt I will get it as bad as she did. I cant miss anymore. school though. On a plus, I have given it to J__[m]. Ha Ha. Today can be a good day if I keep a positive attitude. Until tomarrow...

[page 4]
Tuesday 09/30/97 [in circle:] Tird tired positive tired
Last night, J__[m] got D_____[m] to play "Q____."[online video game] I am really good with the HWguy. The soldier is the hardest to play. They are really slow. The scouts are pretty cool. They are really fats, and can capture the flags. Did u only play the Demoman? What it a gatling gun? That gun belongs to pyros, and Demomen. Pyros shoot fire. And an axe that heals HP. Medics also cannot be poisined by other medics and heal 2 HP every few seconds. HWguys have 300 armour and 200 bullets. ~~You can change we~~ Each guy has certain weapons. Snipers have a sniper rifle and a nail gun

[various stick illustrations of weapons]
gatling
Nailgun
soldiers rocket
snipers gun
medic super nailgun

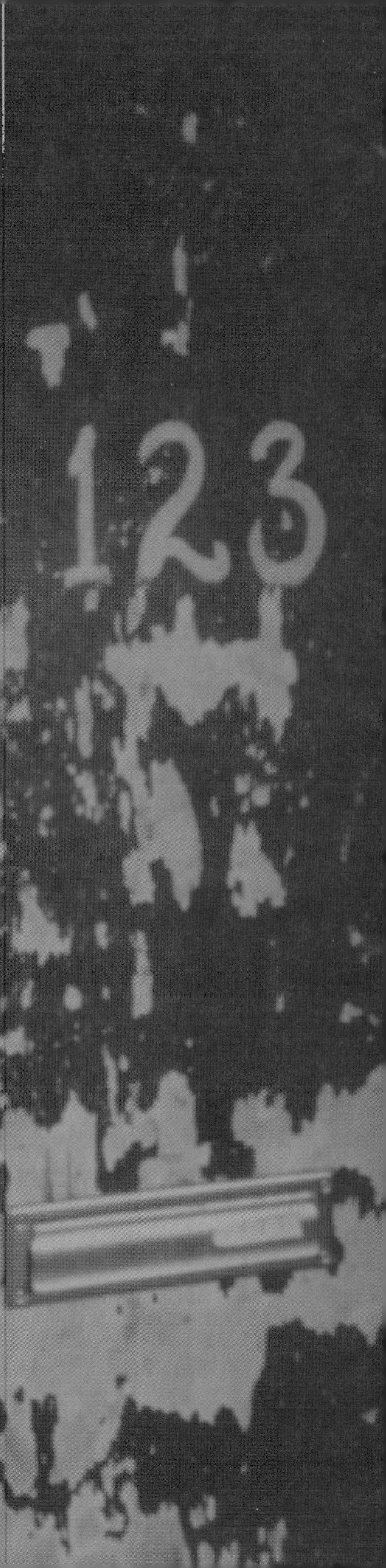

wednesday

9/24/97 Negative | Tired

As you see, I am not a morning person.
We're trying a new way of getting ready

Tuesday

09/30/97 Tired | Positive | Tired

Last night, J[redacted] got D[redacted] to play "Q[redacted]".
I am really good with the HWguy. The soldier is the hardest to play. They are really slow. The scouts are pretty cool. They are really fast, and can capture the flags. Did u only play the Demoman? What is a gatling gun? That gun belongs to pyros, and Demomen. Pyros shoot fire. And an axe that heals HP. Medics also cannot be poisined by other medics and heal 2 HP every few seconds. Hwguys have 300 armour and 200 bullets.
~~You can charge in~~
Each guy has certain weapons. Snipers have a sniper rifle and a nailgun

Thursday

9/25/9

Monday

9/29/97

Wednesday
10/1/97

Ugh. Somebody here has B.O. and I know who it is. But since the teachers will read this, I won't say the name. I am ~~...~~ anxious to play against Dan on [redacted] tonite, and I am going over to his house this weekend. Not much to say today. Until tomarrow......

Thursday
~~Wednesday~~
10/2/97

I kick butt at [redacted] with the HW GUY. I really like the demo man, but I am by far the best with the HW guy. But, I must also take into consideration that there were only 8 people on the server I chose. Hehe..., Ahem. I played [redacted] a long time last night, from 8:00 pm to 11:15 pm. Oh well, I guess I'm just psyched. Until tomarrow...

Monday
10/6/97

AAAAHHH!, [redacted] came today! It is really fun! But I dont wanna talk about that. [redacted] is smelling exceptionally "ripe" this morning. Has he ever heard of deodorant? I love to critizize people. [redacted] and [redacted] are the biggest suck-ups I have ever seen! For some reason the "[redacted] twins" always state the obvious, and that stupid lisp will haunt me for all eternity. [redacted] needs to stop breathing through her mouth, and [redacted] needs a good ass-kicking. AAhh. Until Tomarrow..

well. Daus is ~~a~~ ~~...~~ back to its usual time slot, thank-god. I'm antsy to see what happened yesterday [redacted] rocks, but I can't attack shite! That really bites. ~~...~~ whatever. Until tomarrow...

[page 5]
wednesday 10/1/97 [in circle:] tired anxious tird tired
Ugh. Somebody here has B.O. and I know who it is. But since the teachers will read this, I won't say the name. I am ~~axn~~ anxious to play against D__[m] on q____ tonite, and I am going over to his house this weekend. Not much to say today. Until tomarrow ......

~~Wednesday~~ Thursday 10/2/97 [in circle:] [illegible] Full tired tired
I kick butt at Q____ with the HWGUY. I really like the demo man, but I am by far the best with the HWguy. But, I must also take into consideration that there were only 8 people on the server I chose. Hehe...., Ahem. I played Q____ a long time last night, from 8:00 pm to 11:18pm. Oh well, I guess I'm just psyched. Until tomarrow....

Monday 10/6/97 [in circle:] UO UO UO UO
AAAAHHH! U_____ O_____[online computer service] came today! It is really fun! But I dont wanna talk about that. F____[m] is smelling exceptionally "ripe" this morning. Has he ever heard of deodorant? I love to critizize people. N___[m] and C____[m] are the biggest suck-ups I have ever seen! For some reason the "D_____ twins" always state the obvious, and that stupid lisp will haunt me for all eternity. E____[f] needs to stop breathing through her mouth, and A_____[m] needs a good ass-kicking. AAhh. Until Tomarrow...

[page 6] [next to small drawing] thruster
10/7/97
[in circle:] — tied — stressed
I actually got to bed before 10:30 last night! Omigod! But I am still very tired. I am stressed because I need to work double time this year in math to get into Algebra 2. The Algebra I book which I'm in contains Algebra, Geometry, and a little Algebra 2. If I finish the book this year, I be right back on track. I'm in a weird mood today, not quite irritable, not quite happy. But at least I am not In a bad mood. I might have to kick L____'s[f] ass....Just joking. Until tomarrow

10/8/97 [in circle:] tired inter[illegible] sleepy weird
Uh-Oh! D___ of O__ L____ won't be on at the usual 3:00pm time today. It comes on at 10:30 am today, due to the baseball world series. Damn. Wednesdays are always fairly Ok episodes. Thursdays bite asshole. Fridays kick ass. So do Mondays. Tryed to play U_____-O_____ last night. Spent half the damn time trying to get it to work, and make a stupid character. Ugh. I am also extremely tired today aswell. Whatever. Until tomarrow...

10/9/97 [in circle:] ouch tird ouch in-pain
I got my finger stuck in one of the 3 rigns of my binder! Ouch! Oh well. "Days" is ~~a ba~~ back to its usual time slot, thank-god. I'm antsy to see what happened yesterday. U_____ O_____ rocks, but I can't attack shite! That really bites. ~~Oh w~~ Whatever. Until tomarrow...

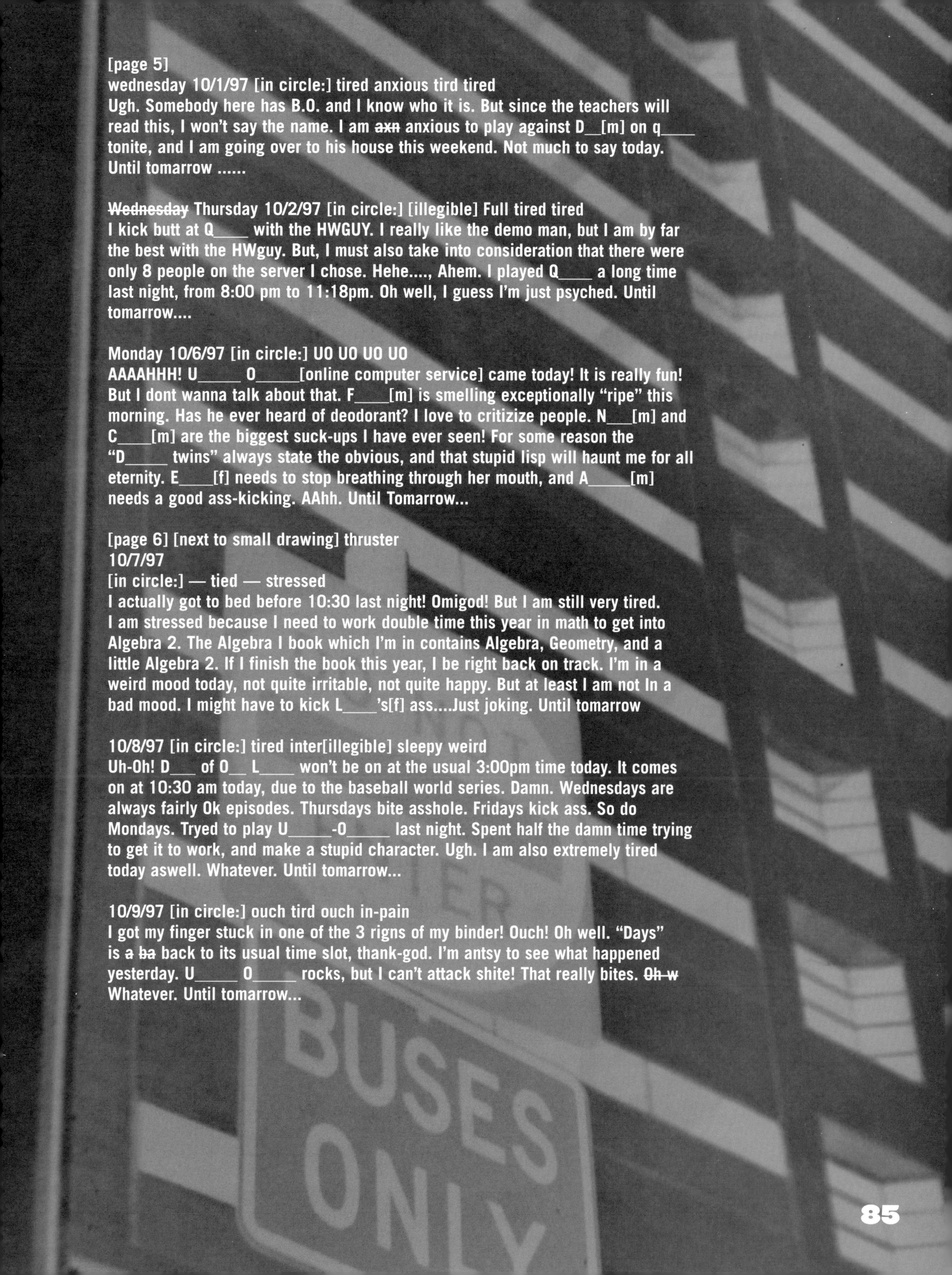

[page 7]
10/13/97 [in circle:] Sore – tired Sick
Man, I have to be coming down with a cold. I am feeling very tired, and I am writing this very slow. Well not very slow but pretty slow. In U_____ news, I made an awesome chacter, but since they have problems with the servers, I kept losing my character. I am not in a very talkitive mood today, or should iI say writive mood today, so this is where I will end. Until tomarrow...

~~10/14/97~~ 10/14/97 [in circle:] Sick tired tire tired
Tired, Tired, Tired, Sick, Sick Sick!!! Godamn! And to top all that shit off, I got some fucking soap in my goddamn, eye!!! And, I have come to an analasis. ~~E~~ Just about every one at this school gets ~~af~~ on my nerves. I would love to write every thing that I don't like about just about everyone here, but, I don't have that much time. Every time I look up, D__[f] has that stupid look on her face, as if D_____ Doughnuts is giving away free food. You know. The one where she looks up with her eyes ~~wid~~ WIDE open and her mouth clenched. Jesucs Christ!! Whatever. Until tomarrow....

[page 8]
10/20/97 [in circle:] tired stuffy – –
Ugh. I'm back. At school. Damn. I had a very unproductive weekend, but I learned a lot about U_____. Jesus, that game kicks ass! Its really addictive. Almost more-so than "Days!" I love to talk about it, and I love thinking about it. I feel awful about J_____'s[f] book. 4 days over-due because of me. *sigh*. GOD!! U_____, U_____, U_____, U_____! Whatever. Until tomarrow...

10/21/97 [illegible notes in circle] Unreadable jambles! Shit. J_____[f] is going to jump ion my shit today, because I didn't go to that stupid P&T meeting. I am tired of this crap. Too many people give me shit. So when asked why I didn't go to that stupid meeting, I'll say, "I had other things to do." When ~~w~~ asked what those "things" were, I'll say, "Just things. Thats my business." Whatever. Until tomarrow...

10/22/97 [illegible notes in circle] More unreadable ~~s~~ jambles! Journal writing time is stupid. All we do is sit on our asses, and write lies and bullshit in these fucking journals. Ha Ha Ha. Not me. I tell it straight. All the girls at this school are fucking dogs. Not one attractive one in the bunch. E____[f] has the potential to be a very pretty girl when she gets older. I can see it in her. I think she has a little ~~cr~~ crush on me, but I can't seem to prove it. Some attractive, ~~a~~older, female students better come to the school this year! Whatever. Until Tomarrow...

[page 9]
10/247/97 [in circle:] – – – – I don't feel like writing at the moment. D__[f] is pissing me off already. For some reason, I feel that I can't write my true feelings in this book, because its at school, and a person could steal it very easily. So, yeah, I don't trust half of the little fucks at this school. Some of the people in this school aren't too bad, but many get on my nerves. D__[m] just farted, looked around, and pretended not to hear it. Yuck! Any way, the day is going to suck, i'm sure, unless something amazing happens. Whatever. Until tommarrow...

10/28/97 [in circle:] Tired Tired Tired I don't know
I am actually not very tired at all. But I couldn't think of anything else to say. It is just getting harder and harder to get up in the morning. I go to bed at a regular time: 11:30, but I can't get up worth shit. D__[f] has definatley replaced C____ S_____ [m/f?] from last-year. They don't have the same voice, but both voice piss me off. Grrr. I am in a fairly bad mood today, probably because I don't wanna bike anywhere. Let alone A____ elementary school. I don't want to be with little 3rd and 4th grade little brats. Talk about awkward.. Whatever. Until tommarrow...

[page 10]
10/29/97 – I don't feel like writing in my journal today whatever. Until tommarrow...

10/30/97 – I'm tired of people in general. D__[f] is the loudest one in this stupid school, as she's the one telling us to be quiet. I have had my fill with damn near every-one at this school. I will list the people: J______[f], h_____[f], O______[m], F____[m], m____[m], b_______[m], m______[f], a____[m], a_____[m], L_____[f], s____[m], s___[m], c____[m/f?], n___[m]. e____[f], s_____[f], b___[f], c_________[f], k_____[f], D__[f], m____[f], l____[f]. Now I will tell you why I very much dislike the "people": J______[f]. Always wanting to bring attention to herself by making loud noises, or doing theatrics. H_____[f]. The biggest follower I have ever met. O______[m]: Stupidest asshole and most incompetent person in the entire school. F____[m]: Smells like shit, and needs to stop flirting with L_____ E.[f] M____[m]: A little shit. B______[m]: He has to win and be the best all the time, even though he sucks. M______[f]: A little slut whore. A____[m]: EEDIN!

10/1

(bore | tired | sick)

Man, I have to be coming down with a cold. I am feeling very tired, and I am writing this very slow. Well not very slow but pretty slow. In [redacted] news, I made an awesome chacter, but since they have problems with the servers, I kept losing my character. I am not in a very talkitive mood today, or should I say writive mood today, so this is where I will end. Until tomarrow...

~~10/14/97~~

10/14/97

(sick | tired | tire | tired)

Tired, Tired, Tired, sick, sick sick!!! Godamn! And to top all that shit off, I got some fucking soap in my goddamn, eye!!! And, I have come to an analasis. ~~I~~ Just about every one at this school gets ~~o~~ on my nerves. I would love to write every thing that I don't like about just about everyone here, but, I don't have that much time. Every time I look up, [redacted] has that stupid look on her face, as if she just heard that [redacted] Doughnuts is giving away free food. You know. The one where she looks up with her eyes ~~wi~~ WIDE open and her mouth clenched. Jesus Christ!! Whatever. Until tomarrow...

those ... whatev...

my business." Whatever.

← More unreadable ~~j~~ jambles! Journal writing time is stupid. All we do is sit on our asses, and write lies and bullshit in these fucking journals. Ha Ha Ha. Not me. I tell it straight. All the girls at this school are fucking dogs. Not one attractive one in the ... [redacted] has the potential to be a very pretty ... older. I can see it in her. I ... me, but I

A[redacted]N

I am not a writer I am...
Fre...

...o Write. Sorry. Me feel no writ...
...ill tommarow...

...alked to [redacted] today. I wa...
go try out that French ...
9:00am. But it was switche...
...use my mom still wants to
[redacted] about it. I think that if
a class at C.H.S. I shoul...
classes at C.H.S. But [redacted]
...eed to be challenged more,
French 3 is extremely cha...
actually getting a C+ in it
...we'll see what ~~ha~~ happens. Wh...
...ll tommarow...

...am not sure if I am in a...
...d or not today. No UO for
...nth now, because we alrea...
... our time. I plan to
... cursive this enti...
...eroid. When one writes i...
...he words tend to be
...rsive always looks g...
...a away, but always ...
...nda shitty up-close. En...
...rsive for now. Whatever. Unt...

11/3/97 - Today, I am really tired. And my eye hurts
hell. So I rub it. It becomes blood-shot. C...
3 day week this... week. Thursday and t...
off. [redacted] and [redacted] dressed-up like
on Thursday, and I am amazed tha...
aren't staying in that skater/punk ou...
[redacted] is making us stop now. Whatever ...
tommarow...

11/4/97 - Geez! I am in the worst mood ...
And I have no idea why. Well, ac...
do know why. French will be no more...
the end of November, and I will [redacted]
bike to C.H.S. everyday. [redacted]
and I think [redacted] will h...
teacher. But I have to go to C.H...
all in the same level of Frenc...
Leslie says I have to go to...
it will be a, "more challenging envi...
I will see if my mom could...
about it. I think I might go to...
[redacted] is. So is [redacted] might t...
know a lot of people there, which...
cool. The only way I could real...
school is if it makes a comp...
around. But I guess I will...
someday. Whatever. Until tomm...

...real a prick. Pete fucking asshole

[page 11]
11/3/97: Today, I am really tired. And my eye hurts like hell. So I rub it. It becomes blood-shot. Only a 3 day week this...week. Thursday and Friday off. L____[f] and M______[f] dressed-up like J______[f] on Thursday, and I am amazed that they aren't staying in that skater/punk outfit. D__[f] is making us stop now. Whatever. Until tommarrow...

11/4/97 – Geez! I am in the worst mood today! And I have no idea why. Well, actually, I do know why. French will be no more as of the end of November, and I will have to hike to C.H.S. everyday. D__[m], A____[m], S_____[f] and I think C________[f] will have a special teacher. But I have to go to C.H.S! They are all in the same level of French as me. L_____[f] says I have to go to C.H.S because it will be a "more challenging enviorment." So I will see if my mom could talk to L_____[f] about it. I think I might go to C.H.S. next-year. M___[m] is. So is D__[m]. A___[m] might too. So I will know a lot of people there, which will be pretty cool. The only way I could really stay at this school is if it makes a complete turn around. But I guess I will figure it out someday. Whatever. Until tommarrow...

[page 12]
11/5/97 – No Write. Sorry. Me feel no write not. Whatever. Until tommarow...

11/13/97 I talked to L_____[f] today. I was supposed to go try out that French class today at 9:00am. But it was switched to Tuesday, because my mom still wants to talk to L_____[f] about it. I think that if I am gunna take a class at C.H.S, I should take all my classes at C.H.S. But L_____[f] says that I need to be challenged more, yet being in French 3 is extremely challenging. I am actually getting a C+ in it right now. So, we'll see what ~~ta~~ happens. Whatever. Until tommarrow...

11/17/97 I am not sure if I am in a bad mood or not today. No UO for 1/2 a month now, because we already used up our time. I plan to write in cursive this entire Journal peroid. When on writes in cursive, the words tend to be longer cursive always looks good from far away, but always but always Kinda shitty up-close. Enough for cursive for now. Whatever. Until tommarrow...

[page 13]
11/18/97 –
I am in a pretty bad mood. And it is certain people that make me in bad moods: J______[f], O______[m], L_____ E.[f], F____[m], B___[f], K_____[f], J_____[m], (A___[m]) occasionally, B______[m], M____[f], M____[m], C____[m/f?]. What's really stupidm is that we keep screwing up this building. I figure we've got about 2 more months here. Whatever. Until tommarrow...

11/21/97
J__[m] is being a complete fucking asshole today. What a prick.

[page 14]
12/1/97
A___ M.[m]
I am not a writer. I am an actor. Everyone is a actor. Noone is who they really think they are. I think that I could write a song, but it would be really stupid. So I won't even try.

Found by M. packed up in his stage gear after a gig in Olympia, WA.
8½" x 11", computer laser print on white paper

Dear Mom,

I felt it was important to write down on paper what I need to tell you. The situation here has reached a climax of sorts, and a conclusion approaches. I am fairly certain what the outcome will be, and have made the necessary shifts in my goals. It is very unlikely I will be allowed to attend Evergreen this fall, as I do not have the funds needed to attend the counseling which I must undergo. I feel very angry and hurt by this, and it is difficult to not see it as unjust. On the one hand, society seems to think I am a threat to myself and others, but it is unable to help provide the services that it thinks will end that threat. Everyone I speak to about it seems to agree that this is contradictory and at worst even harmful to society, but it is doubtful that the situation will change.

For a while I thought that there is justice in society only as much as it doesn't interfere with more fundamental processes that are both structurally formative and inherently unfair. Attending psychiatric counseling in the Olympia area seemed to be an example of this. I can attend counseling and help myself and the rest of society if I have the money, but I can't get the money required unless I learn a skill society finds useful, which I cannot do until I attend counseling.

All of this, from the fight me and N[redacted] had, to the court order, to the fines and psychiatric counseling I never received, leads me to the conclusion that I am very messed up, and am an unwanted, unnecessary member of society. Often, I wonder why this is so. I assume it is because I lack the appropriate guidance, am considered uncontrollable (I like to do things my own way, I like to be noticed for doing things in a new and different manner, I am creative, etc...,) and am poor. It is frustrating to recognize how difficult it is to change these possible causes.

It makes me feel that a mistake had been made somewhere, and that I wasn't ever supposed to be here. Contrary to what you and some others might tell me, I am now fairly certain that it is actually the intention of society to communicate this to me; society *is* telling me that mistakes have been made, and that I was never supposed to be here. Its telling me that I am not useful or productive as I am, and so I must decide whether or not I am willing to change myself in fundamental ways so that I can be what it needs me to be.

There's a lot of trust that comes with that. Trust that I will live through those changes and not be gutted thoroughly in the process. Trust that society is really looking out for my interests. Trust which I don't really possess, because I know both sides of the coin which is society, and I know that it is not always there to help. Sometimes it is there to kill a person's spirit, or take someone's life arbitrarily.

I've done a lot of mean and vicious things in my life. Things I will regret the rest of my life, things that I have to live with and urges I know I have, and have to control. I have a responsibility to myself and every living person in this world to deal with it, which means I have to eradicate them as much as possible.

This day sucks. I can't fucking believe [redacted] is married. Happily married. I thought I found the man. Commissioner at 29 & just brilliant. Fuck. It was such a good crush. For all the right reasons. I'm so exhausted. I had the worst night of sleep in history & spent the morning crazed on caffeine & stressed out about money. Money. Time. I can't seem to find the right balance of the two. God, <u>MARRIED</u>. Married. He is married. I hate being this tired. I get all emotional. I hate my cheap-ass furniture. I hate being broke. Fuck. I just totally lost it & balled my eyes out. I can't do the work/school thing for another quarter. This internship is what I want to be doing. I guess thats not the way shit works.

Found by Rich W. inside a well-known political glossy, which had been left behind at a popular chain submarine sandwich shop in downtown Portland, OR.
8½" x 11", pencil on the back of a black-and-white photocopy on white paper of a "Guest Control Log"

Found by Julian C. on a disk purchased at an Internet cafe in Vancouver, BC.
8½" x 11", computer laser print on white paper

G[redacted] C[redacted]
Class 52
R[redacted] B[redacted]
Sept. 6 1996

-A Biography of Feelings-

I pray the sun shines again, my bones can't take this. I want heat, I want comfort, I want a filtered cigarette. God if I only had a rolling paper I could use some of these butts for a smoke. I need one, it's been two hours. Where is he? He said he'd come by today. I haven't seen him since wednesday, I'm sick of wednesday. He only seems to come by when things are good, not like M[redacted], he was always there, he took care of me. Oh M[redacted], you bastard, why?

Christ sakes, I can smell my hair, or is it my clothes, my breathe? No wonder why things are slow today. Why are you kids starting so young, why aren't you in school? Go courting? Go learn to sew? I quess your learning what it's really about, not to depend on no one, maybe that's the best lesson you could learn.

Hey look at me! Look at me! Look into these eyes! I'm not buggin you. Why are you so concerned about getting where your going. These days, you don't look, and sometimes when you do, you wish you hadn't. Oh well, it's close to time for a coffee. Maybe my ship will return, maybe I'll have a coffee and a smoke by supper time. Maybe he will come by, maybe I'll visit M[redacted] soon, I miss you M[redacted].

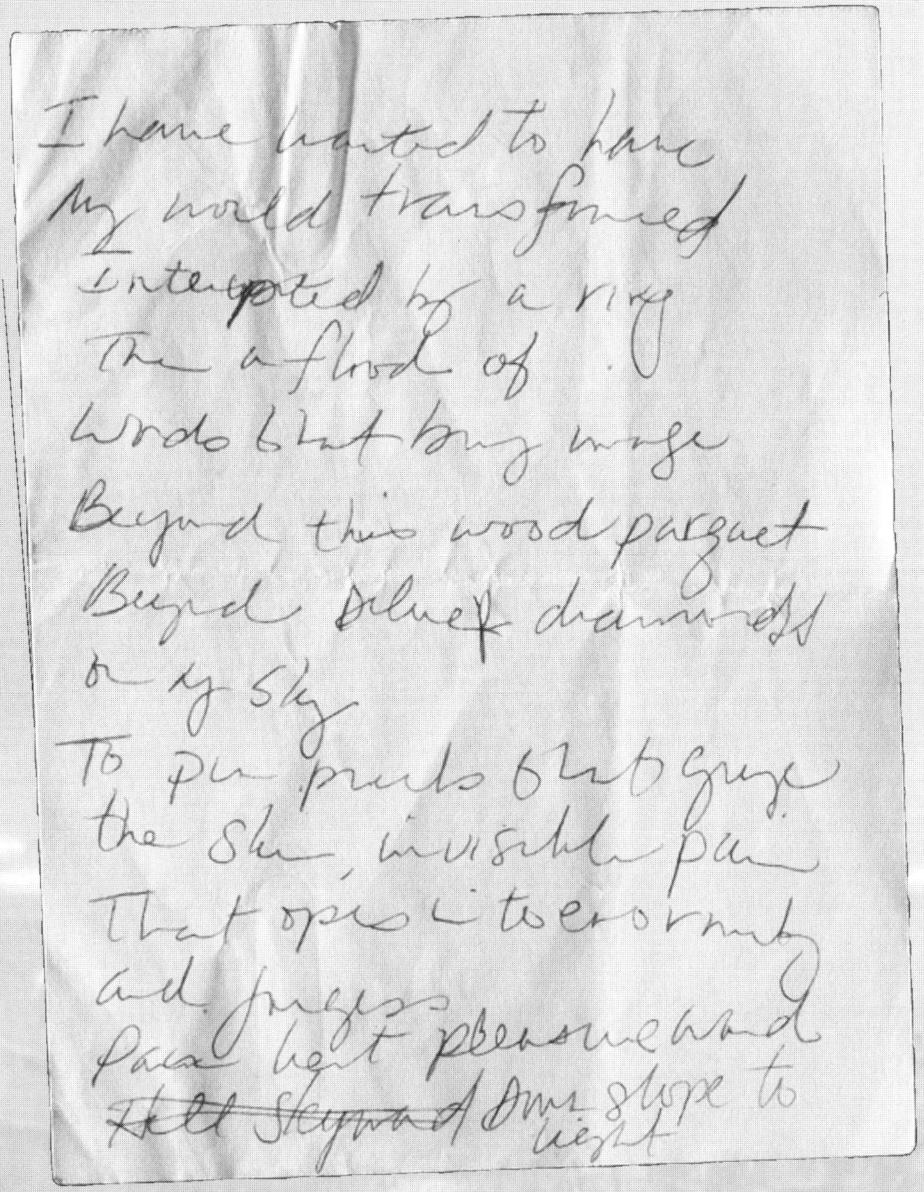
I have wanted to have
My world transformed
Interupted by a ring
Then a flood of .
Words that bring image
Beyond this wood parquet
Beyond silver diamonds
or [illegible] Sky
To pin pricks that graze
the Skin, invisible pain
That opens in to enormity
and largess
Pain bent pleasure wand
~~Hell Skyward~~ [illegible] slope to
light

Found and translated by Kim O. She found this outside a grocery store on 45th Street in the Seattle, WA, neighborhood of Wallingford.
4¼" x 5½", black ballpoint pen on the back of cream-colored notepaper from a private club in downtown Seattle

I have wanted to have
My world transformed
Interupted by a ring
Then a flood of .
Words that bring image
Beyond this wood parquet
Beyond silver diamonds
or [illegible] sky
To pin pricks that graze
the Skin, invisible pain
That opens in to enormity
and largess
Pain bent pleasure wand
Hell Skyward [illegible] slope to
light

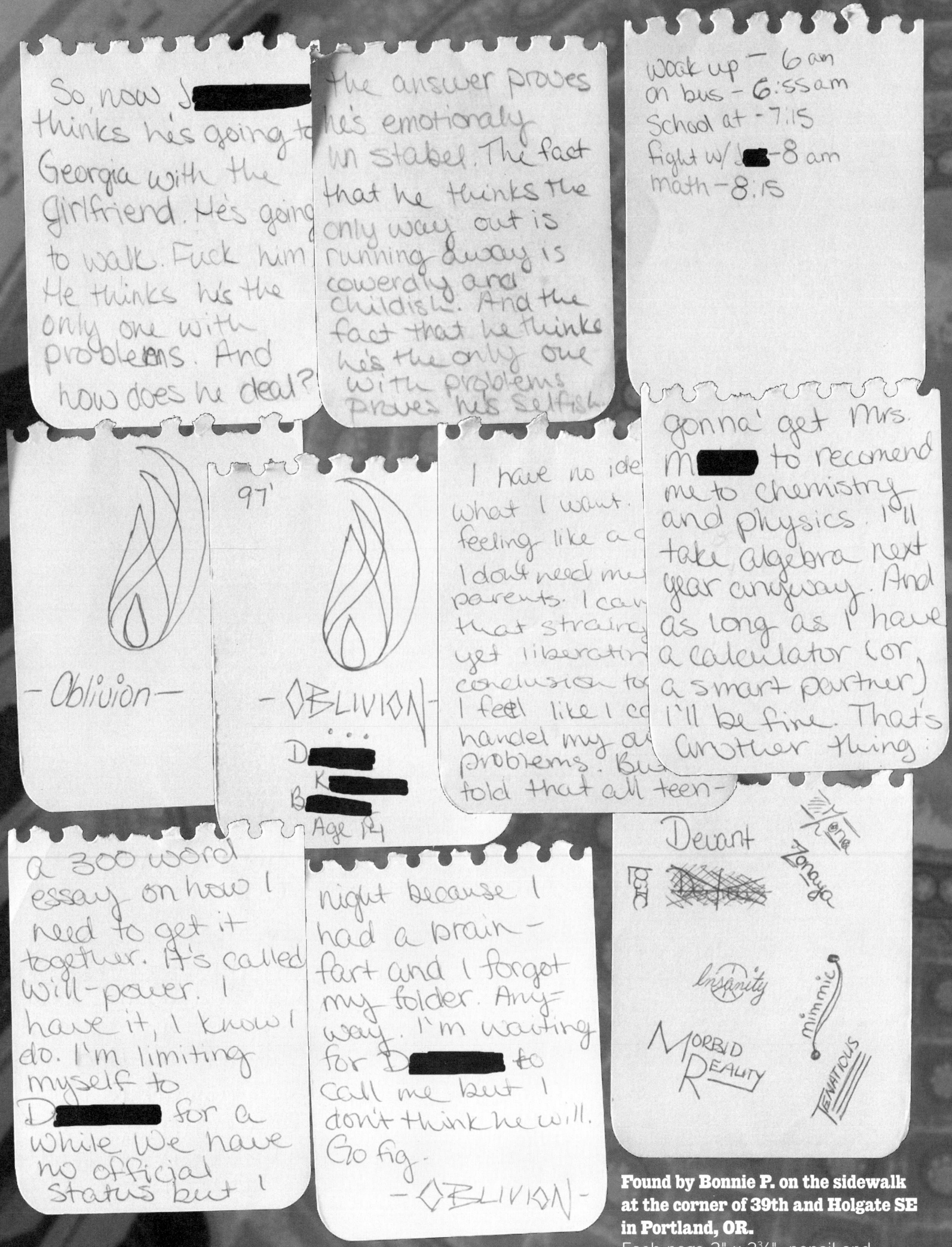

So, now J[redacted] thinks he's going to Georgia with the girlfriend. He's going to walk. Fuck him He thinks he's the only one with problems. And how does he deal?

the answer proves he's emotionaly un stabel. The fact that he thinks the only way out is running away is cowerdly and childish. And the fact that he thinks he's the only one with problems proves he's selfish

Wook up - 6 am
on bus - 6:55am
School at - 7:15
fight w/ [redacted] - 8 am
math - 8:15

- Oblivion -

97'

- OBLIVION -

D[redacted]
K[redacted]
B[redacted]
Age 14

I have no ide
what I want.
feeling like a
I don't need my
parents. I can
that straing
yet liberatin
conclusion to
I feel like I co
handel my ow
problems. Bu
told that all teen-

gonna' get Mrs. M[redacted] to recomend me to chemistry and physics. I'll take algebra next year anyway. And as long as I have a calculator (or a smart partner) i'll be fine. That's another thing.

a 300 word essay on how I need to get it together. It's called will-power. I have it, I know I do. I'm limiting myself to D[redacted] for a while. We have no official status but I

night because I had a brain-fart and I forgot my folder. Any-way. I'm waiting for D[redacted] to call me but I don't think he will. Go fig.
- OBLIVION -

Found by Bonnie P. on the sidewalk at the corner of 39th and Holgate SE in Portland, OR.
Each page 3" x 3¾", pencil and pink and blue ballpoint pen on white notepaper

[page 1] So, now, J_______[m] thinks he's going to Georgia with the girlfriend. He's going to walk. Fuck him. He thinks he's the only one with probleems. And how does he deal?

[page 2, not pictured] He runs away! That is the most juvinile, Childish, immature and the Stupidest thing I have ever herd of! The simple fact that he thought running away was

[page 3]the answer proves he's emotionaly un stabel. The fact that he thinks the only way out is running away is cowerdly and childish. And the fact that he thinks he's the only one with problems proves he's selfish.

[page 4] woak up – 6 am on bus – 6:55 am school at - 7:15 fight w/J__[m]–8 am math–8:15

[page 5] –Oblivion–

[page 6] 97'
–OBLIVION–
D______ K_______ B______[f] Age 14

[page 7] I have no idea what I want. I hate feeling like a child. I don't need my parents. I came to that strainge yet liberating conclusion today. I Felel like I can handel my own problems. But I'm told that all teen-

[page 8, not pictured] agers feel that way. I don't like being clumped w/ the majority. Next year for rotations I'll take KBPS, journalism, transportation II and probably fluid power. I'm

[page 9] gonna' get Mrs. M_____[f] to recomend me to chemistry and physics. I'll take algebra next year anyway. And as long as I have a calculator (or a smart partner) I'll be fine. That's another thing.

[page 10, not pictured] I need to quit spongeing. I have to get it together. As of next week, no more slacking. I always say that but now I have it in writing so I can make myself write

[page 11] a 300 word essay on how I need to get it together. It's called Will-power. I have it, I know I do. I'm limiting myself to D______[m] for a while. We have no official status but I

[page 12-13, not pictured] don't really care. I'm sure he's a good thing for me. But he can't treat me like a child or a whore. I'm neither. And I'll be damned if I ever am. Here's the way tomorow (1-22-97) is going to work: get up @ 6:30, leave at 7:00, be at school by 8:00, Math final @ 8:30, Nothing until 12:10, then P.E. final, then go home. I'm going to do my biology tomorow

[page 14] night because I had a brain-fart and I forgot my folder. Any-way. I'm waiting for D______[m] to call me but I don't think he will. Go fig. –OBLIVION–

[page 15, various words and phrases made into "logos"] [page 16, the word "oblivion" made into different "logos"]

[page 17] Iliad — find that in a libary

[page 18] Some days it's like, if I don't force myself to get up, I won't get up. But deep down in my heart I know I'm just a fuck up. K___[m] tells me that i'm beautyful, smart, fun to be with. Purfect. Why is he so blind?
D______ B______[f] 2-18-97 age 14

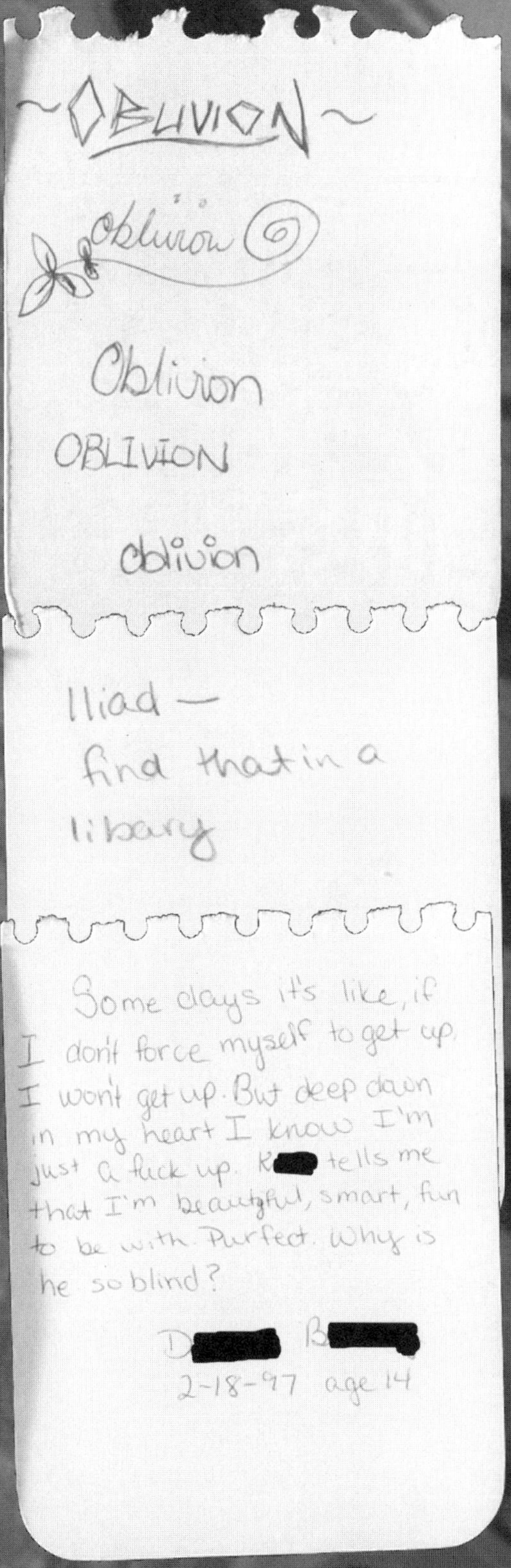

L Loneliness is a disease which affects me like no other. I Try to prevent by using Narcotics but all it does is amplify it. Why can't people accept each other? It's a question that probes my mind. The problem in life is that people think about their own needs instead of others. If we Thought about other people's desires then maybe we could quench our own desires at the same time. Maybe Loneliness is caused by a human phenomenon to strive for something better. The human compulsion is to always strive to better themselves, Why can't The human race strive to make themselves more happy. Humans are destroying this world because they strive to make Their atmosphere more suitable to themselves. When the Homosapien was Evolved it became a dangerous weapon that was unleashed upon this world. We are Just a bunch of Fuck Heads. Why can't we act more like animals. Animals don't hurt there atmosphere because they don't have the compulsion to change their environment. All they do is aclimate themselves to the environment around Them

Loneliness is a disease which affects me like no other. I Try to prevent by using Narcotics but all it does is amplify it. Why Can't people accept each other? IT's a question that probes my mind. The ~~pr~~ problem in life is that people think about their own needs ~~before~~ INSTead of others. If we Thought about other people's desires then maybe we could quench our own desires at the same time. Maybe Loneliness is Caused by a human phenomonon to strive for something better. The human compulsion is to always strive ~~for~~ to better themselves. Why can't the human race ~~to~~ strive to make themselves more happy. Humans are destroying this world because they strive to make their atmosphere more suitable to themselves. When the Homosapien was Evolved it became a dangerous weapon that was unleashed upon this world. Weo are Just a bunch of Fuck Heads. Why can't weo act more like animals. Animals don't hurt their atmosphere because they don't have the compulsion to change their environment. All they do is acclimate themselves to the environment around them.

[back, not pictured]
Basically I'm very distraught about what us humans Call Civiluzation
Loneliness is Cauzed by CivilizatioN.

Berkely, CaliforNia
1992 __ EasTer VacaTioN
aT My BroTher's a ApArTmenT
In T___ S_________'s[m] Room

Found at a gas station by someone who doesn't want us to know who they are or where they've been.
8" x 10⅞", black ballpoint pen on spiral notebook paper

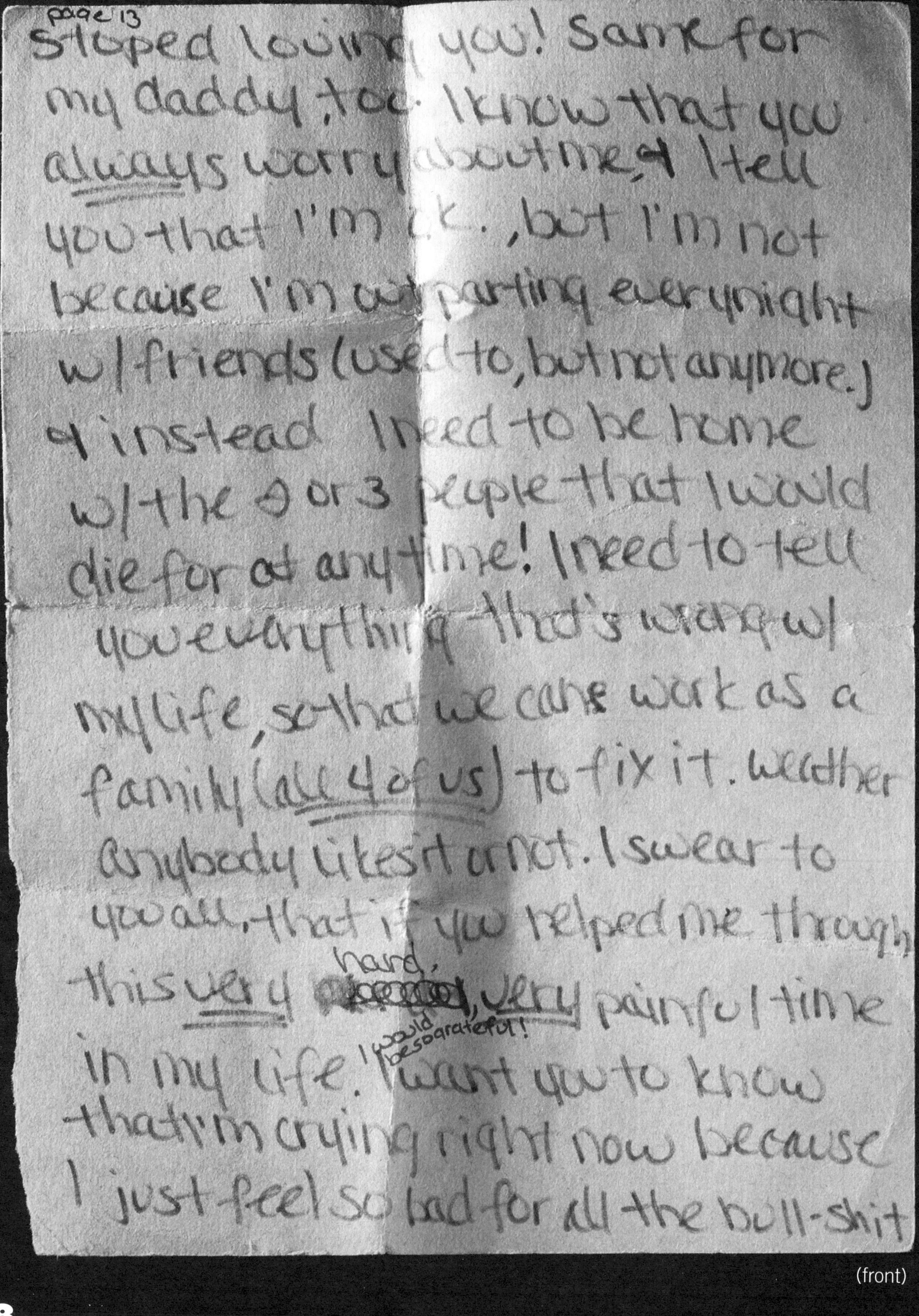
page 13
stoped loving you! Same for
my daddy, too. I know that you
always worry about me, & I tell
you that I'm ok., but I'm not
because I'm out parting every night
w/ friends (used to, but not anymore.)
& instead I need to be home
w/ the 2 or 3 people that I would
die for at any time! I need to tell
you everything that's wrong w/
my life, so that we can work as a
family (all 4 of us) to fix it. weather
anybody likes it or not. I swear to
you all, that if you helped me through
this very hard, very painful time
in my life. I would be so grateful! I want you to know
that I'm crying right now because
I just feel so bad for all the bull-shit

(front)

(back)

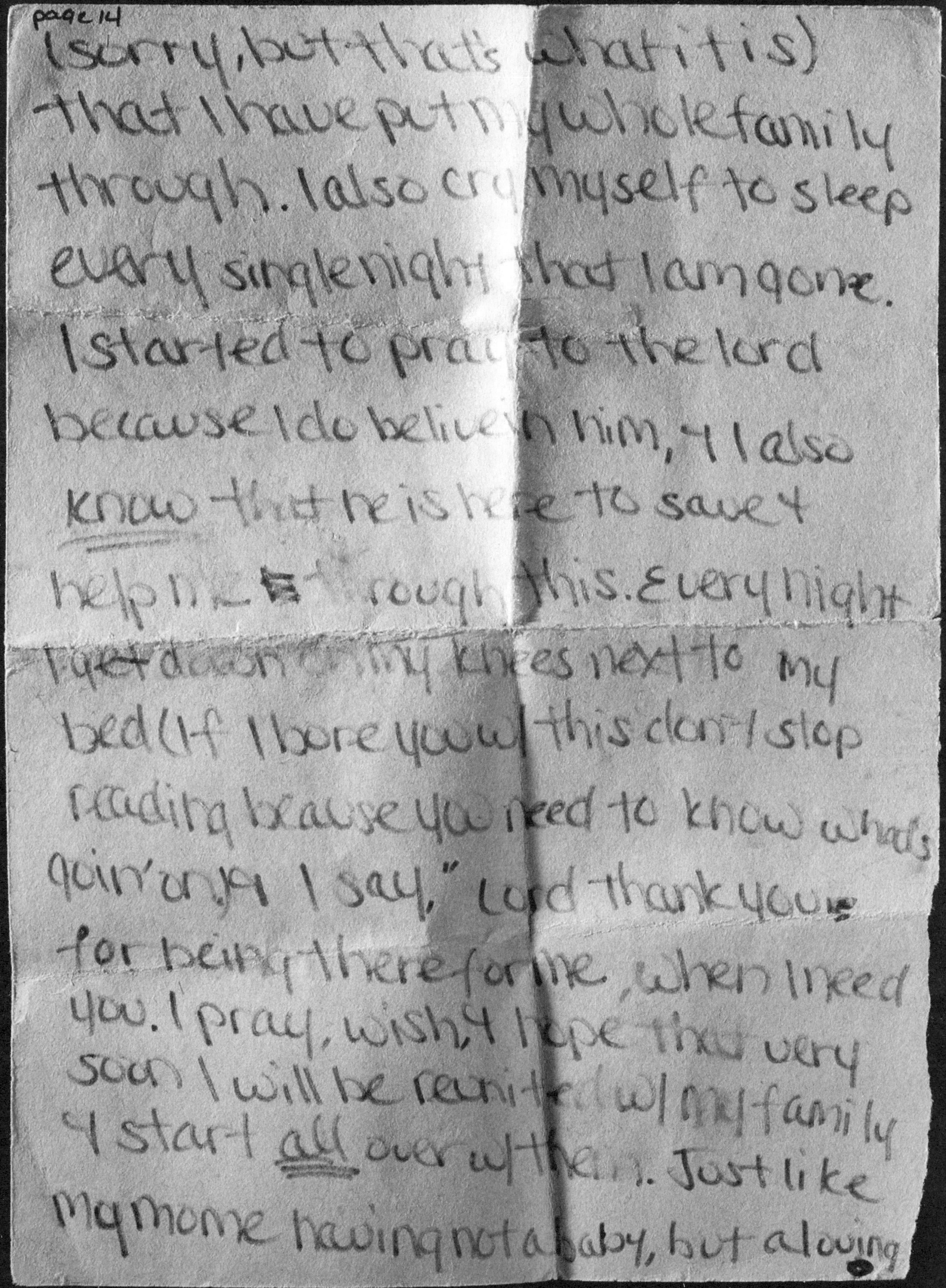
page 14
(sorry, but that's what it is)
that I have put my whole family
through. I also cry myself to sleep
every single night that I am gone.
I started to pray to the lord
because I do belive in him, & I also
know that he is here to save &
help me through this. Every night
I get down on my knees next to my
bed (If I bore you w/ this don't stop
reading because you need to know what's
goin' on.) & I say, "Lord thank you
for being there for me, when I need
you. I pray, wish, & hope that very
soon I will be reunited w/ my family
& start all over w/ them. Just like
my mome having not a baby, but a loving

Found by Ben N. in SE Portland, OR.
9" x 12", blue, red and black felt-tip marker on green construction paper.

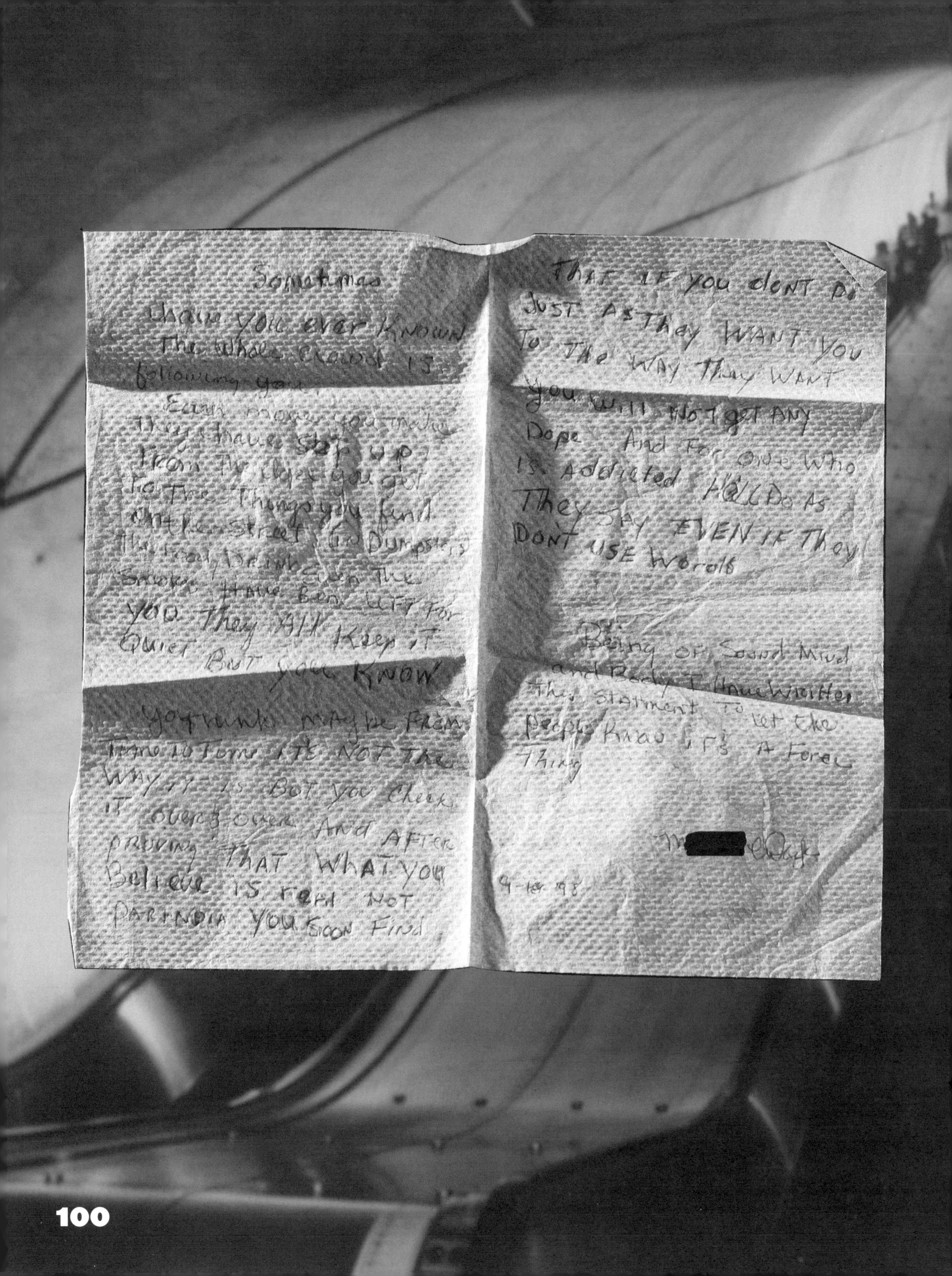
Sometimes
Have you ever known
The whole Crowd is
following you.
Every move you make
they have step up
from the dope you get
to the things you find
on the street in dumpsters
the food, drink even the
smoke have been left for
you they all keep it
quiet but you know

you think maybe from
time to time it's not the
way it is but you check
it over & over and after
proving that what you
believe is real not
paranoia you soon find

That if you dont do
just as they want you
to the way they want
you will not get any
dope and for one who
is addicted he'll do as
they say even if they
dont use words

Being of sound mind
and body I have written
this statment to let the
people know it's a Forec
thing

[redacted]

9-18-98

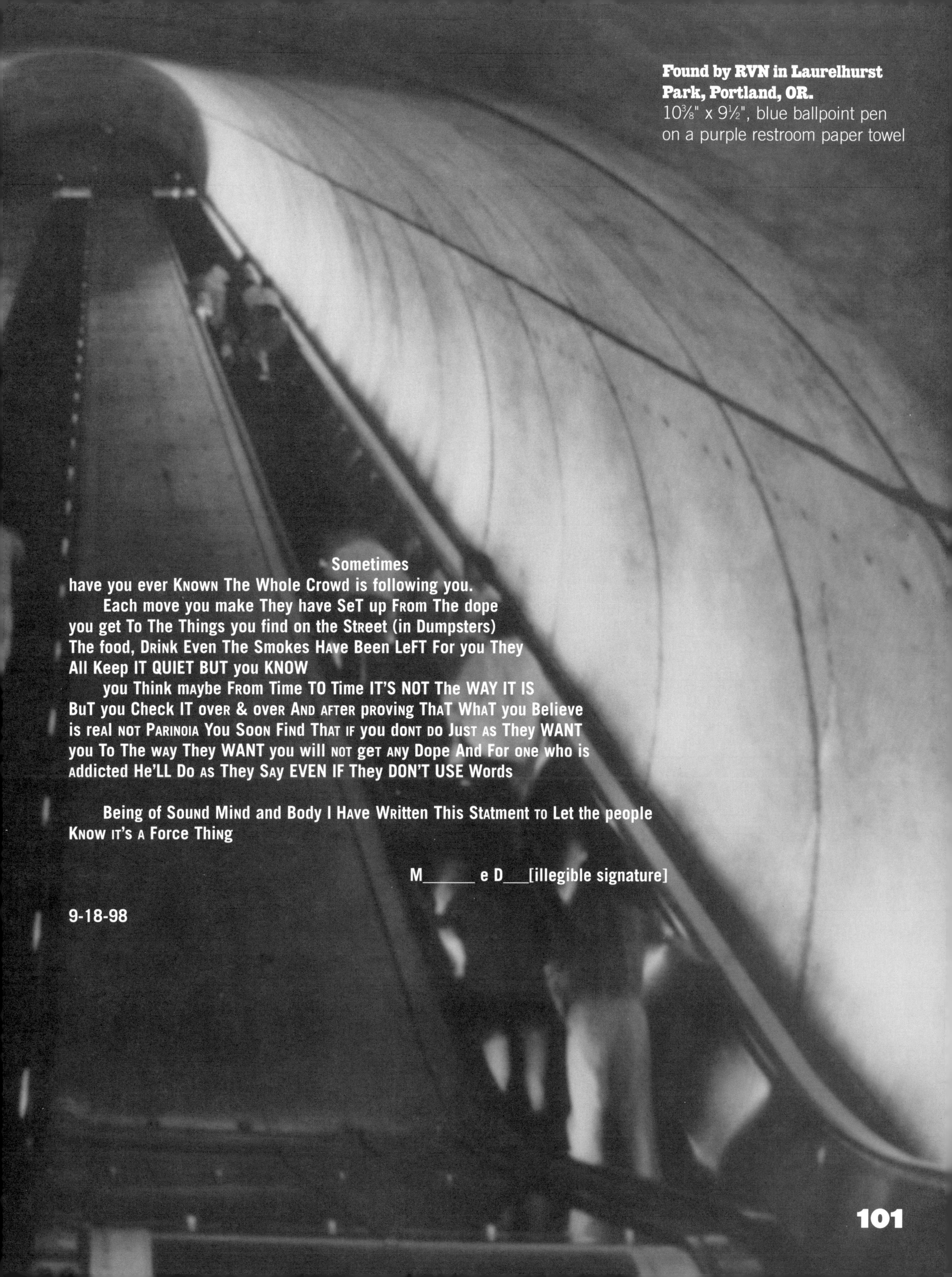

Found by RVN in Laurelhurst Park, Portland, OR.
10⅜" x 9½", blue ballpoint pen on a purple restroom paper towel

Sometimes
have you ever KNOWN The Whole Crowd is following you.
Each move you make They have SeT up FROM The dope you get To The Things you find on the STREET (in Dumpsters) The food, DRINK Even The Smokes HAVE Been LeFT For you They All Keep IT QUIET BUT you KNOW
you Think mAYbe FROM Time TO Time IT'S NOT The WAY IT IS BuT you Check IT OVER & OVER AND AFTER PROVING ThaT WhaT you Believe is real NOT PARINOIA You SOON Find THAT IF you DONT DO JUST AS They WANT you To The WAY They WANT you will NOT get ANY Dope And For ONE who is Addicted He'LL Do AS They SAY EVEN IF They DON'T USE Words

Being of SOUND Mind and Body I HAVE WRITTEN This STATMENT TO Let the people KNOW IT'S A Force Thing

M______ e D___[illegible signature]

9-18-98

like today sucks
I've desided that Im going to act like a complete dumass all day! because It Sucks I think I'll go hide in the closet now. bye that one bleed alot sorry Im Slitting my rists. I must die die die Die my hair black

I'll [illegible] you in my [illegible]

Down with teachers Down with School
FUCK THE WORLD

God make me a bird so I can Fly far far away

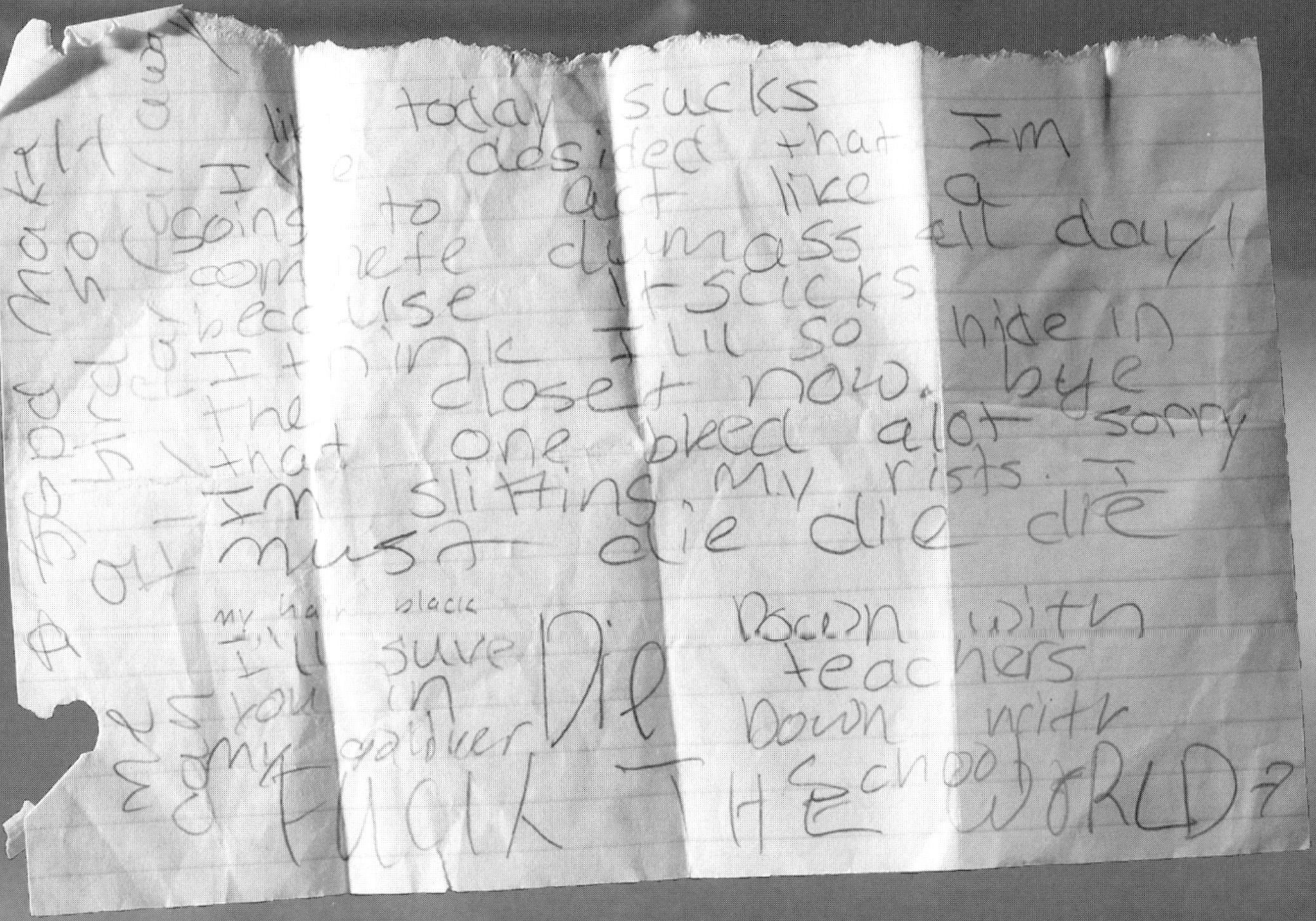

Found by Dumpster Diving in Corvallis, OR.
Approximately 8" x 4⅞", pencil on notebook paper

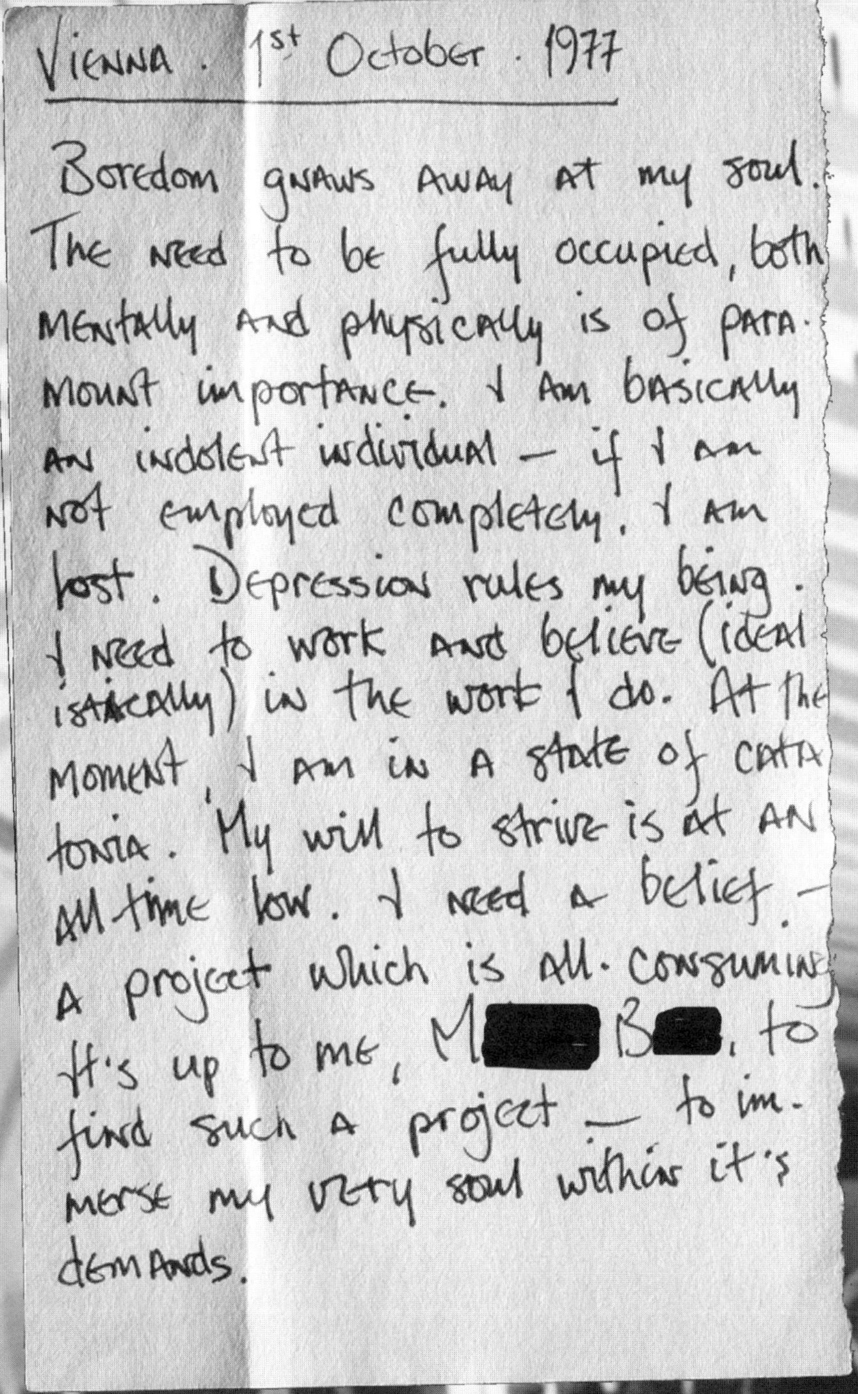

Vienna · 1st October · 1977

Boredom gnaws away at my soul. The need to be fully occupied, both mentally and physically is of para-mount importance. I am basically an indolent individual — if I am not employed completely. I am lost. Depression rules my being. I need to work and believe (ideal istically) in the work I do. At the moment, I am in a state of cata tonia. My will to strive is at an all time low. I need a belief — a project which is all-consuming It's up to me, M[redacted] B[redacted], to find such a project — to im-merse my very soul within it's demands.

Vienna • 1st October • 1977

Boredom gnaws away at my soul. The need to be fully occupied, both mentally and physically is of para-mount importance. I am basically an indolent individual — if I am not employed completely, I am lost. Depression rules my being. I need to work and believe (ideal-istically) in the work I do. At the moment, I am in a state of cata tonia. My will to strive is at an all-time low. I need a belief — a project which is all-consuming It's up to me, M______ B___[m], to find such a project — to im-merse my very soul within it's demands.

Found by Eric S. of Eugene, OR.
4¼" x 7", black felt-tip ink on the back of the last page of the paperback edition of a science fiction novel.

MY FRIEND

[front]
I ran into A__[f] on the Street and I must simply fill you in on the news. Apparently C_____[m] and E___[f] are going to get Married. This is not such a good idea. An alcoholic and a drug addict coming together to make babies. Not a good idea. I sure hope they go to detox first. Plus, do you think C_____[m] knows about E___'s[f] infidelity while he was on tour? I've heard he's stopped since he quit the band, but given her last marraige to that scoundrel M___[m] who was

[back]
always screwing around, I hope for C_____'s[m] sake that E___[f] has really changed. Anyway, that is The lastest news.

call me!
A__[f]

Found by Hillary at a bar in NW Portland, OR.
Approximately 5⅛" x 8½", red ballpoint pen on white paper

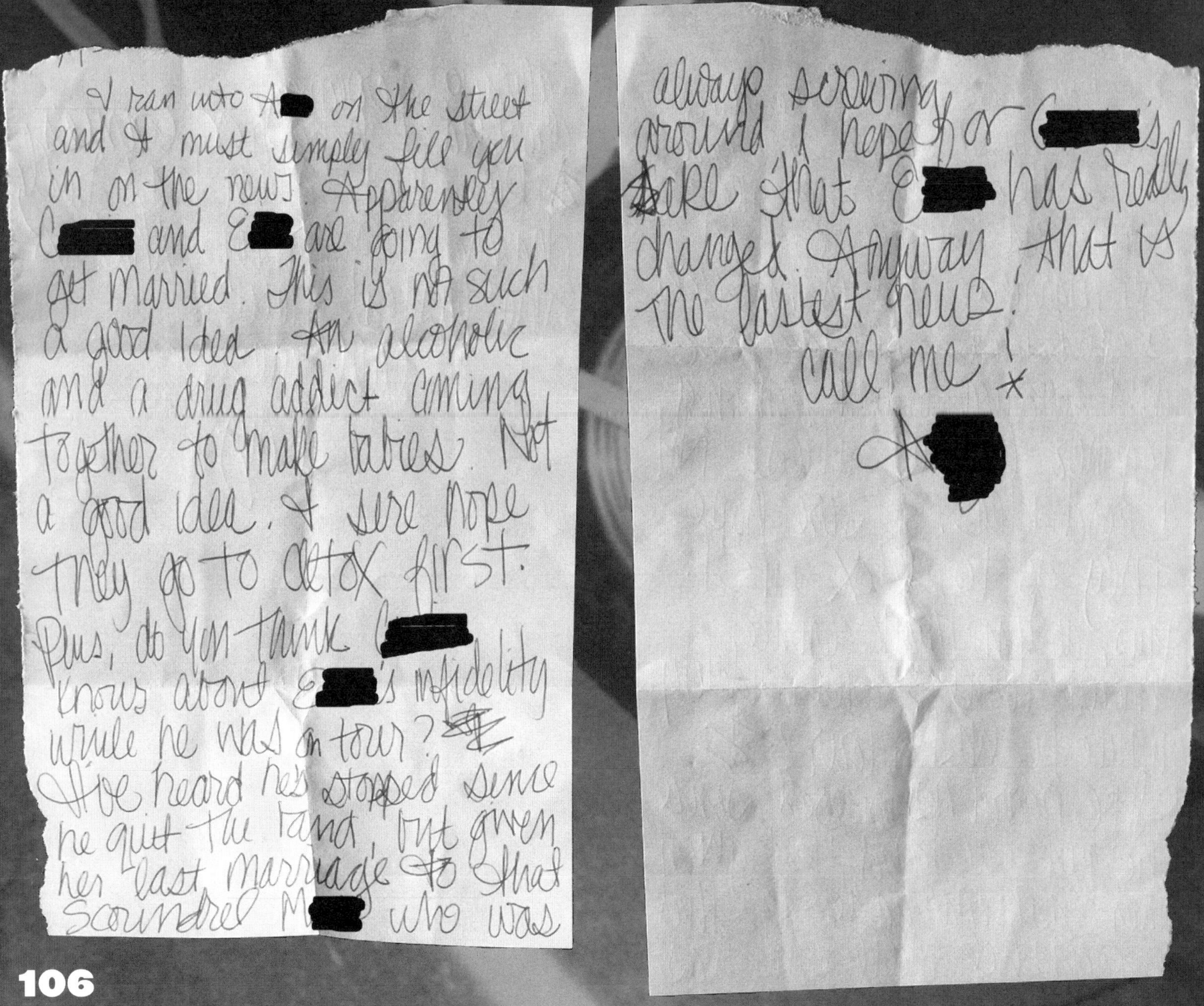
I ran into [redacted] on the street and I must simply fill you in on the news. Apparently [redacted] and [redacted] are going to get Married. This is not such a good idea. An alcoholic and a drug addict coming together to make babies. Not a good idea. I sure hope they go to detox first. Plus, do you think [redacted] knows about [redacted]'s infidelity while he was on tour? I've heard he's stopped since he quit the band, but given her last marriage to that scoundrel [redacted] who was

always screwing around I hope for [redacted]'s sake that [redacted] has really changed. Anyway that is the lastest news!
call me! *
[redacted]

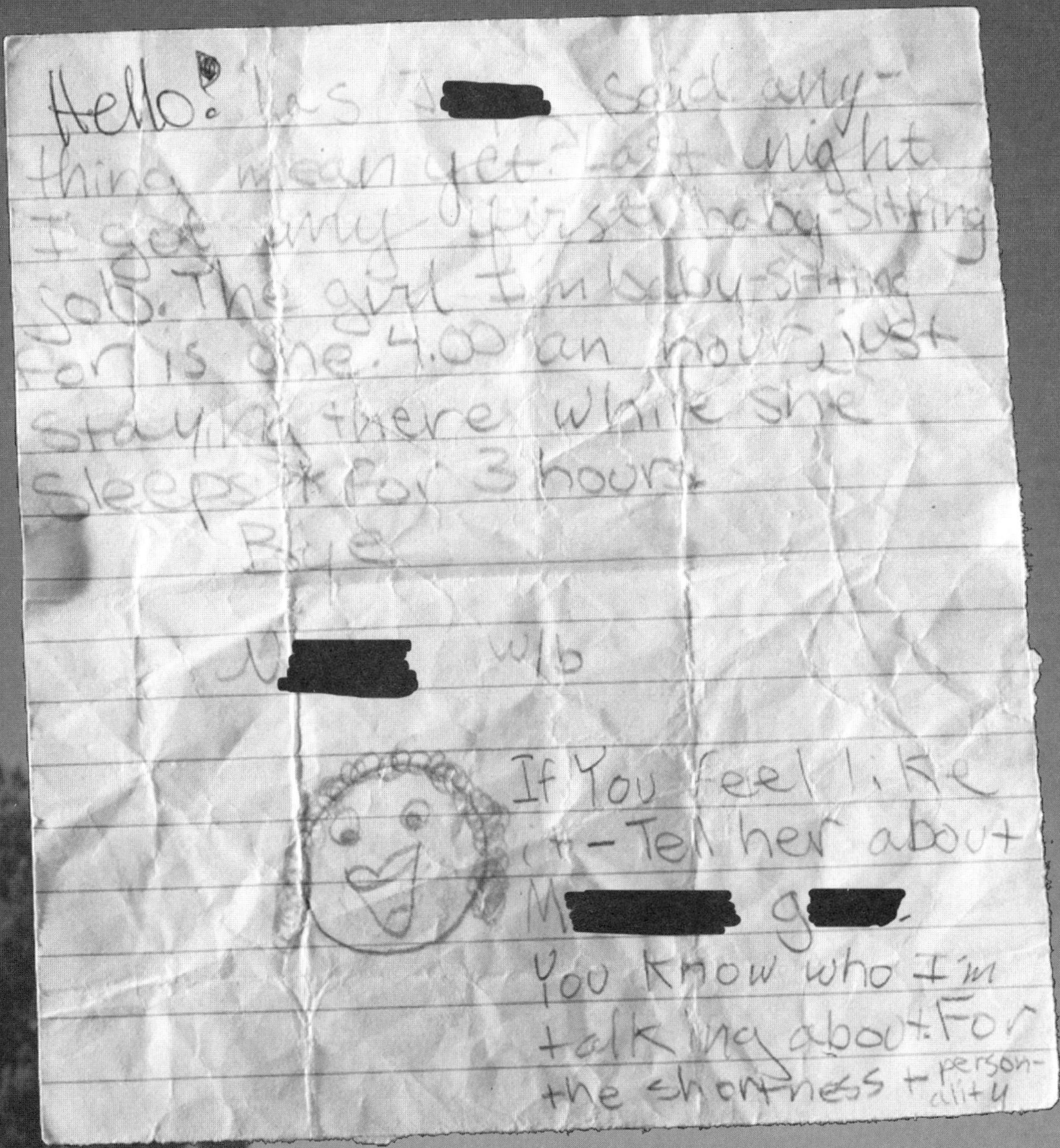
Hello! Has [redacted] said any-
thing mean yet? Last night
I got my first baby-sitting
job. The girl I'm baby-sitting
for is one. 4.00 an hour, just
staying there while she
sleeps + for 3 hours.
Bye

N[redacted] w/b

If You feel like
it - Tell her about
M[redacted] g[redacted]
You Know who I'm
talking about. For
the shortness + person-
ality

[outside]
K_____[f]
[inside]
Hello! Has J___[f] said any-thing mean yet? Last night I got my first baby-sitting job. The girl I'm baby-sitting for is one. 4.00 an hour, just staying there while she sleeps + for 3 hours.

Bye

N_____[f] w/b

[drawing of face]

If You feel like it – Tell her about M______ g___[brand of plant fertilizer]. You Know who I'm talking about. For the shortness + person-ality

Found by Beth and Andy in Portland, OR.
Approximately 5 3/16" x 5 1/2", pencil and black ballpoint pen on lined white notepaper

10/21/97

Hey Brother
What's up? Dude! Whatca
fuckin doin tweekin in
front of what [redacted]
on Lancaster with fuckin
[redacted] and the tweekyfreaks
for? Ya fuck!
Bro, I felt pretty fuckin
bad, that day you got
busted. I left you at the
can-can thinking you ~~had~~
put me on the okey doke and
burnt me.
Well not 20 minutes later
[redacted] calls me up and
makes good.
Then a few hours later,
I hear you got busted,
And [redacted] got busted.
And [redacted]
And [redacted] who was with
[redacted].
Weird fuckin day, Bro
Weerd.
So check it out. I owe
you and apology [redacted].
I had no faith in my
partner. Sorry Brother.
Hey, so whats yer release
date? I'll come get ya,

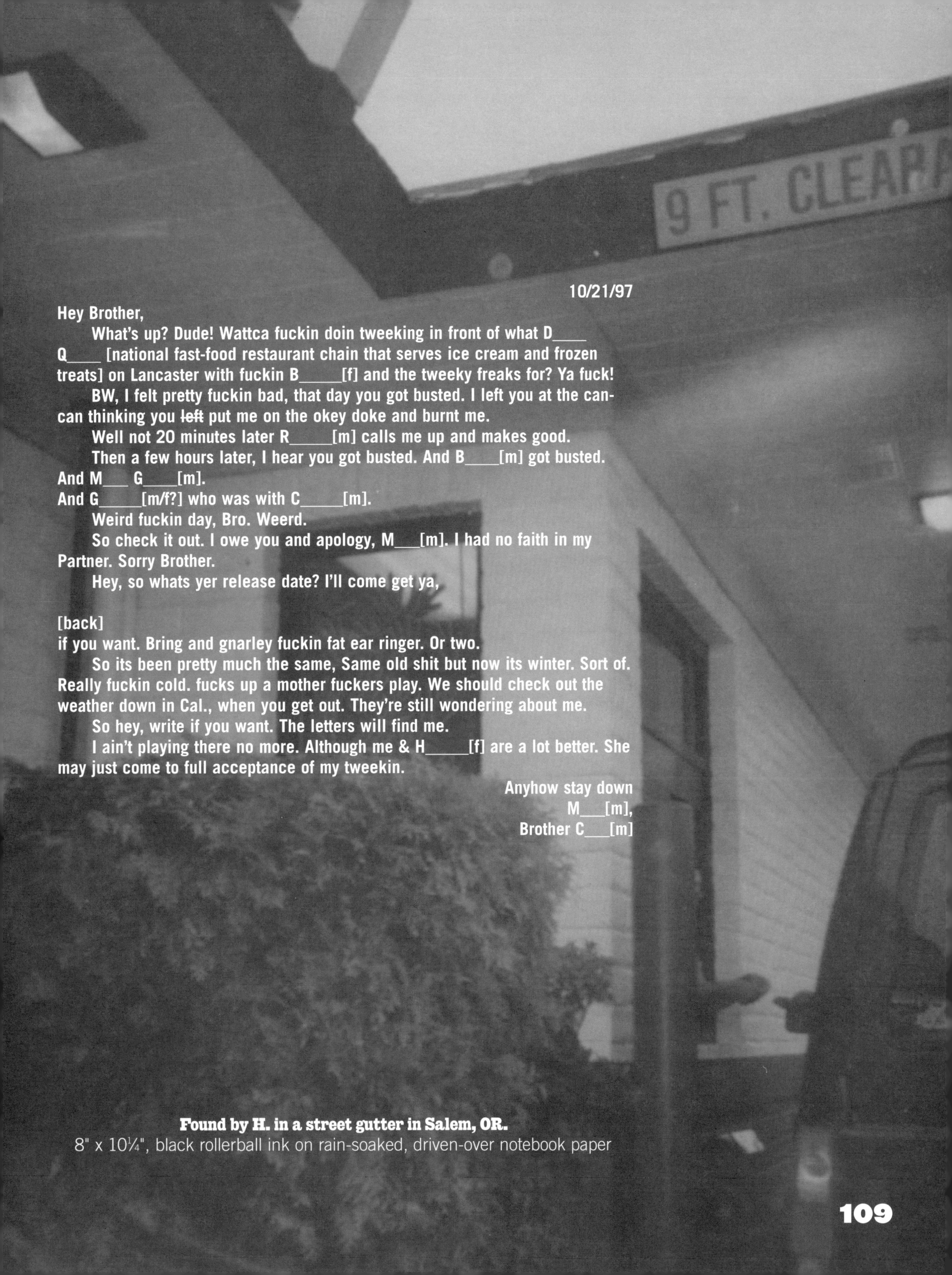

10/21/97

Hey Brother,

What's up? Dude! Wattca fuckin doin tweeking in front of what D____ Q____ [national fast-food restaurant chain that serves ice cream and frozen treats] on Lancaster with fuckin B_____[f] and the tweeky freaks for? Ya fuck!

BW, I felt pretty fuckin bad, that day you got busted. I left you at the can-can thinking you ~~left~~ put me on the okey doke and burnt me.

Well not 20 minutes later R_____[m] calls me up and makes good.

Then a few hours later, I hear you got busted. And B____[m] got busted. And M___ G____[m].
And G_____[m/f?] who was with C_____[m].

Weird fuckin day, Bro. Weerd.

So check it out. I owe you and apology, M___[m]. I had no faith in my Partner. Sorry Brother.

Hey, so whats yer release date? I'll come get ya,

[back]
if you want. Bring and gnarley fuckin fat ear ringer. Or two.

So its been pretty much the same, Same old shit but now its winter. Sort of. Really fuckin cold. fucks up a mother fuckers play. We should check out the weather down in Cal., when you get out. They're still wondering about me.

So hey, write if you want. The letters will find me.

I ain't playing there no more. Although me & H_____[f] are a lot better. She may just come to full acceptance of my tweekin.

Anyhow stay down
M___[m],
Brother C___[m]

Found by H. in a street gutter in Salem, OR.
8" x 10¼", black rollerball ink on rain-soaked, driven-over notebook paper

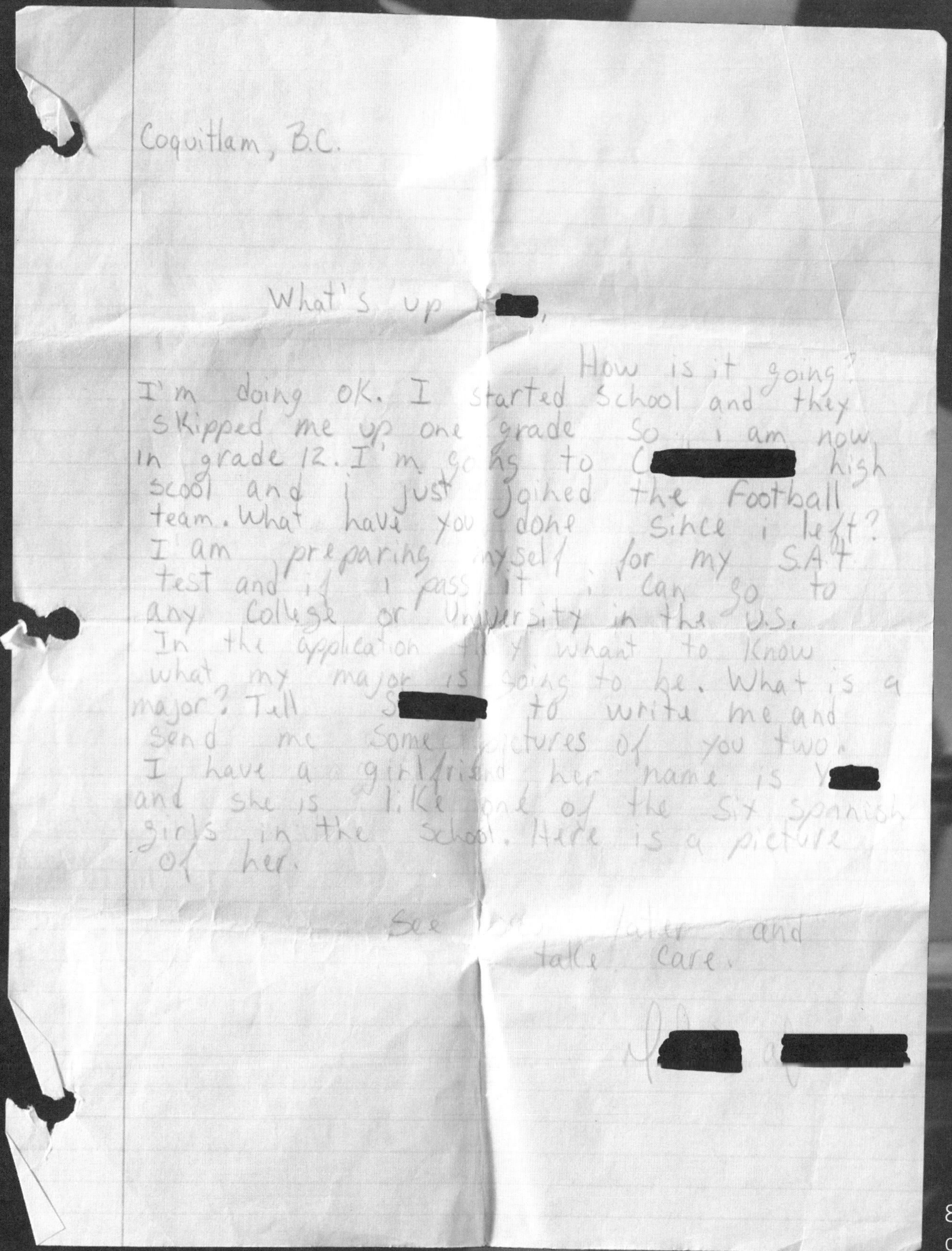

Coquitlam, B.C.

What's up [redacted],

How is it going? I'm doing OK. I started School and they Skipped me up one grade So i am now in grade 12. I'm going to C[redacted] high scool and i just joined the Football team. What have you done Since i left? I am preparing myself for my SAT test and if i pass it i can go to any College or University in the U.S. In the application they whant to Know what my major is going to be. What is a major? Tell S[redacted] to write me and send me Some pictures of you two. I have a girlfriend her name is Y[redacted] and she is like one of the Six Spanish girls in the School. Here is a picture of her.

See You later and take care.

[redacted] [redacted]

8⅜" x 10¾", pencil on notebook paper

Coquitlam, B.C.

What's up F___[m],

How is it going? I'm doing OK. I started School and they Skipped me up one grade So i am now in grade 12. I'm going to C_________ high scool and i just joined the Football team. What have you done Since i left? I am preparing myself for my S.A.t. test and if i pass it i can go to any College or University in the U.S. In the application they whant to Know what my major is going to be. What is a major? Tell S_____[m] to write me and Send me Some pictures of you two. I have a girlfriend, her name is Y____[f] and she is like one of the Six Spanish girls in the school. Here is a picture of her.

See You later and take care.

D_____ A______[m]

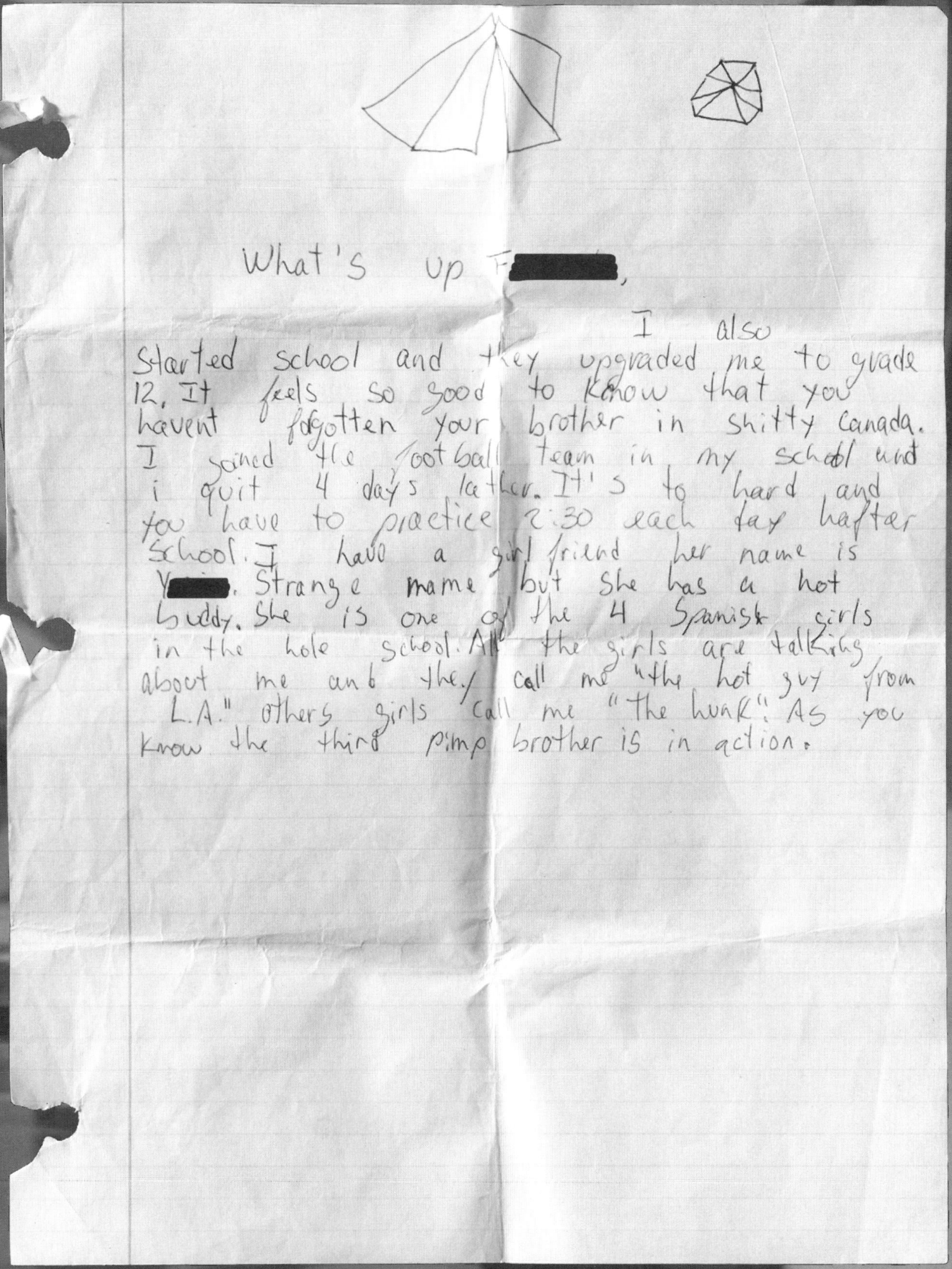
What's up F[redacted],

I also Started school and they upgraded me to grade 12, It feels So good to Know that you havent forgotten your brother in Shitty Canada. I joined the football team in my scholol and i quit 4 days lather. It's to hard and you have to practice 2:30 each day hafter School. I have a girl friend her name is Y[redacted]. Strange mame but She has a hot buddy. She is one of the 4 Spanish girls in the hole school. All the girls are talking about me anb they call me "the hot guy from L.A." others girls call me "the hunk". As you Know the third Pimp brother is in action.

Both letters found by an anonymous contributor, sent in an envelope marked with a Canadian stamp. 8⅜" x 10¾", black ballpoint pen on notebook paper

What's up F_______[m],

I also Started school and they upgraded me to grade 12, It feels So good to Know that you havent forgotten your brother in Shitty Canada. I joined the football team in my scholol and i quit 4 days lather. It's to hard and you have to practice 2:30 each day hafter School. I have a girl friend her name is Y____[f]. Starnge name but She has a hot buddy. She is one of the 4 Spanish girls in the hole school. All the girls are talking about me and they call me "the hot guy from L.A." others girls call me "the hunk." As you Know the third Pimp brother is in action.

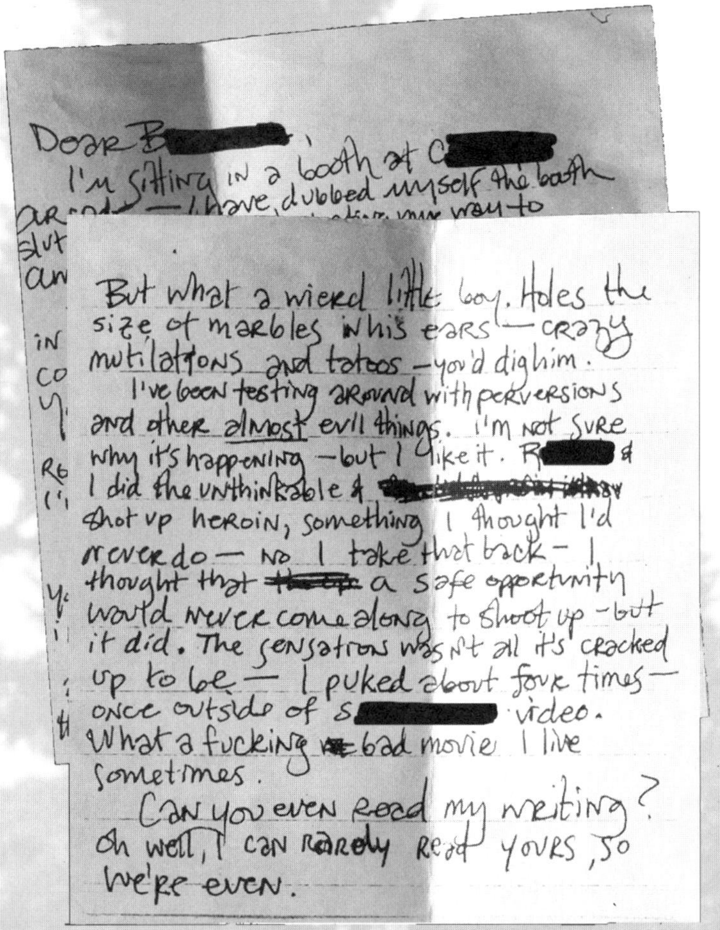

[front]
Dear B______[f],

I'm sitting in a booth at C_____ arcade—I have dubbed myself the booth slut of Seattle. Masterbating my way to amsterdam seems pretty apropriate.

How are you, my lovely and dear friend in arizona? I miss you—I Miss café co-secret & fucked up downtown trips with You.

I wish I was Sitting in Europe Right now–Roasting a big fat fucking bowl!!! Arrgh! I've got to get a fat sack—soooooon!!!

At some point it would be good to hear you elaborate on your interesting interactions—heh heh!

Remember R_____[m]—the desk slave at the L____? [short name for Seattle nude dance parlor] I suppose you could Say that we're kind of Seeing each other

[back]
But what a wierd little boy. Holes the size of marbles in his ears—crazy mutilations and tatoos—you'd dig him.

I've been testing around with perversions and other almost evil things. I'm not Sure why it's happening—but I like it. R_____[m] & I did the unthinkable & ~~tried heroin introv~~ shot up heroin, something I thought I'd never do—no I take that back—I thought that ~~ther~~ a safe opportunity would never come along to shoot up–but it did. The sensation wasn't all it's cracked up to be—I puked about four times—once outside of S_______ video. What a fucking m bad movie I live Sometimes.

Can you even read my writing? Oh well, I can rarely read yours, So we're even.

Found by Mark T. on January 6, 1996, in a notebook left at a book store on 4th Avenue in Seattle, WA.
$4\frac{3}{4}$" x $5\frac{1}{2}$", black ballpoint pen on notepaper

What your name? K______[f]
Where you from. Hedley BC around Merit
B___[m] from Surrey B.C. and Saskatoon a 8 months move Winnipeg soon on November. Nice to meet you. What are you do over? No coke for 8 soon 9 months I smoke weed. We can go 1/2ers. You, I can smoke a joint in Dubia? Dubie? Where Do you live? Do you want buy a weed? I______ Pub My GooD Buddy in Surrey. I have one J at my Place Main & Cordova.

Found by Benj in Vancouver, BC, at the corner of Fraser and 13th, in what he calls the lovely slums of Mt. Pleasant.
$3\frac{3}{8}$" x $8\frac{7}{8}$", blue ballpoint pen on the back of an unfolded king-size cigarette box

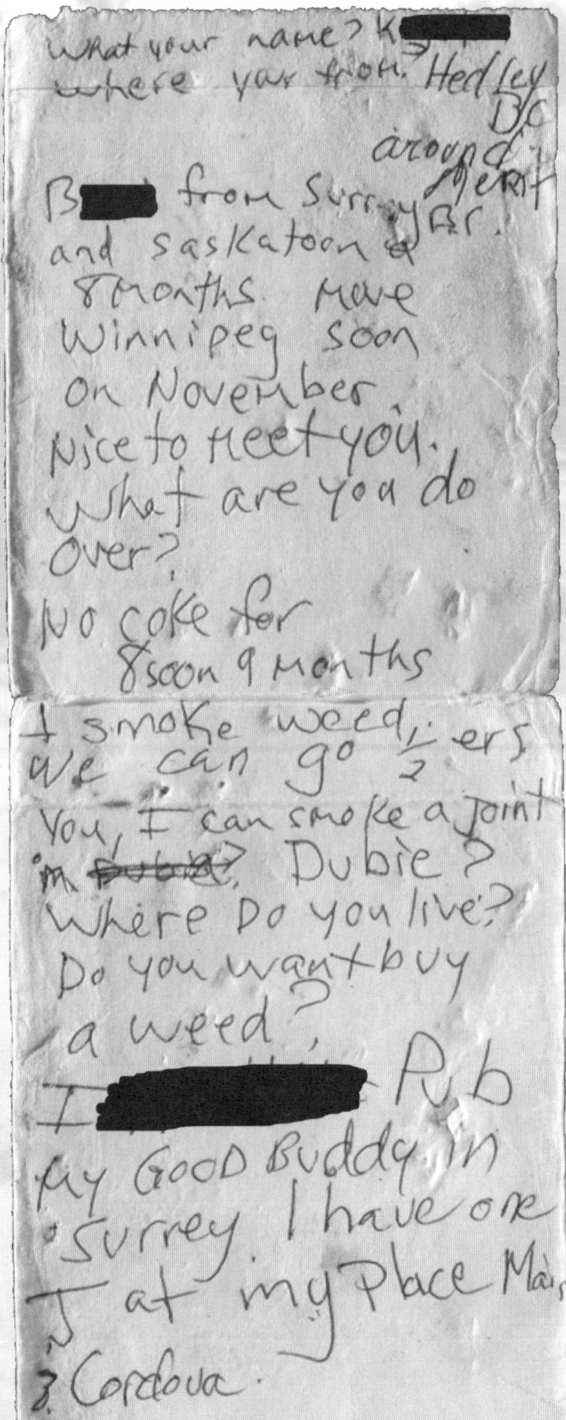

L______[m],

Well Know what I want to say, I just don't know how to say it. Right now I'm really Confused. I went out w/ J____[m], and he forgot he was even going out w/ me cuz he was on acid, I went out w/ D____[m] and broke up w/ him cuz I still had feelings for you, and he decided to try killing himself 10 minutes later because of me. The police and aid car was there. Then I went back out w/ J____[m] and got hurt yet again. I just want you to know I Still have Strong feelings for you.

Found by Gregor G. in Ravenna Park, Seattle, WA.
5⅜" x 8", blue ballpoint pen on spiral notepaper

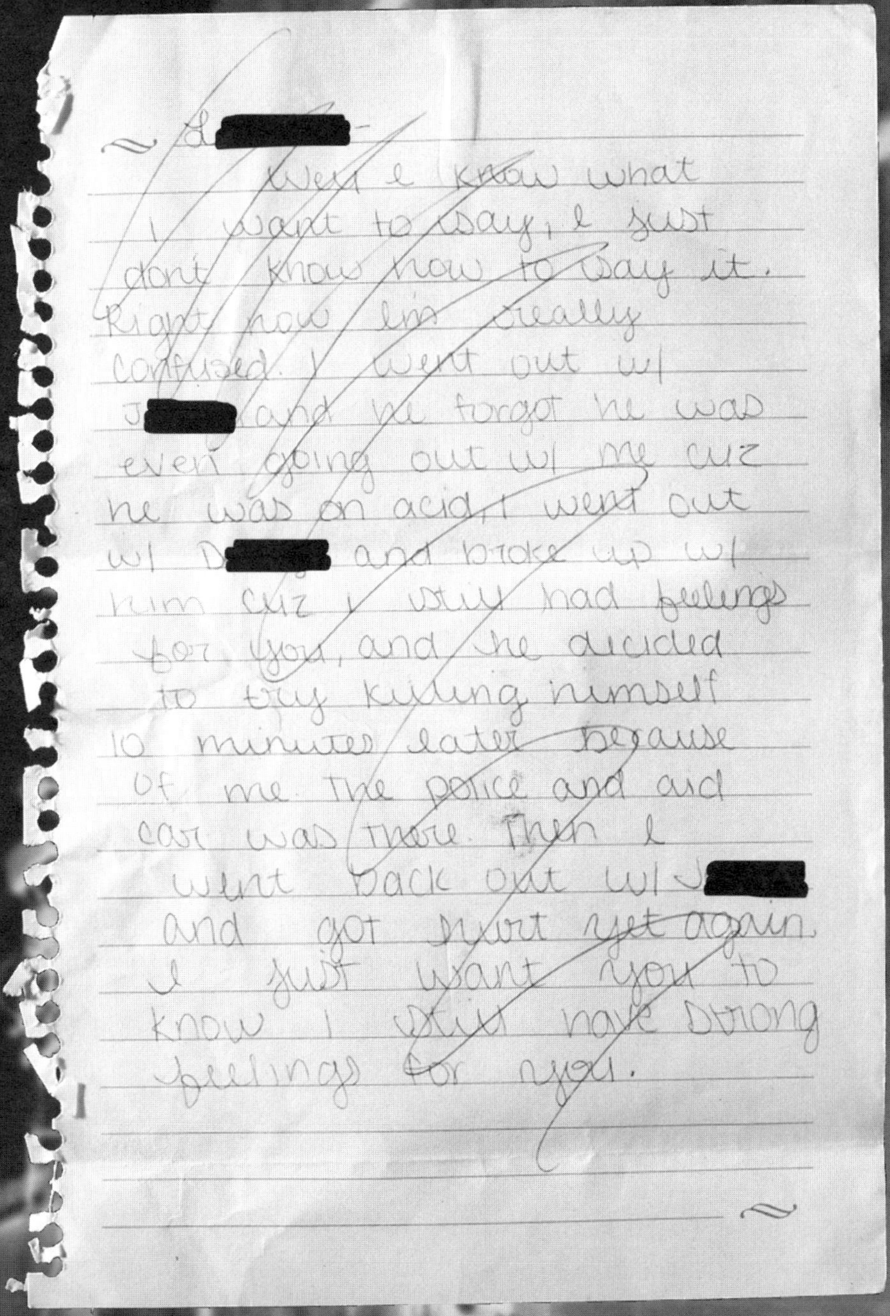
[redacted]
Well I know what I want to say, I just don't know how to say it. Right now I'm really Confused. I went out w/ [redacted] and he forgot he was even going out w/ me cuz he was on acid, I went out w/ [redacted] and broke up w/ him cuz I still had feelings for you, and he decided to try killing himself 10 minutes later because of me. The police and aid car was there. Then I went back out w/ [redacted] and got hurt yet again. I just want you to know I still have Strong feelings for you.

My T.B. Hamster

Punkin

Punkin was my Hamster
And a cute little guy he was
He was full of pep and loved to scamper
All over ~~the~~ my room He was

I would sometimes comb his fur
But Did He mind? not he
He would sit And wait till I was Done
Then He would play, YOU SEE

He Died on an interesting Date.
It was July 4th to be exact
He was like a Big pet
But he was Better Compact

All I have now is memireys
of my small But sweet pet
which I will Charish forever
No pet could top that.

Good-Bye sweet
Pukie
I Love YOU

Born January 3rd 1981 By M.C.
Died July 4th 1981

My T.B. Hamster

punkin

punkin was My Hamster
And a Cute little guy he was
He was Full of pep and Loved to scamper
All over ~~the~~ my room He Was

I would sometimes Comb his Fur
But Did He mind? not he
He would sit And wait till I was Done
Then He would play, you see

He DieD on an interesting Date,
It was July 4th to be exact
He was like a Big pet
But he was Better 'Compact'

All I have now is mem'reys
Of My Small But Sweet pet
Which I will Charish Forever
No pet Could top that.

Good-Bye sweet
pukie
I Love you

Born January 3rd 1981 By M.C.
Died July 4th 1981

Found by Joy H. in Tualatin, OR., in the back of a library book.
8" x 10½", purple felt-tip marker on white notebook paper

M[redacted]

whats up young Native whats your cute butt doing in here, hope nuttin serious that you'll be doing anytime 4. I got pulled in walking wit my girlfreind just being a gangsta. So you still fucking wit [redacted], because i can plug you wit somebody thats real quit fucking wit lil ass boyz im not hating on my homie but i done put him in check 4 acting like a bitch. Youre young do what you wanna do because [redacted] will let you know you got it going on depending on youre age and if i was already in a relationship i might just come at you a lil different you know. I'm in on a P.V. so i might get up to a month who knows. Alright then cutie you take care of your self and think about what i said anything can happen Really doe.

[redacted]

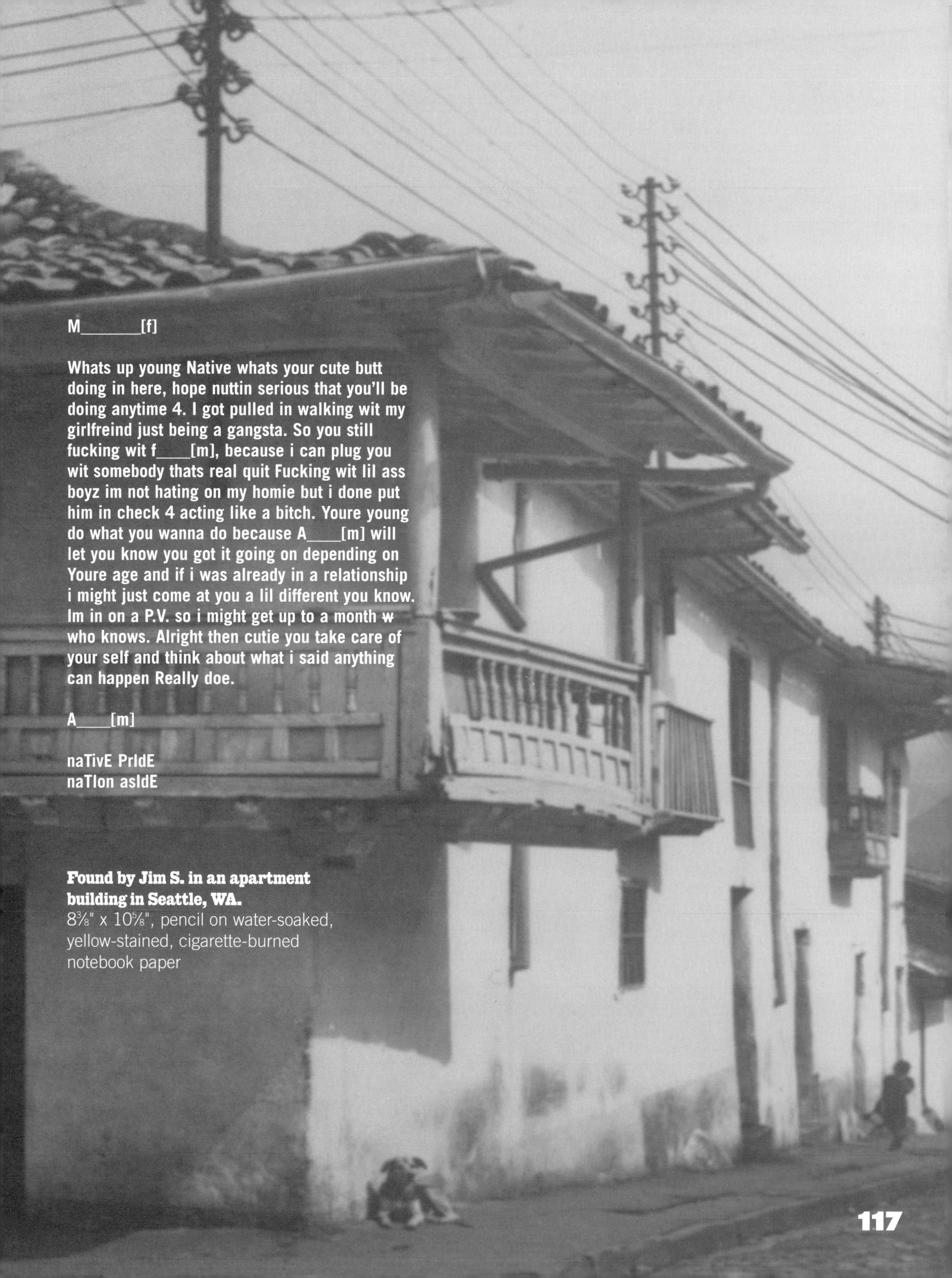

M______[f]

Whats up young Native whats your cute butt doing in here, hope nuttin serious that you'll be doing anytime 4. I got pulled in walking wit my girlfreind just being a gangsta. So you still fucking wit f____[m], because i can plug you wit somebody thats real quit Fucking wit lil ass boyz im not hating on my homie but i done put him in check 4 acting like a bitch. Youre young do what you wanna do because A____[m] will let you know you got it going on depending on Youre age and if i was already in a relationship i might just come at you a lil different you know. Im in on a P.V. so i might get up to a month ~~w~~ who knows. Alright then cutie you take care of your self and think about what i said anything can happen Really doe.

A____[m]

naTivE PrIdE
naTIon asIdE

Found by Jim S. in an apartment building in Seattle, WA.
8⅜" x 10⅝", pencil on water-soaked, yellow-stained, cigarette-burned notebook paper

Found by J. (while eating a burrito) on the corner of NW 85th Street and 15th Avenue NW in the Ballard neighborhood of Seattle, WA.
8⅞" x 11", blue ballpoint pen on spiral notebook paper

T[redacted]

L[redacted]'s

P[redacted] - I haven't seen him in a while. I really want him to find true hope and joy. Maybe the Lord will use someone else to actually bring him to Christ. He knows the truth. Maybe he doesn't know it in his heart.

For us - As we're all trying to graduate this year, The Lord will give us strength, 'cause we are trying to do His will. God is with us. Remember that.

Help in witnessing. I can't believe it! I can't believe some of the things I say and do to witness now, especially since camp. It's not big things or anything, probably anyone else would do it without even thinking about it, but I've never done this. It's really exciting! I praise God. Now there's a lot more I could be doing, but I'm on the right road and I know I will learn.

For us and our husbands. That we can grow closer to God and therefore closer to each other. Like a triangle.

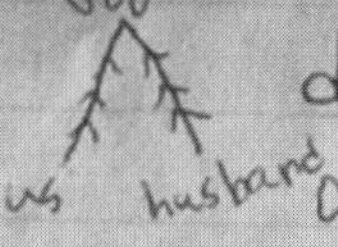

I really need prayer for my relationship with God. As far as prayer goes that is. I love to read my Bible, but for some reason I kind of dread praying. I mean, not dread it, but I don't look forward to it like I should. I haven't been praying for half an hour every day either. So please pray that I could desire talking with God more. Can God give us that desire? I don't know.

Well, you guys, I love you so much. Thank God for you both. May God bless you this week.

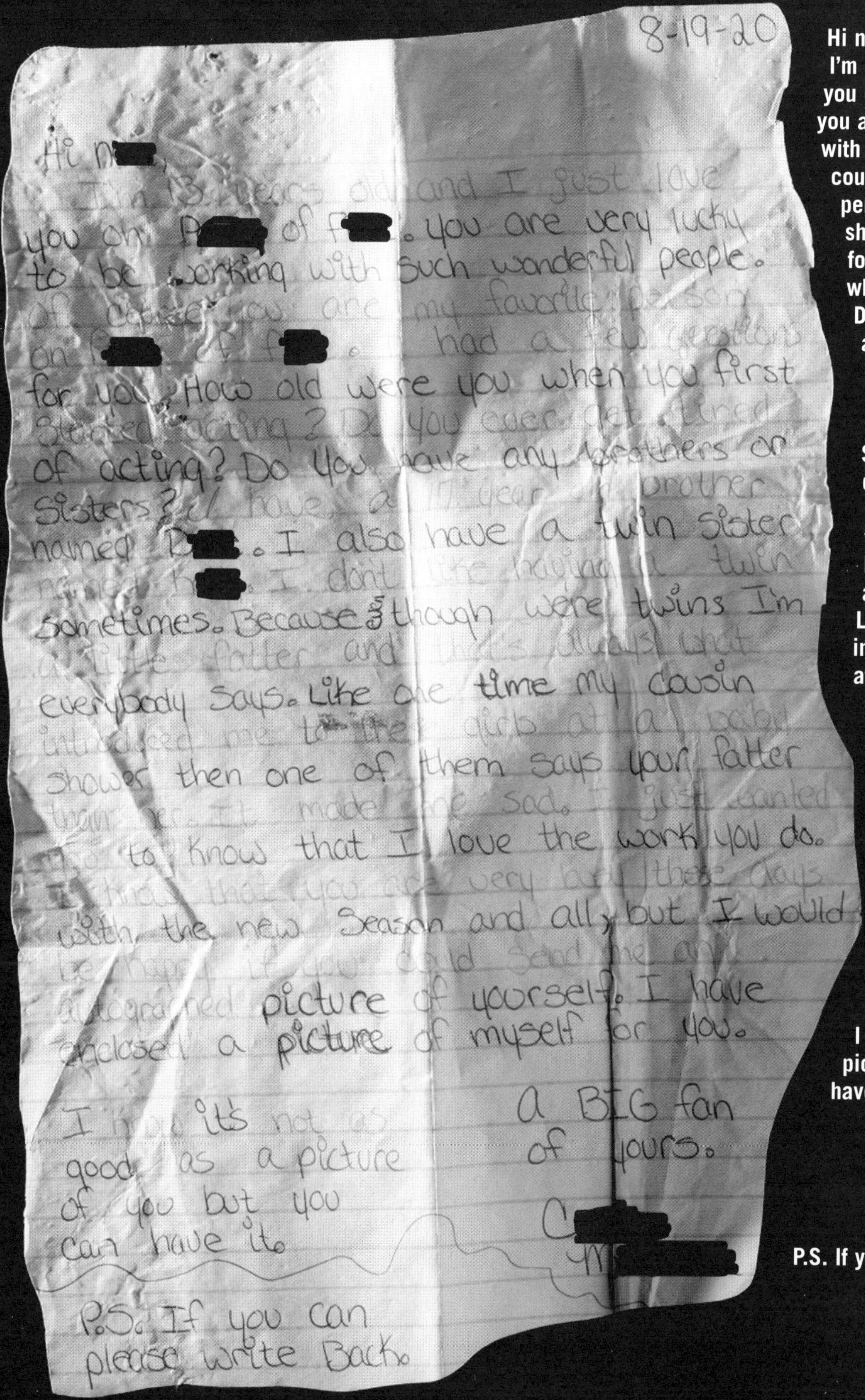
8-19-20
Hi [redacted],
I'm 13 years old and I just love
you on [redacted] of [redacted]. you are very lucky
to be working with such wonderful people.
Of course you are my favorite person
on [redacted] of [redacted]. I had a few questions
for you. How old were you when you first
Started acting? Do you ever get tired
of acting? Do you have any brothers or
Sisters? I have a 17 year old brother
named [redacted]. I also have a twin sister
named [redacted]. I don't like having a twin
sometimes. Because though we're twins I'm
a little fatter and that's always what
everybody says. Like one time my cousin
introduced me to these girls at a baby
shower then one of them says your fatter
than her. It made me sad. I just wanted
you to know that I love the work you do.
I know that you are very busy these days
with the new Season and all, but I would
be happy if you could send me an
autographed picture of yourself. I have
enclosed a picture of myself for you.

I know it's not as good as a picture of you but you can have it.

a BIG fan of yours.
[redacted]

P.S. If you can please write Back.

8-19-20

Hi n___[f],
I'm 13 years old and I just love you on P____ of f___[TV show]. you are very lucky to be working with such wonderful people. Of course you are my favorite person on P____ of f___[TV show]. I had a few questions for you. How old were you when you first started acting? Do you ever get tired of acting? Do you have any brothers or Sisters? I have a 17 year old brother named D___[m]. I also have a twin Sister named K____[f]. I don't like having a twin sometimes. Because even though we're twins I'm a little fatter and that's always what everybody says. Like one time my cousin introduced me to these girls at a baby shower then one of them says your fatter than her. It made me sad. I just wanted you to know that I love the work you do. I know that you are very busy these days with the new Season and all, but I would be happy if you could send me an autographed picture of yourself. I have enclosed a picture of myself for you. I know it's not as good as a picture of you but you can have it.

A BIG fan
of yours.
C_____
M_______[f]

P.S. If you can please write Back.

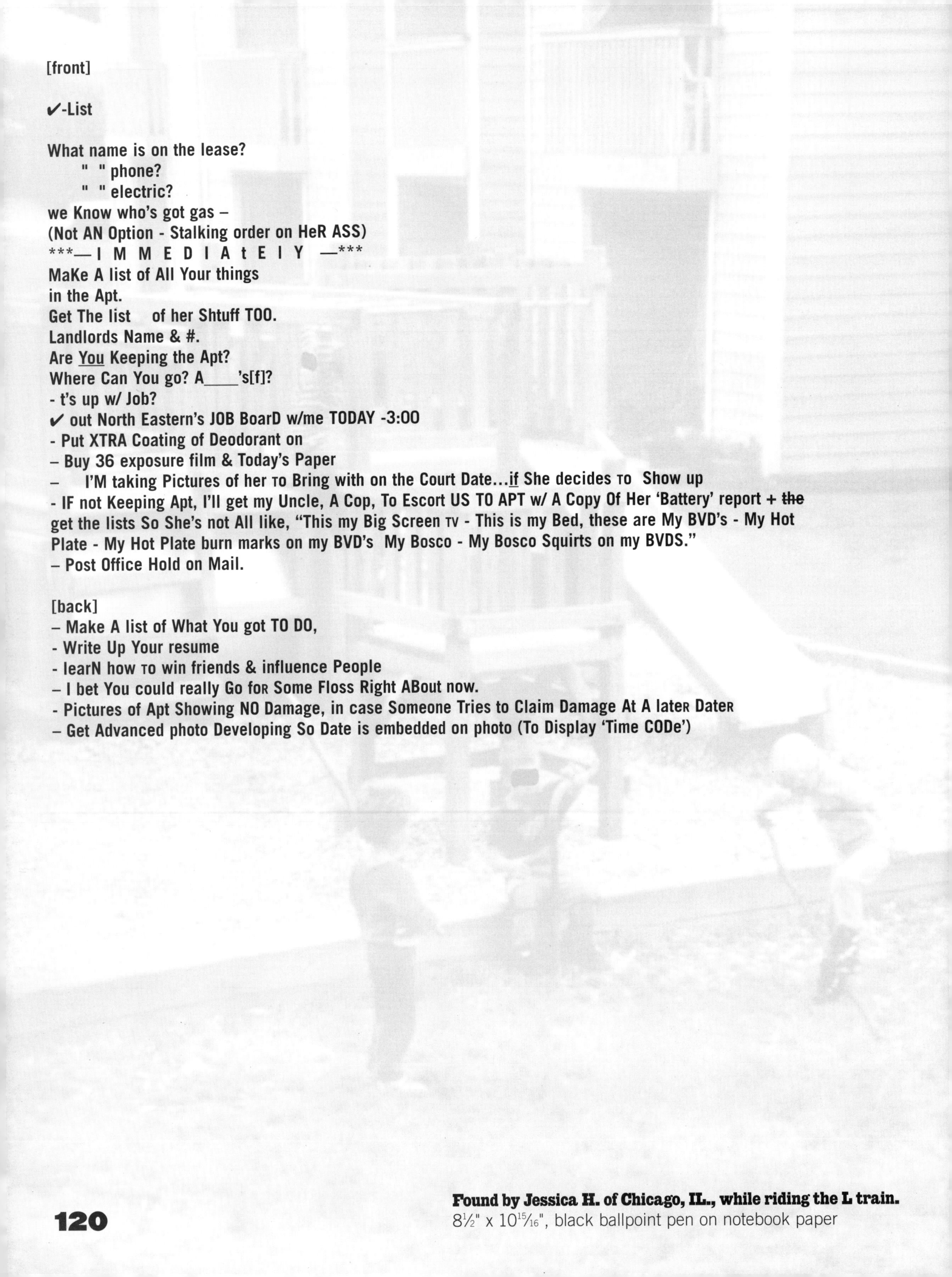

[front]

✔-List

What name is on the lease?
" " phone?
" " electric?
we Know who's got gas –
(Not AN Option - Stalking order on HeR ASS)
— I M M E D I A t E I Y —
MaKe A list of All Your things
in the Apt.
Get The list of her Shtuff TOO.
Landlords Name & #.
Are <u>You</u> Keeping the Apt?
Where Can You go? A____'s[f]?
- t's up w/ Job?
✔ out North Eastern's JOB BoarD w/me TODAY -3:00
- Put XTRA Coating of Deodorant on
– Buy 36 exposure film & Today's Paper
– I'M taking Pictures of her TO Bring with on the Court Date...<u>if</u> She decides TO Show up
- IF not Keeping Apt, I'll get my Uncle, A Cop, To Escort US TO APT w/ A Copy Of Her 'Battery' report + ~~the~~ get the lists So She's not All like, "This my Big Screen TV - This is my Bed, these are My BVD's - My Hot Plate - My Hot Plate burn marks on my BVD's My Bosco - My Bosco Squirts on my BVDS."
– Post Office Hold on Mail.

[back]
– Make A list of What You got TO DO,
- Write Up Your resume
- learN how TO win friends & influence People
– I bet You could really Go foR Some Floss Right ABout now.
- Pictures of Apt Showing NO Damage, in case Someone Tries to Claim Damage At A lateR DateR
– Get Advanced photo Developing So Date is embedded on photo (To Display 'Time CODe')

Found by Jessica H. of Chicago, IL., while riding the L train.
8½" x 10¹⁵⁄₁₆", black ballpoint pen on notebook paper

-Make A list of what you got TO DO,
-write up your resume
- learn how to win friends & influence People
- I ... You could really Go for some
... now.

√-LIST

What name is on the lease?
" " phone?
" " electric?
We know who's got gas -
Not AN option - Stalking order on Her ASS
*** — I M M E D I A T E L Y ***
Make A list of All your things in the Apt.
Get The list of her Sh+uff TOO.
Landlords Name & #.
Are You Keeping the Apt?
Where Can You go? A[redacted]'s?
- +'s up w/ Job?
✓ out North Eastern's JOB BoarD [M]Tue TODAY - 3:00
- Put XtRA Coating of Deodorant on
- Buy 36 exposure film & Today's Paper
- I'm taking Pictures of her to Bring with on the Court Date... if She decides to Show up
- If not Keeping Apt, I'll get my Uncle, A cop, to Escort us to Apt w/ A copy of Her 'Battery' report & ~~our~~ lists So She's not All like, "This my Big Screen TV - This is my Bed, these are my BVD's - my Hot Plate - my Hot Plate burn marks on my BVD's my Bosco - My Bosco Squirts on my BVD's"
- Pa...

THE UNEXPLAINED

Let Me Smell
Your Panites. I Am
Watching, if Yes Raise
Your Left hand out The
Window. I Will Pay you well!

Take Panties off and Leave Them
in Parking lot - Drive away!

Bee Back neck Week 6-20-97
look under Bus Stop Bench $
Money - Money - Money

Found by Kelly M. on the windshield of her car after leaving a popular chain department store in Midway, WA, on June 13, 1997.
6" x 7½", black ballpoint pen on yellow notepaper

Found by Lisa G. in a book from a used bookstore in the Fremont neighborhood of Seattle, WA.
5½" x 8½", pencil and blue ballpoint pen on tan paper

{front)

(back)

WHO OBAYS WHO OVERWELLMING
GROWTH AND TIERD MINDS DOES
THE TOUGHT FADE LIKE LIGHTNING
WICH TRYS TO TOUCH POINTS OF
LEST DESTRUCKTION DOES IT FALL
DOWN TO BRING GOODNESS
AND PEACE AS WE SLEEP
THE GREATER IS POWER
BY HIS WILL AND WILLINGNESS
TO GET ALONG AS HE MOVE
THOUGH IT HAS GIVEN PERSONS
WITH MORE UNDERS[redacted]
WITH NEEDED COMFORTS
WHO WILL IS ALLWAYS BE
REMINDED AS A GRATE
ONE WHO IS TIERLY GROWER

Found by Aimee L. & Clayton C. on March 19, 1997, in a video store parking lot in Lynnwood, WA.
8⅜" x 10¾", black rollerball ink on a Department of Licensing "Vehicle Trip Permit Receipt"

WHO OBAYS WHO OVERWELLMING GroWtH AND TIERD MINDS Does THe TougHt FADe LIKEe LIgHtNIng WICH TrYS TO TOUCH POINtS OF LESt DEStrucktioN DOES It FALL DOWN TO BriNg GOODNeSS AND PeAce AS we SLEEP THe GreAter IS POWER BY HIS WILL AND WILLINgNeSS TO Get ALONg AS He MOVe TrougH It HAS GIVEN PErpuss WITH MOre UNDerStANdS WITH NeeDeD COMFOrtS WHo WILL IS ALLWAYS Be REMIMERD AS A GrAte ONe WHO IS TIERD growth

[upside down at top]
FOLD RIte to tRy AND Be RIte AS we DON't MEEN to MISS

BLINK [drawing of an eye] DON't UNDerStAND WHAtS MADe It IS SEEN AND TOUCHeD

= * for those on The Run

1)-Female only (Hide out

(5[redacted]-3[redacted]) Felon OK - 5.00 (a day

5.00 a day

2)-Safe Place for privatey (Female Felon)

3)-cook your food 2.50 a day.

4)-Female only (Hide) takeout in trade (free) or 20.00 week

5)-Shower (Female only) $1.00

6)-Sleep In (Female) (2.00 a nite

Found wet and slumped over a bush on Center Street NE in Salem, OR, by Adam K.
8½" x 11", purple felt marker on white paper

Get Your Nugs

1/4 $80.00

1/2 $150.00

1oz $225.00

THE BEST IN
THE NORTHWEST
THIS IS THE DANK

CALL 3[redacted]-4[redacted]

ASK FOR
B[redacted]

Found by "The Swedish Mafia" on the bulletin board at a check-cashing store in Bellingham, WA.
2½" x 5¾", blue ballpoint pen on thick pink paper

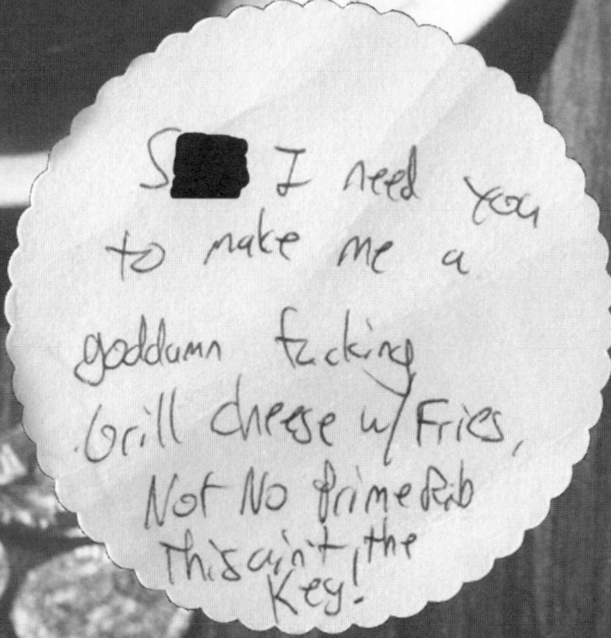
S[redacted] I need you
to make me a
goddamn fucking
Grill cheese w/Fries,
Not No Prime Rib
This ain't the
Key!

Found by Anne outside a restaurant in the Ballard neighborhood of Seattle, WA.
3⅜" in diameter, black ballpoint pen on the back of a paper coaster

[front]

Penalty Judicial Sentencing

(1-card)

1. Receive All-Player Gang-Bang, Immediately
2. Pay, now, every player: Amt, Equal his/her One-time largest loss–This game. You may barter assets, services, moneys, etc: Whatever you can get away with!
3. Pay player across from you Hustler Fee of $$50^{00}$: Get your money's worth!
4. If your Debt/Worth Ratio cannot be reconciled, sell your enslavement to every player you can't not otherwise pay or compensate for: Nego-tiate Total-Service-Rates = 1 now hr., minimum*; 72-hr. weekend service; Next Four, consecutive 72-hr weekend Services: Total, silent, blind, bound servitudes: Max. Indenture.

[written along left side of page] *Min. Indenture

5. Sell 4-hrs. Modeling Services, $[illegible]^{00} 1ST Day 3-hr 75^{00} max., S&M/B&D Leather Gear/Toy/Harnass Mfgr. (all 4-hrs., Required) 1-hr Return when finis-hed mfgr. f/Cat. Illus.
6. Bad Checks To Be Beimbursed: $$750^{00}$, Plus

" " Fines, Accrued = + 350.00

← $1,100.00

To be Worked-Off Modeling →
f/R__ S____[m]. If contracted
with as Prime Model, you are to earn/return the full $1,100 modeling, Leather Mfgr. Asst; Scout-ing; Cheerfully helping in many negotiated ways

7. Bonus Modeling Fees Card: If you've never professionally modeled before, are contractu-ally accepted as a Prime Model with our growing agency, + it is agreeable

[back]

with N________ M_____ M_________ [real or imaginary modeling agency], you will receive, in addition your standard $$25^{00}$ per hr: Nude Photo Sessions, 10% Photo – Profit sharing revenues from our collabora-tions, indefinitely: As long as profits are received.

Advise to New Models: Friendly, companion-ship, helpful assistants in bringing our new business into profit-making mode; Warm caring, sharing, affectionate and, genrally keeping me stimulated + interested in you and your profitability + welfare, above the other many attention + capitol-consuming demands, upcoming, before major cash-flows begin feuling our budget—Around April or May 1997. Every investment-capitol dollar will need to weigh heavily in my mind senses of importance, rapid returns on few, Optimum, investment dollars.

It will, certainly, serve your interests well, to strive to keep me happy, pleasing + serving you. It's easier to take joy in making a "beloved" smile, than to dicker over which photos + photo-products will likely produce a few dollars more, and sooner.

Please, help me thrill, often and for years to come, as I share profits we've earned, together, with you.

Unless, it's your joy to seduce me, understand: A sexual relationship is not a requirement, with me, but, when we share good times and our labor's rewards I can become resentful and quit caring for you, personally,

Found by Erik S. in NW Portland, OR.

8½" x 10$\frac{15}{16}$", pencil, and nearly-dry felt-tip marker and ballpoint pen, on white paper

Penalty Judicial Sentencing

(1-card)

1. Receive ...-Player Gang-Bang, Immediately

2. Pay, most every player: Amt. Equal his/her Any-time largest loss This game: You may barter assets, services, moneys, etc: whatever you can get away with!

3. Pay player across from you ... Fee of $50.00: Get your money's worth!

4. If your Debt/Worth Ratio cannot be reconciled Sell your enslavement to every player you can not otherwise pay or compensate for: Negotiate Total-Service-Rates = 1-hr. (now) minimum; 72-hr. weekend service; Next Four, consecutive 72-hr weekend services: Total, silent, blind, bound servitudes: Max. Indenture

1st Day ... 00

X Min. Indenture

5. Sell 4-hrs. Modeling Services, ... max.; S+M/B+D Leather Gear/Toy/Harness Mfgr. (All 4-hrs., Required.) (1-hr) Return when finished mfgr. f/Cat. Illus.

6. Bad Checks To Be Reimbursed: $50.00 Plus Fines, Accrued = + $50.00

$100.00

To be Worked-Off Modeling → ←$ f/R[redacted]. If contrasted, you are to earn/return with as prime model, your Leather mfgr. asst; Scouting the full $100 modeling; helping in many negotiated ing; cheerfully helping ways

7. Bonus Modeling Fees Card: If you've never professionally modeled before, are contracted with our growing & accepted as a prime model ... & it is agreeable

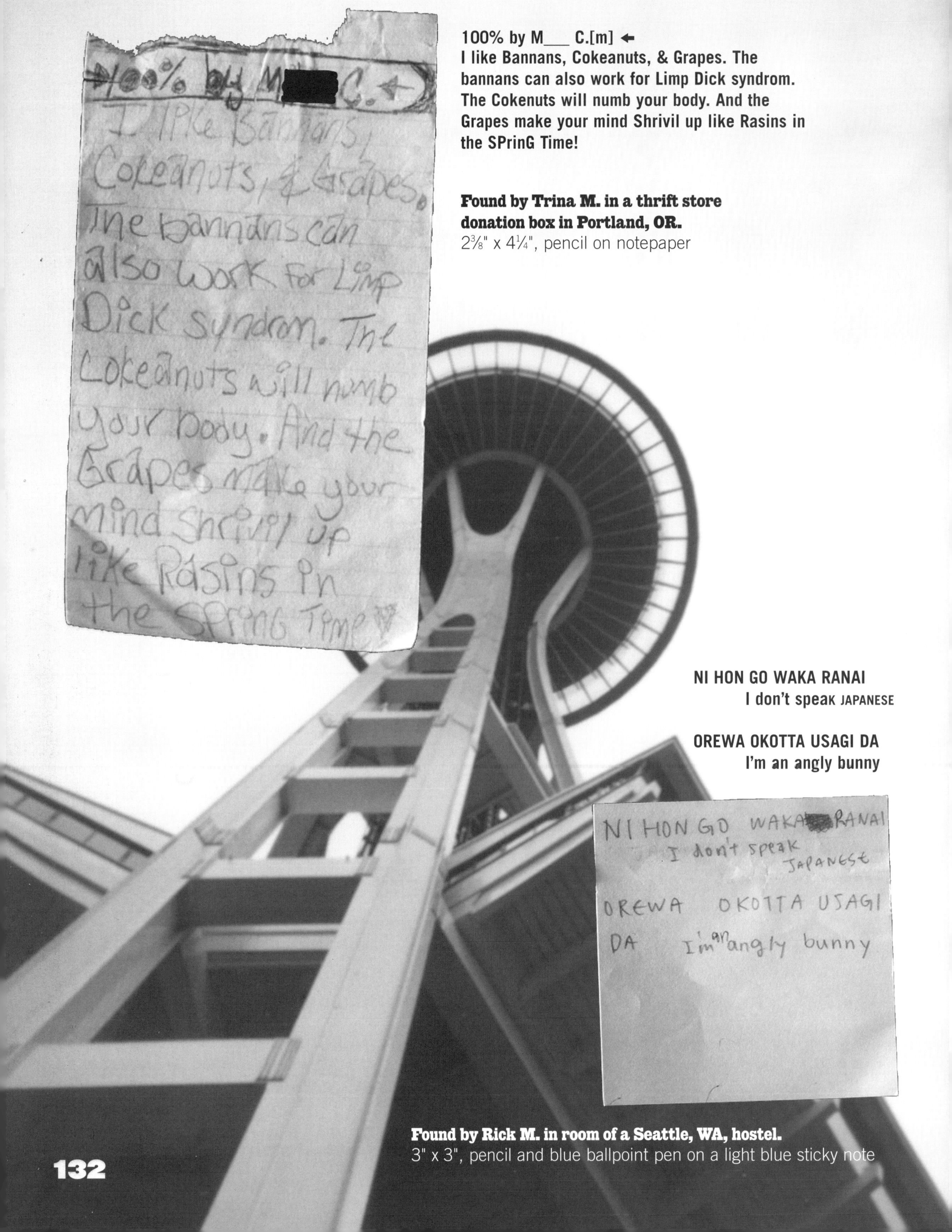

100% by M[redacted]C.

I like Bannans, Cokeanuts, & Grapes. The bannans can also work for Limp Dick syndrom. The Cokeanuts will numb your body. And the Grapes make your mind Shrivil up like Rasins in the SPrinG Time

NI HON GO WAKA RANAI
I don't speak JAPANESE

OREWA OKOTTA USAGI DA I'm an angly bunny

100% by M___ C.[m] ←

I like Bannans, Cokeanuts, & Grapes. The bannans can also work for Limp Dick syndrom. The Cokenuts will numb your body. And the Grapes make your mind Shrivil up like Rasins in the SPrinG Time!

Found by Trina M. in a thrift store donation box in Portland, OR.
2⅜" x 4¼", pencil on notepaper

NI HON GO WAKA RANAI
I don't speak JAPANESE

OREWA OKOTTA USAGI DA
I'm an angly bunny

Found by Rick M. in room of a Seattle, WA, hostel.
3" x 3", pencil and blue ballpoint pen on a light blue sticky note

SOCIETY FOR THE
PROMOTION OF
RACIAL PURITY
P.O. BOX [redacted]
SEATTLE, WA, 98[redacted]

July 9, 1997

G[redacted] M[redacted]
[redacted] [redacted] Avenue Southwest
Seattle, Washington, 98[redacted]

Dear Mr. M[redacted],

We would like to take this opportunity to thank you for your generous donation and your willingness to volunteer your time and expertise to this important cause. Your prior commitment and involvement with Ku Klux Klan should prove to be a great asset to our organization.

You have only to look around you to see the sad results of our country's racial tolerance—Increased drug use, gang violence, robberies and burglaries, sex crimes, mixed-race marriages resulting in impure bloodlines—problems once limited to the less intelligent races are now occuring in white communities more frequently. We are working to put those races which are detrimental to our society back where their influence will not be felt in white America.

Only through monetary and volunteer contributions such as yours can we hope to destroy the idea of "racial equality" which has swept the country. Without your continuing support we could not even hope to erradicate these problems.

Very truely yours,

[redacted]

N[redacted] B. A[redacted]
Secretary, SPRP

Enclosure

Found by David Anthony in Seattle, WA.
8½" x 11", black-and-white laser print on white paper

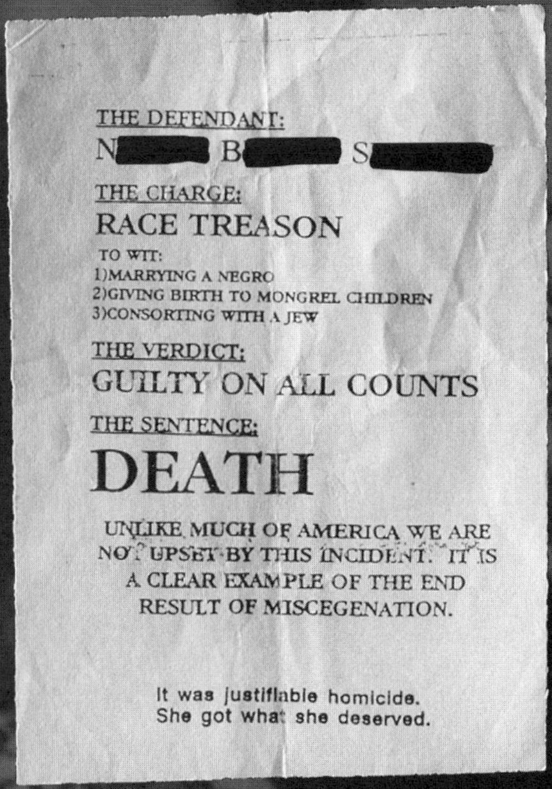

THE DEFENDANT:
N[redacted] B[redacted] S[redacted]
THE CHARGE:
RACE TREASON
TO WIT:
1)MARRYING A NEGRO
2)GIVING BIRTH TO MONGREL CHILDREN
3)CONSORTING WITH A JEW
THE VERDICT:
GUILTY ON ALL COUNTS
THE SENTENCE:
DEATH
UNLIKE MUCH OF AMERICA WE ARE NOT UPSET BY THIS INCIDENT. IT IS A CLEAR EXAMPLE OF THE END RESULT OF MISCEGENATION.

It was justifiable homicide. She got what she deserved.

THE DEFENDANT:
N_____ B____ S______ [former wife of a former professional football player; she was mrdered in 1994 and he was accused, then in 1996 acquitted, for the crime]
THE CHARGE:
RACE TREASON
TO WIT:
1)MARRYING A NEGRO
2)GIVING BIRTH TO MONGREL CHILDREN
3)CONSORTING WITH A JEW
THE VERDICT:
GUILTY ON ALL COUNTS
THE SENTENCE:
DEATH
UNLIKE MUCH OF AMERICA WE ARE NOT UPSET BY THIS INCIDENT. IT IS A CLEAR EXAMPLE OF THE END RESULT OF MISCEGENATION.
It was justifiable homicide. She got what she deserved.

Found by W. Spencer on the floor in the housewares section of a thrift store on SE 6th in Portland, OR.
Approximately 3⅜" x 4¼", photocopy on white paper

(front)

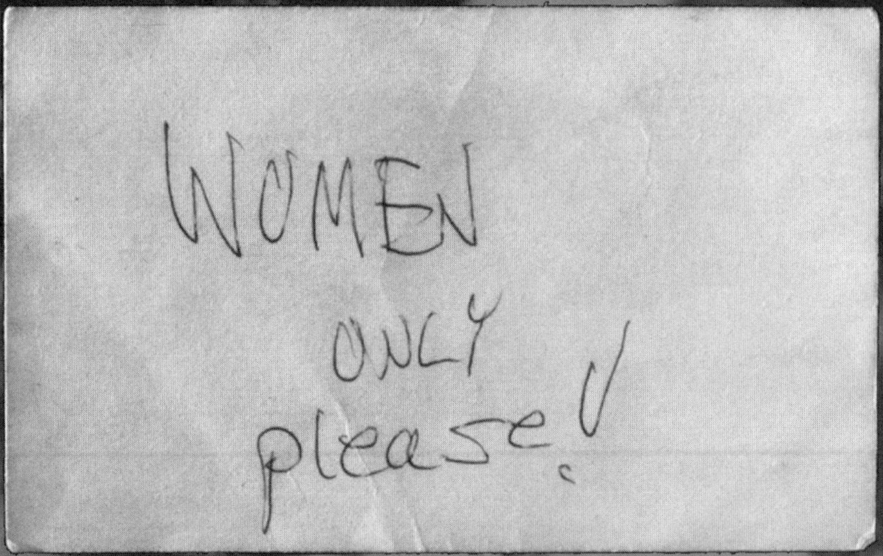

WOMEN
ONLY
please!

[front]
WOMEN ONLY please!

[back]
KinKy white Single male, 34.
Loves watching A Legal AGED
Single womAN Go to the bathroom
will help you, if you Need so.
"NO SEX involved
I CAN Be Beached AT 9__-0___
Anytime.

Found by Gene P. while walking his dog across the Ferry Street bridge in Eugene, OR.
5" x 3", black ballpoint pen on a white index card

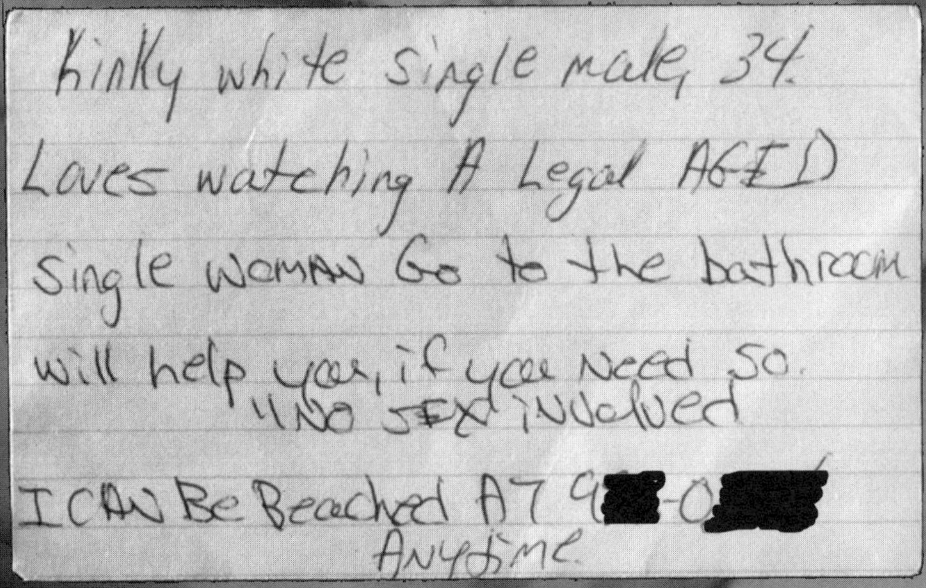

Kinky white single male, 34.
Loves watching A Legal AGED
Single WOMAN Go to the bathroom
will help you, if you Need so.
"NO SEX involved
ICAN Be Beached AT 9[redacted]-0[redacted]
Anytime.

(back)

2__-5___
I hate men especially N_____ H_____[m]. He's a bitch and not a man. And I'm sure by now he hates me! but I Love that man so much. What the hell I'm I going to do!!!!! Survive I guess w/o Love and who cares, not me. I wish I would die. Thats what I really want. No pain no gain.
2__-5___

Found by Kate and Anthony in their front yard in Portland, OR.
9½" x 4¾", blue ballpoint pen on a dirty napkin

There are 3 I would possibly consider, K____[m], E___[m], B__[m], in that order. J___[m] is no where on my list But he is totally gone and it is my fault. I worked the Fucking system and I worked it well and now I have him wrapped around my Finger, trouble is I don't want him there. So why don't I just add him to my list? He doesn't belong there. Why? #1 he isn't a Christian, #2 he has more expirience than doc #3 he isn't as oh I don't know. The other 3 are all Catholic, all 3. E___[m] has tons of "expirience" K____[m] has none and B__[m] has at least a little. K____[m] is sweet, alone, he tries hard, he doesn't get mad, he is smart, he is Funny. E___[m] is Funny, writes poetry, is well rounded, has a well paying job, is interesting, is sweet. B__[m] is sweet, Funny, smart, and cute. By their own right K____[m] is obviously 1st then E___[m] then B__[m]. J___[m] only has Fun, he is not mature, he has no idea what he is talking about, he thinks he understands me, he thinks he can have me. But no one can own me unless I first chose them and I haven't chosen him yet not anywhere close to choosing him yet. But I don't want to hurt him. B__[m] is macho so is E___[m] a bit, K____[m] is not entirely but J___[m] is too emotional too insecure. I need stability, I need a strong tall shoulder to cry on. His is a weak scrawny shoulder barely able to Function with its own problems let alon all of mine. It is not him I want. Not even a little. I was playing a game and he took it serious. He could never be all I need and I refuse to accept less just because I Feel bad.

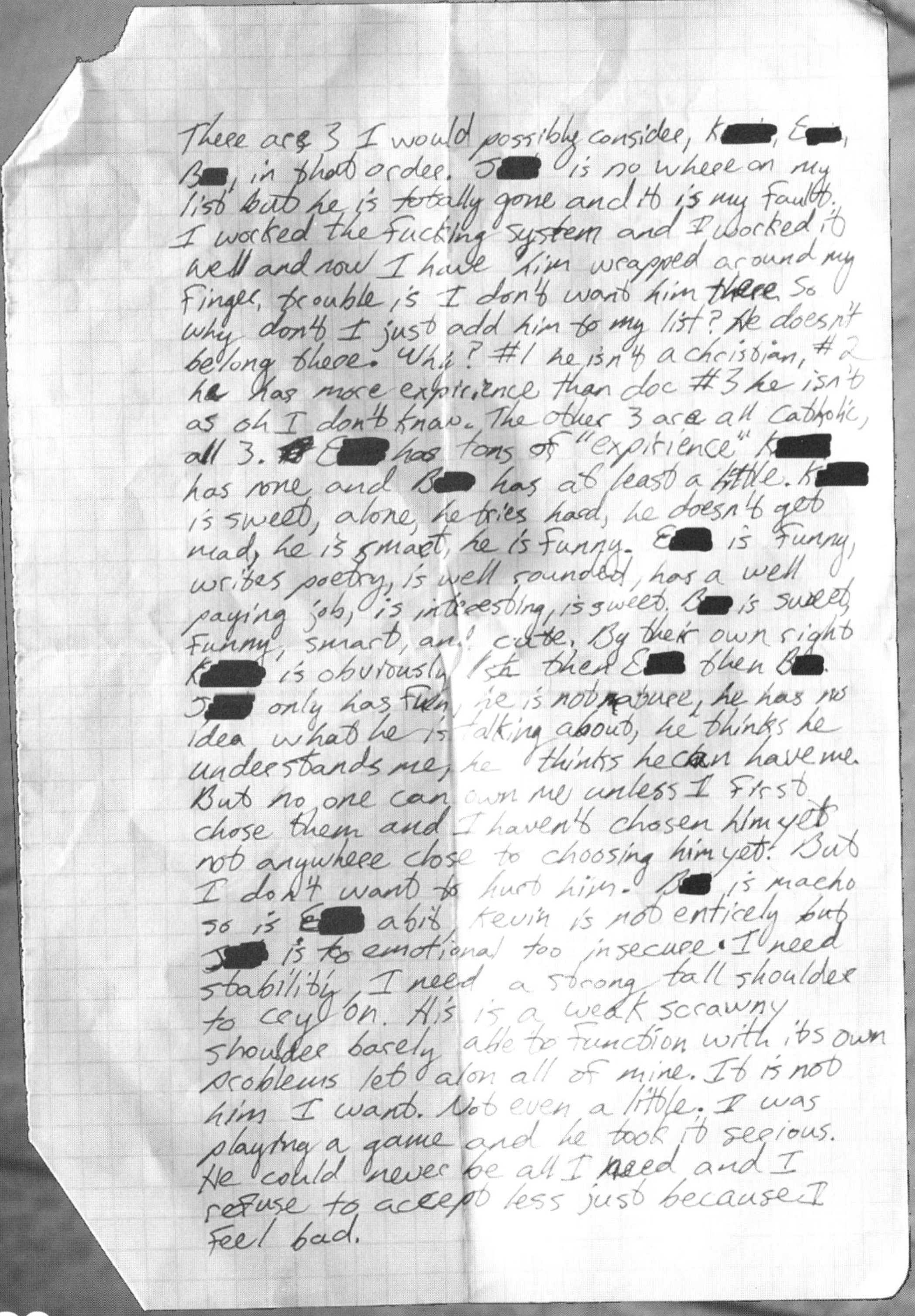

There are 3 I would possibly consider, K[redacted], E[redacted], B[redacted], in that order. J[redacted] is no where on my list but he is totally gone and it is my fault. I worked the Fucking system and I worked it well and now I have him wrapped around my Finger, trouble is I don't want him there. So why don't I just add him to my list? He doesn't belong there. Why? #1 he isn't a christian, #2 he has more expirience than doc #3 he isn't as oh I don't know. The other 3 are all Catholic, all 3. [redacted] E[redacted] has tons of "expirience" K[redacted] has none and B[redacted] has at least a little. K[redacted] is sweet, alone, he tries hard, he doesn't get mad, he is smart, he is Funny. E[redacted] is Funny, writes poetry, is well rounded, has a well paying job, is interesting, is sweet. B[redacted] is sweet, Funny, smart, and cute. By their own right K[redacted] is obviously 1st then E[redacted] then B[redacted]. J[redacted] only has Fun, he is not mature, he has no idea what he is talking about, he thinks he understands me, he thinks he can have me. But no one can own me unless I first chose them and I haven't chosen him yet not anywhere close to choosing him yet. But I don't want to hurt him. B[redacted] is macho so is E[redacted] a bit, Kevin is not entirely but J[redacted] is too emotional too insecure. I need stability, I need a strong tall shoulder to cry on. His is a weak scrawny shoulder barely able to function with its own problems let alon all of mine. It is not him I want. Not even a little. I was playing a game and he took it serious. He could never be all I need and I refuse to accept less just because I Feel bad.

Found Tyler L. of Eugene, OR.
5¾" x 8¼", black rollerball ink on graph paper

Found by Wendy C. outside a Redmond, WA, teen center.
8½" x 14", black-and-white photocopy, green felt marker and invisible tape on white paper

Wanna be on the PULP! mailing list? Send us your name, address, phone number, email address… Oh!—and any comments or thoughts—and we'll send you some FREE shtuff!

PULP!

P.O. Box 70584
Seattle WA 98107

Watch for the PULP! website, www.pulpnet.com, coming soon! More found objects (updated weekly), an online catalog, and more! It's all juicy!